William Taylor Adams

Up the Baltic

Or, Young America in Norway, Sweden, and Denmark

William Taylor Adams

Up the Baltic
Or, Young America in Norway, Sweden, and Denmark

ISBN/EAN: 9783337107604

Printed in Europe, USA, Canada, Australia, Japan

Cover: Foto ©ninafisch / pixelio.de

More available books at **www.hansebooks.com**

YOUNG AMERICA ABROAD—SECOND SERIES.

UP THE BALTIC;

OR,

YOUNG AMERICA IN NORWAY, SWEDEN, AND DENMARK.

A Story of Travel and Adventure.

BY

WILLIAM T. ADAMS.
(*OLIVER OPTIC*),
AUTHOR OF "OUTWARD BOUND," "SHAMROCK AND THISTLE," "RED CROSS,"
"DIKES AND DITCHES," "PALACE AND COTTAGE,"
"DOWN THE RHINE," ETC.

BOSTON:
LEE AND SHEPARD, PUBLISHERS.
NEW YORK:
LEE, SHEPARD AND DILLINGHAM,
Nos. 47 AND 49 GREENE ST.
1871.

TO

MY EVER-CHEERFUL AND GOOD-NATURED FRIEND

SHEPARD K. MATTISON,

WHOM I MET FOR THE FIRST TIME AT TROLHÄTTEN, ON THE
GÖTA CANAL, AND WITH WHOM I JOURNEYED THROUGH
SWEDEN, RUSSIA, AUSTRIA, SPAIN, AND PORTUGAL,

This Volume

IS RESPECTFULLY DEDICATED.

YOUNG AMERICA ABROAD.

By OLIVER OPTIC.

A Library of Travel and Adventure in Foreign Lands. First and Second Series; six volumes in each Series. 16mo. Illustrated.

First Series.

I. *OUTWARD BOUND;* or, Young America Afloat.

II. *SHAMROCK AND THISTLE;* or, Young America in Ireland and Scotland.

III. *RED CROSS;* or, Young America in England and Wales.

IV. *DIKES AND DITCHES;* or, Young America in Holland and Belgium.

V. *PALACE AND COTTAGE;* or, Young America in France and Switzerland.

VI. *DOWN THE RHINE;* or, Young America in Germany.

Second Series.

I. *UP THE BALTIC;* or, Young America in Norway, Sweden, and Denmark.

II. *NORTHERN LANDS;* or, Young America in Russia and Prussia. In preparation.

III. *CROSS AND CRESCENT;* or, Young America in Turkey and Greece. In preparation.

IV. *SUNNY SHORES;* or, Young America in Italy and Austria. In preparation.

V. *VINE AND OLIVE;* or, Young America in Spain and Portugal. In preparation.

VI. *ISLES OF THE SEA;* or, Young America Homeward Bound. In preparation.

PREFACE.

UP THE BALTIC, the first volume of the second series of "YOUNG AMERICA ABROAD," like its predecessors, is a record of what was seen and done by the young gentlemen of the Academy Squadron on its second voyage to Europe, embracing its stay in the waters of Norway, Sweden, and Denmark. Agreeably to the announcement made in the concluding volume of the first series, the author spent the greater portion of last year in Europe. His sole object in going abroad was to obtain the material for the present series of books, and in carrying out his purpose, he visited every country to which these volumes relate, and, he hopes, properly fitted himself for the work he has undertaken.

In the preparation of UP THE BALTIC, the writer has used, besides his own note-books, the most reliable works he could obtain at home and in Europe, and he believes his geographical, historical, and political matter is correct, and as full as could be embodied in a story. He has endeavored to describe the appearance of the country, and the manners and customs of the people, so as to make them interesting to young readers. For this purpose these descriptions are often interwoven with the story, or brought out in the comments of the boys of the squadron.

The story is principally the adventures of the crew of the second cutter, who attempted "an independent excursion without running away," which includes the career of a young Englishman, spoiled by his mother's indulgence, and of a Norwegian waif, picked up by the squadron in the North Sea.

The author is encouraged to enter upon this second series by the remarkable and unexpected success which attended the publication of the first series. Difficult as it is to work the dry details of geography and history into a story, the writer intends to persevere in his efforts to make these books instructive, as well as interesting; and he is confident that no reader will fail to distinguish the good boys from the bad ones of the story, or to give his sympathies to the former.

HARRISON SQUARE, BOSTON,
    May 10, 1871.

CONTENTS.

		PAGE
I.	A Waif on the North Sea.	11
II.	Off the Naze of Norway.	27
III.	An Accident to the Second Cutter.	43
IV.	Norway in the Past and the Present.	59
V.	Mr. Clyde Blacklock and Mother.	76
VI.	A Day at Christiansand.	92
VII.	Up the Christiania Fjord.	110
VIII.	Sights of Christiania, and other Matters.	128
IX.	The Excursion without Running Away.	146
X.	Gottenburg and Finkel.	164
XI.	On the Way to the Rjukanfos.	181
XII.	The Boatswain and the Briton.	201
XIII.	The Meeting of the Absentees.	218
XIV.	Through the Sound to Copenhagen.	237

CONTENTS.

XV.	Copenhagen and Tivoli.	255
XVI.	Excursion to Klampenborg and Elsinore.	274
XVII.	To Stockholm by Göta Canal.	292
XVIII.	Up the Baltic.	310
XIX.	The Cruise in the Little Steamer. . . .	329
XX.	Stockholm and its Surroundings.	349

UP THE BALTIC;

OR,

YOUNG AMERICA IN NORWAY, SWEDEN, AND DENMARK.

CHAPTER I.

A WAIF ON THE NORTH SEA.

"BOAT on the weather bow, sir!" shouted the lookout on the top-gallant forecastle of the Young America.

"Starboard!" replied Judson, the officer of the deck, as he discovered the boat, which was drifting into the track of the ship.

"Starboard, sir!" responded the quartermaster in charge of the wheel.

"Steady!" added the officer.

"Steady, sir," repeated the quartermaster.

By this time a crowd of young officers and seamen had leaped upon the top-gallant forecastle, and into the weather rigging, to obtain a view of the little boat, which, like a waif on the ocean, was drifting down towards the coast of Norway. It contained only a single person, who was either a dwarf or a boy, for he was small in stature. He lay upon a seat near the stern of the boat, with his feet on the gunwale. He was either asleep or dead, for though the ship had approached within hail, he neither moved nor made any sign. The wind was light from the southward, and the sea was quite calm.

"What do you make of it, Ryder?" called the officer of the deck to the second master, who was on duty forward.

"It is a flat-bottomed boat, half full of water, with a boy in it," answered Ryder.

"Hail him," added the officer of the deck.

"Boat, ahoy!" shouted Ryder, at the top of his lungs.

The person in the boat, boy or man, made no reply. Ryder repeated the hail, but with no better success. The officers and seamen held their breath with interest and excitement, for most of them had already come to the conclusion that the occupant of the boat was dead. A feeling akin to horror crept through the minds of the more timid, as they gazed upon the immovable body in the dilapidated craft; for they felt that they were in the presence of death, and to young people this is always an impressive season. By this time the ship was within a short distance of the water-logged bateau. As the waif on the ocean exhibited no signs of life, the first lieutenant, in charge of the vessel, was in doubt as to what he should do.

Though he knew that it was the first duty of a sailor to assist a human being in distress, he was not sure that the same effort was required in behalf of one who had already ceased to live. Captain Cumberland, in command of the ship, who had been in the cabin when the excitement commenced, now appeared upon the quarter-deck, and relieved the officer of the responsibility of the moment. Judson reported the cause of the unwonted scene on deck, and as the captain discovered the little boat, just on the weather bow, he promptly directed the ship to be hove to.

"Man the main clew-garnets and buntlines!" shouted the first lieutenant; and the hands sprang to their several stations. "Stand by tack and sheet."

"All ready, sir," reported the first midshipman, who was on duty in the waist.

"Let go tack and sheet! Up mainsail!" continued Ryder.

The well-trained crew promptly obeyed the several orders, and the mainsail was hauled up in much less time than it takes to describe the manœuvre.

"Man the main braces!" proceeded the officer of the deck.

"Ready, sir," reported the first midshipman.

"Let go and haul."

As the hands executed the last order; all the yards on the mainmast swung round towards the wind till the light breeze caught the sails aback, and brought them against the mast. The effect was to deaden the headway of the ship.

"Avast bracing!" shouted the first lieutenant, when the yards on the mainmast were about square.

In a few moments the onward progress of the Young America was entirely checked, and she lay motionless on the sea. There were four other vessels in the squadron, following the flag-ship, and each of them, in its turn, hove to, or came up into the wind.

"Fourth cutters, clear away their boat!" continued the first lieutenant, after he had received his order from the captain. "Mr. Messenger will take charge of the boat."

The young officer indicated was the first midshipman, whose quarter watch was then on duty.

"All the fourth cutters!" piped the boatswain's mate, as Messenger crossed the deck to perform the duty assigned to him.

"He's alive!" shouted a dozen of the idlers on the rail, who had not removed their gaze from the waif in the small boat.

"He isn't dead any more than I am!" added a juvenile tar, springing into the main rigging, as if to demonstrate the amount of his own vitality.

The waif in the bateau had produced this sudden change of sentiment, and given this welcome relief to the crew of the Young America, by rising from his reclining posture, and standing up in the water at the bottom of his frail craft. He gazed with astonishment at the ship and the other vessels of the squadron, and did not seem to realize where he was.

"Avast, fourth cutters!" interposed the first lieutenant. "Belay, all!"

If the waif was not dead, it was hardly necessary to lower a boat to send to his relief; at least not till it appeared that he needed assistance.

"Boat, ahoy!" shouted Ryder.

"On board the ship," replied the waif, in tones not at all sepulchral.

"What are you doing out here?" demanded the first lieutenant.

"Nothing," replied the waif.

"Will you come on board the ship?"

"Yes, if you will let me," added the stranger, as he picked up a broken oar, which was floating in the water on the bottom of his boat.

"Yes, come on board," answered the first lieutenant, prompted by Captain Cumberland, who was quite as much interested in the adventure as any of his shipmates.

The waif, using the broken oar as a paddle, worked his water-logged craft slowly towards the ship. The accommodation ladder was lowered for his use, and in a few moments, with rather a heavy movement, as though he was lame, or much exhausted, he climbed up the ladder, and stepped down upon the ship deck.

"Fill away again!" said the captain to the first lieutenant, as a curious crowd began to gather around the stranger. Ryder gave the necessary orders to brace up the main yards, and set the mainsail again, and the ship was soon moving on her course towards the Naze of Norway, as though nothing had occurred to interrupt her voyage.

"What are you doing out here, in an open boat, out of sight of land?" asked Captain Cumberland, while the watch on deck were bracing up the yards.

The waif looked at the commander of the Young America, and carefully examined him from head to foot. The elegant uniform of the captain seemed to produce a strong impression upon his mind, and he evidently regarded him as a person of no small consequence. He did not answer the question put to him, seeming to be in doubt whether it was safe and proper for him to do so. Captain Cumberland was an exceedingly comely-looking young gentleman, tall and well formed in person, graceful and dignified in his manners; and if he had been fifty years old, the stranger before him could not have been more awed and impressed by his bearing. So far as his personal appearance was concerned, the waif appeared to have escaped from the rag-bag, and to have been out long enough to soil his tatters with oil, tar, pitch, and dirt. Though his face and hands, as well as other parts of his body, were very dirty, his eye was bright, and, even seen through the disguise of filth and rags that covered him, he was rather prepossessing.

"What is your name?" asked Captain Cumberland, finding his first question was not likely to be answered.

"Ole Amundsen," replied the stranger, pronouncing his first name in two syllables.

"Then you are not English."

"No, sir. Be you?"

"I am not; we are all Americans in this ship."

"Americans!" exclaimed Ole, opening his eyes, while a smile beamed through the dirt on his face. "Are you going to America now?"

"No; we are going up the Baltic now," replied Captain Cumberland; "but we shall return to America in the course of a year or two."

"Take me to America with you — will you?" continued Ole, earnestly. "I am a sailor, and I will work for you all the time."

"I don't know about that. You must speak to the principal."

"Who's he?"

"Mr. Lowington. He is in the cabin now. Where do you belong, Ole?"

"I don't belong anywhere," answered the waif, looking doubtfully about him.

"Where were you born?"

"In Norway, sir."

"Then you are a Norwegian."

"I reckon I am."

"In what part of Norway were you born?"

"In Bratsberg."

"That's where all the brats come from," suggested Sheridan.

"This one came from there, at any rate," added Mayley. "But where is Bratsberg, and what is it?"

"It is an *amt*, or province, in the south-eastern part of Norway."

"I came from the town of Laurdal," said Ole.

"Do the people there speak English as well as you do?" asked the captain.

"No, sir. I used to be a *skydskarl*, and —"

"A what?" demanded the crowd.

"A *skydskarl* — a boy that goes on a cariole to take back the horses. I learned a little English from the Englishmen I rode with; and then I was in England almost a year."

"But how came you out here, alone in an open boat?" asked the captain, returning to his first inquiry.

Ole put one of his dirty fingers in his mouth, and looked stupid and uncommunicative. He glanced at

2

the young officers around him, and then over the rail at the sea.

"Were you wrecked?" inquired the captain.

"No, sir; not wrecked," replied Ole. "I never was wrecked in my life."

"What are you doing out here, out of sight of land, in a boat half full of water?" persisted the captain.

"Doing nothing."

"Did you get blown off from the shore?"

"No, sir; a southerly wind wouldn't blow any-body off from the south coast of Norway," answered Ole, with a smile which showed that he had some perception of things absurd in themselves.

"You are no fool."

"No, sir, I am not; and I don't think you are," added Ole, again glancing at Captain Cumberland from head to foot.

The young tars all laughed at the waif's retort, and the captain was not a little nettled by the remark. He pressed Ole rather sharply for further information in regard to his antecedents; but the youth was silent on this point. While the crowd were anxiously waiting for the stranger to declare himself more definitely, eight bells sounded at the wheel, and were repeated on the large bell forward by the lookout. From each vessel of the fleet the bells struck at nearly the same moment, and were followed by the pipe of the boat-swain's whistle, which was the signal for changing the watch. As the officers of the ship were obliged to attend to their various duties, Ole Amundsen was left alone with the captain. The waif still obstinately refused to explain how he happened to be alone in a water-logged boat, asleep, and out of sight of land, though he promptly answered all other questions which were put to him."

Mr. Lowington, the principal of the Academy Squadron, was in the main cabin, though he had been fully informed in regard to the events which had transpired on deck. The young commander despaired of his own ability to extort an explanation from the waif, and he concluded to refer the matter to the principal.

"How long have you been in that boat?" asked Captain Cumberland, as he led the way towards the companion ladder.

"Eighteen hours," answered Ole, after some hesitation, which, perhaps, was only to enable him to count up the hours.

"Did you have anything to eat?"

"No, sir."

"Nothing?"

"Not a thing."

"Then you are hungry?"

"I had a little supper last night — not much," continued Ole, apparently counting the seams in the deck, ashamed to acknowledge his human weakness.

"You shall have something to eat at once."

"Thank you, sir."

Captain Cumberland therefore conducted the stranger to the steerage, instead of the main cabin, and directed one of the stewards to give him his supper. The man set half a cold boiled ham on one of the mess tables, with an abundant supply of bread and butter. Cutting off a large slice of the ham, he placed it on the plate before Ole, whose eyes opened wide with astonishment, and gleamed with pleasure. Without paying much attention to the forms of civilization, the boy began to devour it, with the zeal of one who had not tasted food for twenty-four hours. Captain Cumberland smiled, but with becoming dignity, at the greediness of the guest, before whom the whole slice of ham and half a brick loaf disappeared almost in a twinkling. The steward appeared with a pot of coffee, in time to cut off another slice of ham, which the waif attacked with the same voracity as before. When it was consumed, and the young Norwegian glanced wistfully at the leg before him, as though his capacity for cold ham was not yet exhausted, the captain began to consider whether he ought not to consult the surgeon of the ship before he permitted the waif to eat any more. But the steward, like a generous host, seemed to regard the quantity eaten as complimentary testimony to the quality of the viands, and helped him to a third slice of the ham. He swallowed a pint mug of coffee without stopping to breathe.

As the third slice of ham began to wax small before the voracious Norwegian, Captain Cumberland became really alarmed, and determined to report at once to the principal and the surgeon for instructions. Knocking at the door of the main cabin, he was admitted. Dr. Winstock assured him there was no danger to the guest; he had not been without food long enough to render it dangerous for him fully to satisfy himself. The quantity eaten might make him uncomfortable, and even slightly sick, but it would do the gourmand no real injury. The captain returned to the steerage, where Ole had broken down on his fourth slice of ham; but he regarded it wistfully, and seemed to regret his inability to eat any more.

"That's good," said he, with emphasis. "It's the best supper I ever ate in my life. I like this ship; I like the grub; and I mean to go to America in her."

"We will see about that some other time; but if you don't tell us how you happened to be off here, I am afraid we can do nothing for you," replied the captain. "If you feel better now, we will go and see the principal."

"Who's he?" asked Ole.

"Mr. Lowington. You must tell him how you happened to be in that leaky boat."

"Perhaps I will. I don't know," added Ole, doubtfully, as he followed the commander into the main cabin.

Captain Cumberland explained to the principal the circumstances under which Ole had come on board, and that he declined to say anything in regard to the strange situation in which he had been discovered.

"Is the captain here?" asked the midshipman of the watch, at the steerage door.

"Yes," replied Captain Cumberland.

"Mr. Lincoln sent me down to report a light on the lee bow, sir."

"Very well. Where is Mr. Beckwith?"

"In the cabin, sir."

The captain left the main cabin, and entered the after cabin, where he found Beckwith, the first master, attended by the second and third, examining the large chart of the North Sea.

"Light on the lee bow, sir," said the first master.

"Do you make it out?"

"Yes; we are all right to the breadth of a hair," added the master, delighted to find that his calculations had proved to be entirely correct. "It is Egero Light, and we are about fifty miles from the Naze of Norway. We are making about four knots, and if the breeze holds, we ought to see Gunnarshoug Light by one o'clock."

Captain Cumberland went on deck to see the light reported. Though it was half past eight, the sun had but just set, and the light, eighteen miles distant, could be distinctly seen. It created a great deal of excitement and enthusiasm among the young officers and seamen, who had read enough about Norway to be desirous of seeing it. For weeks the young gentlemen on board the ship had been talking of Norway, and reading up all the books in the library relating to the country and its people. They had read with interest the accounts of the various travellers who had visited it, including Ross Brown, in Harper's Monthly, and Bayard Taylor, and had studied Harper, Murray, Bradshaw, and other Guides on the subject. The more inquiring students had read the history of Norway, and were well prepared to appreciate a short visit to this interesting region.

They had just come from the United States, having sailed in the latter part of March. The squadron had had a fair passage, and the students hoped to be in Christiansand by the first day of May; and now nothing less than a dead calm for forty-eight hours could disappoint their hopes. Five years before, the Young

America and the Josephine, her consort, had cruised in the waters of Europe, and returned to America in the autumn. It had been the intention of the principal to make another voyage the next year, go up the Baltic, and winter in the Mediterranean; but the war of 1866 induced him to change his plans. Various circumstances had postponed the cruise until 1870, when it was actually commenced.

The Young America was the first, and for more than a year the only, vessel belonging to the Academy. The Josephine, a topsail schooner, had been added the second year; and now the Tritonia, a vessel of the same size and rig, was on her first voyage. The three vessels of the squadron were officered and manned by the students of the Academy. As on the first cruise, the offices were the rewards of merit bestowed upon the faithful and energetic pupils. The highest number of merits gave the highest office, and so on through the several grades in the cabin, and the petty offices in the steerage. The routine and discipline of the squadron were substantially the same as described in the first series of these volumes, though some changes had been made, as further experience suggested. Instead of quarterly, as before, the offices were given out every month. Captains were not retired after a single term, as formerly, but were obliged to accept whatever rank and position they earned, like other students.

There was no change from one vessel to another, except at the end of a school year, or with the permission of the principal. The ship had six instructors, three of whom, however, lectured to all the students in the squadron, and each of the smaller vessels had two teachers. Mr. Lowington was still the principal. He was the founder of the institution; and his high moral and religious principles, his love of justice, as well as his skill, firmness, and prudence, had made it a success in spite of the many obstacles which continually confronted it. As a considerable portion of the students in the squadron were the spoiled sons of rich men, who had set at defiance the rules of colleges and academies on shore, it required a remarkable combination of attributes to fit a gentleman for the difficult and trying position he occupied.

Mr. Fluxion was the first vice-principal in charge of the Josephine. He was a thorough seaman, a good disciplinarian, and a capital teacher; but he lacked some of the high attributes of character which distinguished the principal. If any man was fit to succeed Mr. Lowington in his responsible position, it was Mr. Fluxion; but it was doubtful whether, under his sole administration, the institution could be an entire success. His love of discipline, and his energetic manner of dealing with delinquents, would probably have increased the number of "rows," mutinies, and runaways.

The second vice-principal, in charge of the Tritonia, was Mr. Tompion, who, like his two superiors in rank, had formerly been an officer of the navy. Though he was a good sailor, and a good disciplinarian, he lacked that which a teacher needs most — a hearty sympathy with young people.

The principal and the two vice-principals were instructors in mathematics and navigation in their respective vessels. Mr. Lowington had undertaken this task himself, because he felt the necessity of coming more in contact with the student than his position as mere principal required. It tended to promote friendly relations between the governor and the governed, by creating a greater sympathy between them.

The Rev. Mr. Agneau still served as chaplain. In port, and at sea when the weather would permit, two services were held in the steerage every Sunday, which were attended, at anchor, by the crew of all the vessels. Prayers were said morning and evening, in the ship by the chaplain, in the schooners by the vice-principal or one of the instructors.

Dr. Winstock was the instructor in natural philosophy and chemistry, as well as surgeon and sanitary director. He was a good and true man, and generally popular among the students. Each vessel had an adult boatswain and a carpenter, and the ship a sail-maker, to perform such work as the students could not do, and to instruct them in the details of practical seamanship.

After the lapse of five years, hardly a student remained of those who had cruised in the ship or her consort during the first voyage. But in addition to the three vessels which properly constituted the squadron, there were two yachts, each of one hundred and twenty tons. They were fore-and-aft schooners, of beautiful model, and entirely new. The one on the weather wing of the fleet was the Grace, Captain Paul Kendall, whose lady and two friends were in the cabin. Abreast of her sailed the Feodora, Captain

Robert Shuffles, whose wife was also with him. Each of these yachts had a first and second officer, and a crew of twenty men, with the necessary complement of cooks and stewards. They were part of the fleet, but not of the Academy Squadron.

CHAPTER II.

OFF THE NAZE OF NORWAY.

MR. LOWINGTON examined Ole Amundsen very carefully, in order to ascertain what disposition should be made of him. He told where he was born, how he had learned English, and where he had passed the greater portion of his life, just as he had related these particulars to Captain Cumberland.

"But how came you out here in an open boat?" asked the principal.

Ole examined the carpet on the floor of the cabin, and made no reply.

"Won't you answer me?" added Mr. Lowington.

The waif was still silent.

"You have been to sea?"

"Yes, sir; I was six months in a steamer, and over two years in sailing vessels," answered Ole, readily.

"What steamer were you in?"

"I was in the Drammen steamer a while; and I have been three trips down to Copenhagen and Gottenburg, one to Lübeck, one to Stettin, and one to Stockholm."

"Have you been in a steamer this season?"

"No, sir."

"Then you were in a sailing vessel."

Ole would not say that he had been in any vessel the present season.

"Where is your home now?" asked the principal, breaking the silence again.

"Haven't any."

"Have you a father and mother?"

"Both dead, sir."

"Have you any friends?"

"Friends? I don't believe I have."

"Any one that takes care of you?"

"Takes care of me? No, sir; I'm quite certain I haven't any one that takes care of me. I take care of myself, and it's heavy work I find it, sometimes, I can tell you."

"Do you ever go fishing?"

"Yes, sir, sometimes."

"Have you been lately?"

Ole was silent again.

"I wish to be your friend, Ole."

"Thank you, sir," added Ole, bowing low.

"But in order to know what to do for you, I must know something about your circumstances."

"I haven't any circumstances, sir. I lost 'em all," replied Ole, gravely and sadly, as though he had met with a very serious loss.

Dr. Winstock could not help laughing, but it was impossible to decide whether the boy was ignorant of the meaning of the word, or was trying to perpetrate a joke.

"How did you happen to lose your circumstances, Ole?" asked Mr. Lowington.

"When my mother died, Captain Olaf took 'em."

"Indeed; and who is Captain Olaf?"

Ole looked at the principal, and then returned his gaze to the cabin floor, evidently not deeming it prudent to answer the question.

"Is he your brother?"

"No, sir."

"Your uncle?"

"No, sir."

Ole could not be induced to say anything more about Captain Olaf, and doubtless regretted that he had even mentioned his name. The waif plainly confounded "circumstances" and property. Mr. Lowington several times returned to the main inquiry, but the young man would not even hint at the explanation of the manner in which he had come to be a waif on the North Sea, in an open boat, half full of water. He had told the captain that he was not wrecked, and had not been blown off from the coast. He would make no answer of any kind to any direct question relating to the subject.

"Well, Ole, as you will not tell me how you came in the situation in which we found you, I do not see that I can do anything for you," continued Mr. Lowington. "The ship is bound to Christiansand, and when we arrive we must leave you there."

"Don't leave me in Christiansand, sir. I don't want to be left there."

"Why not?"

Ole was silent again. Both the principal and the surgeon pitied him, for he appeared to be a friendless orphan; certainly he had no friends to whom he wished to go, and was only anxious to remain in the ship, and go to America in her.

"You may go into the steerage now, Ole," said the principal, despairing of any further solution of the mystery.

"Thank you, sir," replied Ole, bowing low, and backing out of the cabin as a courtier retires from the presence of a sovereign.

"What do you make of him, doctor?" added Mr. Lowington, as the door closed upon the waif.

"I don't make anything of him," replied Dr. Winstock. "The young rascal evidently don't intend that we should make anything of him. He's a young Norwegian, about fifteen years old, with neither father nor mother; for I think we may believe what he has said. If he had no regard to the truth, it was just as easy for him to lie as it was to keep silent, and it would have been more plausible."

"I am inclined to believe that he is a runaway, either from the shore or from some vessel," said the principal. "He certainly cannot have been well treated, for his filthy rags scarcely cover his body; and he says that the supper he had to-night was the best he ever ate in his life. It was only coffee, cold ham, and bread and butter; so he cannot have been a high liver. He seems to be honest, and I pity him."

"But he is too filthy to remain on board a single hour. I will attend to his sanitary condition at once," laughed the doctor. "He will breed a leprosy among the boys, if he is not taken care of."

"Let the purser give you a suit of clothes for him, for we can't do less than this for him."

The doctor left the cabin, and Ole was taken to the bath-room by one of the stewards, and compelled to scrub himself with a brush and soap, till he was made into a new creature. He was inclined to rebel at first, for he had his national and inborn prejudice against soap and water in combination; but the sight of the suit of new clothes overcame his constitutional scruples. The steward was faithful to his mission, and Ole left dirt enough in the bath-tub to plant half a dozen hills of potatoes. He looked like a new being, even before he had donned the new clothes. His light hair, cut square across his forehead, was three shades lighter when it had been scrubbed, and deprived of the black earth, grease, and tar, with which it had been matted.

The steward was interested in his work, for it is a pleasure to any decent person to transform such a leper of filth into a clean and wholesome individual. Ole put on the heavy flannel shirt and the blue frock which were handed to him, and smiled with pleasure as he observed the effect. He was fitted to a pair of seaman's blue trousers, and provided with socks and shoes. Then he actually danced with delight, and evidently regarded himself as a finished dandy; for never before had he been clothed in a suit half so good. It was the regular uniform of the crew of the ship.

"Hold on a moment, my lad," said Muggs, the steward, as he produced a pair of barber's shears. "Your barber did not do justice to your figure-head, the last time he cut your hair."

"I cut it myself," replied Ole.

"I should think you did, and with a bush scythe."

"I only hacked off a little, to keep it out of my eyes. Captain Olaf always used to cut it."

"Who's Captain Olaf?" asked Muggs.

Ole was silent, but permitted the steward to remove at will the long, snarly white locks, which covered his head. The operator had been a barber once, and received extra pay for his services on board the ship in this capacity. He did his work in an artistic manner, parting and combing the waif's hair as though he were dressing him for a fashionable party. He put a sailor's knot in the black handkerchief under the boy's collar, and then placed the blue cap on his head, a little on one side, so that he looked as jaunty as a dandy man-of-war's-man.

"Now put on this jacket, my lad, and you will be all right," continued the steward, as he gazed with pride and pleasure upon the work of his hands.

"More clothes!" exclaimed Ole. "I shall be baked. I sweat now with what I have on."

"It's hot in here; you will be cool enough when you go on deck. Here's a pea-jacket for you, besides the other."

"But that's for winter. I never had so much clothes on before in my life."

"You needn't put the pea-jacket on, if you don't want it. Now you look like a decent man, and you can go on deck and show yourself."

"Thank you, sir."

"But you must wash yourself clean every morning."

"Do it every day!" exclaimed Ole, opening his eyes with astonishment.

"Why, yes, you heathen," laughed Muggs. "A

man isn't fit to live who don't keep himself clean. Why, you could have planted potatoes anywhere on your hide, before you went into that tub."

"I haven't been washed before since last summer," added Ole.

"You ought to be hung for it."

"You spend half your time washing yourselves — don't you?"

"We spend time enough at it to keep clean. No wonder you Norwegians have the leprosy, and the flesh rots off the bones!"

"But I always go into the water every summer," pleaded Ole.

"And don't wash yourself at any other time?"

"I always wash myself once a year, and sometimes more, when I get a good chance."

"Don't you wash your face and hands every morning."

"Every morning? No! I haven't done such a thing since last summer."

"Then you are not fit to live. If you stay in this ship, you must wash every day, and more than that when you do dirty work."

"Can I stay in the ship if I do that?" asked Ole, earnestly.

"I don't know anything about it."

"I will wash all the time if they will only let me stay in the ship," pleaded the waif.

"You must talk with the principal on that subject. I have nothing to do with it. Now, go on deck. Hold up your head, and walk like a man."

Ole left the bath-room, and made his way up the

forward ladder. The second part of the starboard watch were on duty, but nearly every person belonging to the ship was on deck, watching the distant light, which assured them they were on the coast of Norway. The waif stepped upon deck as lightly as a mountain sylph. The influence of his new clothes pervaded his mind, and he was inclined to be a little "swellish" in his manner.

"How are you, Norway!" shouted Sanford, one of the crew.

"How are you, America," replied Ole, imitating the slang of the speaker.

"What have you done with your dirt?" added Rodman.

"Here is some of it," answered Muggs, the steward, as he came up the ladder, with Ole's rags on a dust-pan, and threw them overboard.

"If you throw all his dirt overboard here, we shall get aground, sure," added Stockwell, as Ole danced up to the group of students.

"No wonder you feel light after getting rid of such a load of dirt," said Sanford.

"O, I'm all right," laughed Ole, good-naturedly; for he did not seem to think that dirt was any disgrace or dishonor to him.

"How came you in that leaky boat, Norway?" demanded Rodman; and the entire party gathered around the waif, anxious to hear the story of his adventure.

"I went into it."

"Is that so?" added Wilde.

"Yes, sir."

"I say, Norway, you are smart," replied Rodman.

"Smart? Where?"

"All over."

"I don't feel it."

"But, Norway, how came you in that old tub, out of sight of land?" persisted Rodman, returning to the charge again.

"I went into it just the same as one of you Americans would have got into it," laughed Ole, who did not think it necessary to resort to the tactics he had used with the principal and the captain. "You could have done it if you had tried as hard as I did."

"After you got in, then, how came the boat out here, so far from land?"

"The wind, the tide, and the broken oar brought it out here."

"Indeed! But won't you tell us your story, Ole?"

"A story? O, yes. Once there was a king of Norway whose name was Olaf, and half the men of his country were named after him, because —"

"Never mind that story, Ole. We want to hear the story about yourself."

"About myself? Well, last year things didn't go very well with me; the crop of potatoes was rather short on my farm, and my vessels caught but few fish; so I decided to make a voyage up the Mediterranean, to spend the winter."

"What did you go in, Norway?" asked Wilde.

"In my boat. We don't make voyages on foot here in Norway."

"What boat?"

"You won't let me tell my story; so I had better finish it at once. I got back as far as the North Sea, and almost into the Sleeve, when a gale came down upon me, and strained my boat so that she leaked badly. I was worn out with fatigue, and dropped asleep one afternoon. I was dreaming that the King of Sweden and Norway came off in a big man-of-war, to welcome me home again. He hailed me himself, with, " Boat, ahoy ! " which waked me ; and then I saw this ship. You know all the rest of it."

" Do you mean to say you went up the Mediterranean in that old craft ? "

" I've told my story, and if you don't believe it, you can look in the almanac, and see whether it is true or not," laughed Ole. " But I must go and show myself to the captain and the big gentleman."

" He's smart — isn't he ? " said Sanford, as the young Norwegian went aft to exhibit himself to the officers on the quarter deck.

" Yes; but what's the reason he won't tell how he happened out here in that leaky tub ? " added Rodman.

" I don't know; he wouldn't tell the captain, nor the principal."

" I don't understand it."

" No one understands it. Perhaps he has done something wrong, and is afraid of being found out."

" Very likely."

" He's just the fellow for us," said Stockwell, in a low tone, after he had glanced around him, to see that no listeners were near. " He speaks the lingo of this country. We must buy him up."

" Good ! " exclaimed Boyden. " We ought not to have let him go till we had fixed his flint."

"I didn't think of it before; but there is time enough. If we can get hold of his story we can manage him without any trouble."

"But he won't tell his story. He wouldn't even let on to the principal."

"No matter; we must have him, somehow or other. Sanford can handle him."

"I don't exactly believe in the scrape," said Burchmore, shaking his head dubiously. "We've heard all about the fellows that used to try to run away from the ship and from the Josephine. They always got caught, and always had the worst of it."

"We are not going to run away, and we are not going to make ourselves liable to any punishment," interposed Sanford, rather petulantly. "We can have a good time on shore without running away, or anything of that sort."

"What's the use?" replied Burchmore.

"The principal isn't going to let us see anything at all of Norway. We are going to put in at Christiansand, and then go to Christiania. We want to see the interior of Norway, for there's glorious fishing in the lakes and rivers — salmon as big as whales."

"I like fishing as well as any fellow, but I don't want to get into a scrape, and have to stay on board when the whole crowd go ashore afterwards. It won't pay."

"But I tell you again, we are not going to run away."

"I don't see how you can manage it without running away. You are going into the interior of Norway on your own hook, without the consent or knowledge of the principal. If you don't call this running away, I don't know what you can call it."

"No matter what we call it, so long as the principal don't call it running away," argued Sanford.

"How can you manage it?" inquired Burchmore.

"I don't know yet; and if I did, I wouldn't tell a fellow who has so many doubts."

"I shall not go into anything till I understand it."

"We don't ask you to do so. As soon as we come to anchor, and see the lay of the land, we can tell exactly what and how to do it. We have plenty of money, and we can have a first-rate time if you only think so. Leave it all to me, and I will bring it out right," continued the confident Sanford, who appeared to be the leader of the little squad.

The traditions of the various runaways who had, at one time and another, attempted to escape from the wholesome discipline and restraint of the Academy, were current on board all the vessels of the squadron. The capture of the Josephine, and her cruise in the English Channel, had been repeated to every new student who joined the fleet, till the story was as familiar to the present students as to those of five years before. There were just as many wild and reckless boys on board now as in the earlier days of the institution, and they were as sorely chafed by the necessary restraints of good order as their predecessors had been. Perhaps it was natural that, visiting a foreign country, they should desire to see all they could of its wonders, and even to look upon some things which it was the policy of the principal to prevent them from seeing.

Whenever any of the various stories of the runaways were related, Sanford, Rodman, Stockwell, and others of similar tendencies, were always ready to point out the defects in the plan of the operators. They could tell precisely where Wilton, Pelham, and Little had been weak, as they termed it, and precisely what they should have done to render the enterprise a success. Still, running away, in the abstract, was not a popular idea in the squadron at the present time; but Sanford believed that he and his companions could enjoy all the benefits of an independent excursion without incurring any of its perils and penalties. Let him demonstrate his own proposition.

Ole Amundsen walked aft, and was kindly greeted by the officers on the quarter-deck, who commented freely upon his improved personal appearance, though they did it in more refined terms than their shipmates on the forecastle had done. Some of them tried to draw from him the explanation of his situation in the leaky boat, but without any better success than had attended the efforts of others. He yielded an extravagant deference to the gold lace on the uniforms of the officers, treating them with the utmost respect.

"Well, Ole, you look better than when I saw you last," said Mr. Lowington.

"Yes, sir; and I feel better," replied Ole, bowing low to the "big gentleman."

"And you speak English very well, indeed."

"Thank you, sir."

"Can you speak Norwegian as well?"

"Yes, sir; better, I hope."

"Monsieur Badois, will you ask him a question or

two in Norwegian," added the principal, turning to the professor of modern languages, who prided himself on being able to speak fourteen different tongues; "I begin to doubt whether he is a Norwegian."

"I will, sir," replied monsieur, who was always glad of an opportunity to exhibit his linguistic powers. "*Hvor staae det til?*" (How do you do?)

"*Jeg takker, meget vel*" (Very well, I thank you), replied Ole.

"*Forstaaer De mig?*" (Do you understand me?)

"*Ja, jeg forstaaer Dem meget vel.*" (Yes, I understand you very well.)

"That will do," interposed Mr. Lowington.

"He speaks Norsk very well," added the professor.

"So do you, sir," said Ole, with a low bow to Monsieur Badois.

"*Meget vel*," laughed the professor.

"I am satisfied, Ole. Now, have you concluded to tell me how you happened to be in that boat, so far from the land."

The waif counted the seams in the quarter-deck, but nothing could induce him to answer the question.

"I have given you a suit of clothes, and I desire to be of service to you."

"I thank you, sir; and a good supper, the best I ever had, though I have often fished with English gentlemen, even with lords and sirs."

"If you will tell me who your friends are —"

"I have no friends, sir."

"You lived on shore, or sailed on the sea, with somebody, I suppose."

Ole looked down, and did not deny the proposition.

"Now, if you will tell me whom you lived with, I may be able to do something for you."

Still the waif was silent.

"Berth No. 72 in the steerage is vacant, and I will give it to you, if I can be sure it is right for me to do so."

But Ole could not, or would not, give any information on this point, though he was earnest in his desire to remain in the ship.

"Very well, Ole; as you will not tell me your story, I shall be obliged to leave you on shore at Christiansand," said the principal, as he walked away.

Dr. Winstock also tried to induce the youth to reveal what he plainly regarded as a secret, but with no different result. Ole passed from the officers to the crew again, and with the latter his answers were like those given to Sanford and his companions. He invented strange explanations, and told wild stories, but not a soul on board was the wiser for anything he said. The waif was permitted to occupy berth No. 72, but was distinctly assured that he must leave the ship when she arrived at Christiansand.

The wind continued light during the night, but at four o'clock in the morning the squadron was off Gunnarshoug Point, and not more than four miles from the land. The shore was fringed with innumerable islands, which made the coast very picturesque, though it was exceedingly barren and desolate. Most of the islands were only bare rocks, the long swells rolling completely over some of the smaller ones. The students on deck watched the early sunrise, and studied the contour of the coast with deep interest, till it became an old story, and then whistled for a breeze to take them along more rapidly towards their port of destination. The fleet was now fully in the Skager Rack, or Sleeve, as it is also called on the British nautical charts.

At eight bells, when, with the forenoon watch, commenced the regular routine of study in the steerage, all the students had seen the Naze, or Lindersnaes, as the Norwegians call it — the southern cape of Norway. It is a reddish headland, beyond which were some hills covered with snow in the spring time. Ole Amundsen remained on deck all day, and had a name for every island and cliff on the coast. He declared that he was competent to pilot the ship into the harbor, for he had often been there. But when the fleet was off Ox-Oe, at the entrance to the port, a regular pilot was taken, at three o'clock in the afternoon. The Josephine and the Tritonia also obtained pilots soon after. The recitations were suspended in order to enable the students to see the harbor.

Ole was wanted to explain the various objects which were presented to the view of the young mariners, but no one had seen him since the pilot came on board. All the habitable parts of the vessel were searched, and the stewards even examined the hold; but he could not be found. Mr. Lowington was anxious to see him, to ascertain whether he had changed his mind in regard to his secret; but Ole had disappeared as strangely as he had come on board of the ship.

CHAPTER III.

AN ACCIDENT TO THE SECOND CUTTER.

THE gentle breeze from the southward enabled the fleet to proceed without delay up the fjord to the town of Christiansand; and, as there was very little ship's duty to be done under such circumstances, the students had an excellent opportunity to examine the islands and the main shore. On board the ship and her two consorts the boys swarmed like bees in the rigging, eagerly watching every new object that was presented to their view. As nautical young gentlemen, they criticised the Norwegian boats and vessels that sailed on the bay, comparing them with those of their own country. The two yachts, which were not restrained by any insurance restrictions, stood boldly up the fjord, following closely in the wake of the two schooners.

The course of the vessels up the fjord was through an archipelago, or "garden of rocks," as it is styled in the Norwegian language. The rocky hills in the vicinity were of a reddish color, with a few fir trees upon them. The country was certainly very picturesque, but the students did not regard it as a very desirable place of residence. The fleet passed between the Island of Dybing and the light on Odderö, and came to anchor in the western harbor. For half an hour the several crews were occupied in furling sails, squaring yards, hauling taut the running rigging, and putting everything in order on board.

The accommodation ladder of the ship, which was a regular flight of stairs, had hardly been rigged before a white barge, pulled by four men, came alongside. The oarsmen were dressed in blue uniform, and wore tarpaulin hats, upon which was painted the word "Grace," indicating the yacht to which they belonged. The bowman fastened his boat-hook to the steps, and the rest of the crew tossed their oars in man-of-war style. In the stern-sheets, whose seats were cushioned with red velvet plush, were three persons, all of whom were old friends of our readers. Captain Paul Kendall, the owner and commander of the Grace, though he is a few inches taller and a few pounds heavier than when we last saw him, was hardly changed in his appearance. Even his side whiskers and mustache did not sensibly alter his looks, for his bright eye and his pleasant smile were still the key to his expression. The Grace carried the American yacht flag, and her commander wore the blue uniform of the club to which he belonged.

Three years before, Paul Kendall had experienced a heavy loss in the death of his mother. She had inherited a very large fortune, which, however, was held in trust for her son, until he reached his majority. At the age of twenty-one, therefore, Paul came to an inheritance bequeathed by his grandfather, which made him a *millionnaire*. His fortune had been carefully invested by the trustees, and now all he had to do was to collect and spend his income, of which there was a considerable accumulation when he attained his majority. Paul was a young man of high moral and religious principle. He had never spent a dollar in dissipation of any kind, and though he knew the world, he was as child-like and innocent as when he was an infant.

His tastes were decidedly nautical, and the first large expenditure from his ample wealth was in the building of the yacht Grace, which was now anchored near the Young America. She was a beautiful craft in every respect, constructed as strong as wood and iron could make her. As her cabin was to be Paul's home during a portion of the year, it was fitted up with every appliance of comfort, convenience, and luxury. It contained a piano, a large library, and every available means of amusement for the hours of a long passage. At the age of twenty-one, Paul was more mature in experience and knowledge than many young men at twenty-five; and hardly had he been placed in possession of his inheritance than he sailed for Europe, and, of course, hastened from Queenstown to Belfast, where Mr. Arbuckle, father of the lady who occupied the stern-sheets of the barge, resided. Six months later he was married to Grace, who still regarded him as "the apple of her eye."

On his return to New York his yacht was finished, though too late in the season for use that year. Her first voyage in the spring was to Brockway, which was the residence of Mr. Lowington, and the headquarters of the Academy Squadron. Learning that his old friend the principal was about to sail for

Europe with his charge, he promptly decided to accompany him, and the Grace was one of the fleet that crossed the Atlantic in April.

Mrs. Kendall was dressed in a plain travelling suit. She was taller and more mature than when she went down the Rhine with the Young Americans, but she was not less beautiful and interesting.

If Fortune had been very kind to Paul Kendall, she had not been so constant to all who formerly sailed in the Young America, and who had then basked in her sunny smile. The third person in the stern-sheets of the barge was Mr. Augustus Pelham. He was a fine-looking fellow, with a heavy mustache, dressed like his commander, in the uniform of the yacht club. By one of those disasters common in American mercantile experience, Pelham's father had suddenly been hurled from apparent affluence to real poverty. Being well advanced in years, he could do nothing better for himself and his family that to accept a situation as secretary of an insurance company, which afforded him a salary only sufficient to enable him to live in comfort. Augustus had completed his course in the Academy ship when the change of circumstances compelled him to abandon all luxurious habits, and work for his own living. This was by no means a calamity to him, any more than to other young men. Doubtless it was annoying to have his allowance of pocket money suddenly stopped, and to find himself face to face with one of the sternest realities of life. His training in the Academy ship had been a blessing to him, for it had reformed his life, and elevated his tastes above the low level of dissipation. It had made a new man of him, besides preparing him for a useful calling. He was competent, so far as nautical skill and knowledge were concerned, to command any vessel to any part of the world, though he lacked the necessary experience in the management of a miscellaneous crew, and in the transaction of business. He was ready to accept a situation as chief or second mate of a ship, when he happened to meet Paul Kendall, and was immediately engaged as chief officer of the Grace, at a salary of one hundred dollars a month. Another ex-student of the ship, Bennington, upon whose father fickle Fortune had not continued to smile, had been appointed second officer. Pelham had shipped the crew of the Grace, and no better set of men ever trod a deck.

The barge came up to the steps, and Paul and Pelham assisted Mrs. Kendall out of the boat, and the three went upon the deck of the ship. Mr. Lowington, who had not seen them, except at a distance, since the fleet sailed from Brockway harbor, gave them a warm greeting, shaking hands heartily with the lady first, and then with her companions.

"I am glad to see you looking so well, Mrs. Kendall," said the principal.

"I have enjoyed myself every moment of the voyage, and have never been sick a single hour," she replied.

"We have had a fine passage, and there was no excuse for an old salt like you to be sick," laughed the principal.

"But I think we shall go on shore, and stay at a hotel a few days, just for a change," added Paul.

"That's a good plan; of course you will see more of the town and the people, than if you remain in your yacht."

"I am sure I like the cabin of the yacht better than any hotel I ever visited," laughed Mrs. Kendall.

"But a change will do you good, my dear," suggested Paul.

"What did you pick up last evening, when you hove to, Mr. Lowington?"

"We picked up a young Norwegian, about sixteen years old," answered the principal, detailing the circumstances under which Ole had been taken on board.

"Where is he now?" asked Paul, looking about him to obtain a sight of the stranger.

"We clothed and fed him, and had become quite interested in him; but just as the pilot came alongside we missed him. I have had the ship searched for him, but we have not been able to find him, though he must be concealed somewhere on board."

"That's strange!" exclaimed Mrs. Kendall, glancing at her husband.

"Perhaps not very strange," continued the principal. "The boy refused to tell us how he came in an open boat, half full of water, and out of sight of land. Probably he has run away from his friends, and has concealed himself to avoid being recognized by the pilot, or other Norwegian people who may come on board. I judged by his appearance that he had some reason for running away from his master or his friends, for he was only half clothed, in the filthiest rags that ever covered a human being."

"I should like a Norwegian in my yacht, to act as interpreter for us," added Paul.

"I intended to keep him for that purpose myself, if I could ascertain who his friends were, and make an arrangement with them, for I will not encourage any boy in running away from his employers. Very likely we shall find him again in the course of the day."

"Very well, sir; if you want him, I will look out for some one on shore," added Paul. "At what time do you pipe to lecture, Mr. Lowington?"

"Not before to-morrow forenoon, at two bells."

"I want to hear the lecture."

"So do I," laughed Mrs. Kendall. "I think it is a capital idea to have a professor tell us all about a country before we attempt to see it. I used to read about the Norsemen, but I have forgotten all about them now, and I want to refresh my memory."

"I wish all our boys had the same view of the matter," said Mr. Lowington.

"We will come on board before nine to-morrow morning, sir," added Paul, as he handed his lady up the steps over the rail.

Descending to the boat, the three oarsmen shoved off, and pulled for the shore, where they landed. The boat had not reached the land, before another barge, the counterpart of the first, and similarly manned, left the Feodora, and pulled alongside the ship. Mr. Robert Shuffles, the owner and commander of the second yacht, assisted his wife up the ladder to the deck of the ship, where they were cordially received by the principal. The yacht Feodora was only six months older than the Grace, for which she had served as the model. Shuffles had not come into possession of any inheritance yet, but his father was as liberal as he was wealthy, and gave his son an annual allowance, which enabled him to marry and keep a yacht. He and Paul had been intimate friends since they were graduated from the Academy ship, and they had made their plans in concert. He had married Lady Feodora a year before, and she had now dropped her aristocratic title, and become a republican lady. Like her husband, she had acquired nautical tastes, and was even more enthusiastic than he in anticipating the pleasures of a yacht cruise up the Baltic, and up the Mediterranean. Shuffles had not been so fortunate as Paul in finding needy graduates of the Academy to officer his yacht, and a fat old shipmaster served as first officer in the Feodora, while the second mate was a young tar, not yet of age. Having paid their respects to the principal, the young couple returned to the boat, and followed Paul to the hotel on shore.

"That's the way to go about Europe," said Sanford, who was sitting on the rail with several of his shipmates.

"What's the way?" asked Stockwell.

"Why, as Kendall and Shuffles do it — in a yacht, with no Latin and geometry to bother their heads, and no decks to wash down on a cold morning."

"That's so; but those fellows were the lambs of the squadron, we are told," laughed Stockwell. "They didn't have black marks; didn't pick upon the professors, and didn't run away from the ship."

"What has all that to do with yachting?" asked Rodman.

"They were good boys, and therefore they have

yachts as their reward," replied Stockwell, laughing.

"Pelham was as good as Shuffles, but he has no yacht, and has to work on a salary for his living."

"He has the fun of it all the same, and Paul Kendall will not overwork him. But I haven't a word to say against them. They were all good fellows, if they were the ship's lambs."

"All the second cutters!" shouted the boatswain's mate, after his pipe had sounded through the ship.

"That means us," said Sanford. "Take your money and pea-jackets, fellows. Something may turn up before we come back."

"Ay, ay," replied Stockwell. "Pass the word to all our fellows."

In a few moments the fourth cutters appeared in the waist, with pea-jackets on their arms, and touched their caps to De Forrest, the fourth lieutenant, who appeared as the officer detailed to go in the boat, which now, as formally, was called the professors' barge, because it was generally appropriated to the use of the instructors. It was pulled by eight oarsmen, and Sanford was the coxswain. The party who had been considering the plan for an independent excursion on shore without incurring the perils and penalties of running away, were the crew of the second cutter. The fact of being together so much in the boat, had united them so that they acted and plotted in concert.

"What are you going to do with those pea-jackets?" asked De Forrest, when he saw their extra clothing.

"It's rather chilly up here in the evening, and we thought we might want them, while we were waiting," replied Sanford.

"I don't think it is very cold, and as to the evening, the sun don't set till about eight o'clock," added the officer, as he went aft to the professors who were going on shore, and reported that the boat was ready; for it had already been lowered into the water, and made fast to the swinging boom.

Her crew went over the side, and seated themselves in the cutter.

"Ready!" said the coxswain, as the stern-sheets of the barge ranged alongside the little stage at the foot of the ladder. "Up oars!"

Up went the eight oars to a perpendicular position, where they were held till the boat should be ready to go.

"I wonder where Ole is," said Sanford.

"Sh!" whispered Stockwell, who pulled the bow oar, shaking his head with energy.

"What do you mean?" demanded the coxswain, in a low tone, for he was very much mystified by the pantomime of the bow oarsman.

"Don't say a word."

"Where is he?" persisted Sanford, who was not willing to have a secret kept from him even for a moment.

Stockwell pointed into the bottom of the boat, and then looked up at the sky, with an affectation of cunning, while the rest of the crew smiled as though they were in possession of the secret. Sanford said no more, and joined the bowman in studying the aspect of the sky. Ole was in the boat to act as guide and interpreter, and if they chose to leave without running away, everything seemed to be favorable to the enterprise. Mr. Mapps and Dr. Winstock presently descended the steps, and seated themselves in the boat, followed by De Forrest.

"All ready, coxswain," said the latter.

"Ready! Let fall!" said Sanford, as he shoved off the stern of the cutter. "Give way — together!"

The well-trained crew bent to their oars, and the boat shot away from the ship towards the shore. Mr. Mapps was going to the town to obtain some additional material for his lecture the following morning, and the surgeon intended to call on Paul Kendall and lady at the hotel.

"This is a very picturesque town, doctor," said Mr. Mapps, as he gazed at the high, rocky steeps which surround Christiansand.

"Very; and I am rather sorry we are not to see more of the environs of the place," replied the surgeon. "I understand we sail to-morrow night."

"I dare say the students will see enough of Norway before they leave it."

"We want to go into the interior," said De Forrest. "There is fine fishing in the streams of Norway."

"Very likely Mr. Lowington will take you into the interior from Christiania," suggested Dr. Winstock.

"I don't exactly see how it is possible to do so," added Mr. Mapps. "The only conveyance of the country is the cariole, which seats but one person — perhaps two boys; and our squadron has nearly two hundred students. I am afraid there are not carioles enough in Christiania to carry the whole of them."

"I think it's too bad we can't have a trial at the salmon," pouted De Forrest.

"Perhaps, if you waited till July, you might catch them," replied Mr. Mapps.

"We should be contented with trout, then."

"I have no doubt Mr. Lowington will do the best he can for you," said Dr. Winstock, as the boat neared the pier.

"In, bows!" called the coxswain; and the two bowmen tossed and boated their oars, taking their stations in the fore-sheets, one of them with the boat-hook in his hand. "Way enough!" added Sanford; and the rest of the crew tossed their oars, and then dropped them upon the thwarts, with a precision which seemed to astonish the group of Norwegians on the wharf, who were observing them.

The two gentlemen landed, and walked up to the town together, leaving the barge to wait for them.

"Part of you may go on shore for half an hour, if you wish, and walk about," said De Forrest to his crew.

"I don't care about going ashore," replied Sanford.

"Nor I either," added Stockwell; and so they all said, very much to the astonishment of the fourth lieutenant, who naturally supposed that boys who had been at sea about four weeks would like to stretch their legs on the solid land for a short time.

"Don't any of you wish to go on shore?" he inquired.

"Not yet," replied Sanford. "If you wish to take a walk, I will push off from the shore, and wait till you return," said Sanford, very respectfully.

"What's up? You won't go on shore, and you wish me to do so!" exclaimed the suspicious officer.

"Nothing, sir," protested Sanford. "We don't intend to run away. We think that is played out."

"If you wanted to do so in this desolate country, I would let you do it, if I were the principal. But you are up to some trick, I know."

"What trick, sir?" demanded the coxswain, innocently.

"I don't know, but it is your next move," replied De Forrest, as he seated himself, and seemed confident of his ability to check any mischief which might be in the minds of his crew. "Shove off, bowman! Up oars! Let fall! Give way together!"

The oarsmen, rather vexed at the turn of events, obeyed the several orders, and the boat was again cutting the still waters of the fjord. All around them were rocks, with several large and small islands in sight. In various places on the rocks were affixed iron rings, to which vessels could make fast in warping out of the bay when the wind was light or foul. A portion of the rock to which they were attached was whitewashed, so that the rings could easily be found, even in the night. To one of these rings, on a small island near Odderö, which commanded a full view of the landing-place, De Forrest directed the coxswain to steer the boat.

"Make fast to that ring," said the officer.

"Ay, ay, sir," replied the bowman.

"Perhaps you would like to land here," added the lieutenant, in a jeering tone, as though he felt that he had checkmated his crew in any evil purpose they entertained. "Whether you do or not, I think I shall stretch my legs on these rocks."

De Forrest leaped from thwart to thwart, and then over the bow upon the island, as though he felt nothing but contempt for the power of the boat's crew to do mischief. He walked up the rough rocks to the summit of the islet, where he paused, and for the first time glanced at his companions, whom he suspected of harboring some design against the peace and dignity of the ship. As he did so, he discovered a steamer, which had just passed through the narrow opening between Odderö and the main land, and whose course lay close to the point of the island where the cutter was moored. He saw that the swash of the steamer was likely to throw the boat on the rocks, and grind her planking upon the sharp points of the island.

"In the boat!" he shouted, lustily. "Shove off!"

Sanford saw the danger which the lieutenant wished to avert, and promptly obeyed the orders.

"Shove off, Stockwell!" he promptly shouted. "Up oars! Stern, all! Give way!"

Stockwell gave a tremendously hard push when he shoved off, and the cutter shot far out upon the still waters; in fact, so far that she was forced directly into the way of the approaching steamer.

THE ACCIDENT TO THE SECOND CUTTER. Page 57.

"Oars!" yelled the coxswain furiously, when he saw that he had overdone the matter. "Hold water! Go ahead! Give way!"

The crew, even in this moment of deadly peril, — for it looked as though, in another instant, they would all be under the wheels of the steamer, — obeyed every command with their wonted precision. But it was a second too late to take the back track. If the boat had continued to back as at first, she would probably have escaped, for the steamer put her helm a-starboard a little, in order to favor her manœuvre. When a collision seemed inevitable, the steamer's bell was rung to stop her, and then to back her.

She struck the cutter; but as her progress had been powerfully checked, the blow did not carry her under, though it stove in the side of the boat. The water poured in through the broken broadside, and the crew sprang for their lives. They leaped upon the guys and bob-stays of the steamer, and were hauled in by the people on the bow.

"Come out of there, Ole," said Stockwell, as he pulled the boat's sail from the extended form of the waif, who was concealed in the bottom of the boat.

Ole lost not a moment in following the example of his companions. As the steamer's headway had now been entirely checked, Stockwell held the wrecked cutter in her position, while Rodman passed the pea-jackets up to the forecastle of the steamer. Having done this, they abandoned the boat, and followed the example of their companions. No one was drowned, or even wet above his knees, for the steamer had struck the boat just hard enough to stave in her side, without carrying her under.

The Norwegians hooked up the boat's painter, and taking it in tow, proceeded on her course; for the captain — as interpreted by Ole — declared that his boat carried the mail, and he could not wait for anything.

CHAPTER IV.

NORWAY IN THE PAST AND THE PRESENT.

"CLEAR away the first cutter!" shouted the first lieutenant of the Young America, from whose deck the catastrophe to the second cutter had been observed,

"All the first cutters!" piped the boatswain, with an energy inspired by the stirring occasion.

"That was very carelessly done," said Mr. Lowington, whose attention had been called to the scene.

"The steamer ran within a couple of rods of the island," added Captain Cumberland. "I saw the fourth lieutenant order the boat to shove off; I suppose he did it to prevent the swash of the steamer from grinding the cutter on the rocks."

"What is he doing among those rocks?" asked the principal.

"I don't know, sir. He landed Mr. Mapps and the doctor, and was ordered to wait for them. I don't see why he went over to that island."

The second lieutenant was directed to take charge of the first cutter; Peaks, the adult boatswain, and Bitts, the carpenter, were ordered to go also, to render any assistance which might be required in succoring the stove boat. The cutter shoved off, her twelve oars struck the water together, and the crew gave way with an energy which caused their oars to bend like twigs, while the barge leaped through the water as though it was some monster of the deep goaded to his utmost to escape the wrath of a more potent pursuer.

"With a will, my lads!" shouted the coxswain. "Steady! Keep the stroke, but use your muscle!"

"There's a job for you, Bitts," said the boatswain, as the Norwegian took the second cutter in tow.

"And a heavy job it will be, too," replied Bitts. "I wonder there is anything left of the boat."

"The steamer stopped her wheels, and backed some time before she struck, or there would not have been much left of the boat, or her crew," added Peaks. "Thank God, the boys are all safe."

"It's a lucky escape for them."

"So it was; and we needn't say anything about the boat."

"The steamer is going ahead," said the carpenter.

"No matter for that, so long as the boys are all safe," replied Peaks.

The people in the steamer seemed to take no notice of the first cutter, appearing not to understand that it had come out for the wrecked crew. But as the boat pulled towards her, she cast off the cutter in tow.

"Steamer, ahoy!" shouted Norwood, the second lieutenant, as he saw the cutter cast adrift.

She made no reply, but hoisted a flag, on which appeared the word "Post," with something else which none in the first cutter could understand.

"She's a mail boat," said the boatswain; "and I suppose she intends to say she is in a hurry."

"Does she mean to carry off the crew of that boat?" demanded the second lieutenant, not a little vexed at the conduct of the Norwegians.

"She will not carry them far," suggested Dunlap, the coxswain.

"She may take them to Bergen."

"I think not, sir. If she is a mail steamer, she stops at all the ports on the coast. I don't think she will carry them far. Very likely they will be sent back, on some other steamer, before night," added Dunlap, who had studied the coast of Norway more carefully than the lieutenant in command.

"First cutter, ahoy!" shouted De Forrest, on the island.

"On shore!" replied Norwood. "We can't catch the steamer — that is certain; steer for the island, coxswain."

The first cutter ran up to the rocky island, and as soon as the bow touched the rocks, De Forrest leaped into the fore-sheets. He was nervous and excited, feeling, perhaps, that he had failed in his duty, and was, therefore, responsible for the accident to the second cutter. From feeling that he had circumvented his crew in carrying out some unexplained trick, he realized that he had led them into a trap, from which they had narrowly escaped with their lives.

"What are you doing on this island, De Forrest?" asked Norwood, as the discomfited officer took his place in the stern-sheets, and the boat shoved off again.

The second lieutenant declared that he had come over

to the island to prevent his crew from running away, or from carrying out some trick whose existence he suspected, but whose nature he could not comprehend.

"Sanford wanted I should go ashore at the town, and offered to look out for the crew while I did so," he continued. "Of course I wouldn't leave my crew: but I told them that half of them might go on shore and take a walk. None of them wanted to go, and then I was satisfied they were up to something. I went on the island for the sole purpose of watching them. I wanted to know what their plan was."

"Well, what did you discover?"

"Nothing at all. I saw that steamer coming, and I ordered Sanford to shove off, so that her swash should not damage the boat."

"I don't believe they intended to play any trick," added Norwood. "You are too suspicious, De Forrest."

"Perhaps I am; but fellows that have been at sea for a month are rather glad of a chance to stretch their legs on shore. They wouldn't do so, when I told them they might; and I don't believe such a thing was ever heard of before. Besides, they all looked as though they were up to something, and just as though they had a big secret in their heads."

"Perhaps you were right, but I don't believe you were," said Norwood, too bluntly for good manners, and too bluntly for the harmony of the officers' mess.

"I suppose I am responsible for the smashing of the second cutter, but I was trying to do my duty," replied De Forrest, vexed at the implied censure of his superior.

"If you had staid at the pier this could not have happened."

"But something else might have happened; and if my crew had run away, I should have been blamed just as much," growled the second lieutenant.

"You were too sharp for your own good — that is all. But I don't mean to blame you, De Forrest," said Norwood, with a patronizing smile. "Perhaps I should have done the same thing if I had been in your place."

"Stand by to lay on your oars!" shouted the coxswain, as the boat approached the water-logged second cutter. "Oars!"

The crew stopped pulling, and levelled their oars.

"In, bows! Stand by the boat-hooks!" continued the coxswain; and the two forward oarsmen grasped the boat-hooks, and took their station in the fore-sheets. "Hold water." And the ten oars dropped into the water as one, checking the onward progress of the cutter.

The bowmen fastened to the second cutter, and recovering her painter, passed it astern to the coxswain, who made it fast to a ring on the stern-board. By this time the steamer, with the luckless crew of the stove boat, had disappeared behind an island. The first cutter pulled back to the ship, and De Forrest immediately reported to the first lieutenant, and explained his conduct in presence of the principal and the captain. He detailed his reasons for supposing his crew intended to run away, or to play some trick upon him.

"I think you have done all that a careful and vigilant officer could, De Forrest; and so far as I can see, you are free from blame," replied Mr. Lowington.

The fourth lieutenant glanced at Norwood.

"Just what I said," added the latter, in a low tone.

"If you made any mistake, it was in leaving your boat at the island," continued the principal.

"Just exactly my sentiments," whispered Norwood. "I don't blame the fourth lieutenant, but I shouldn't have done just as he did."

"Where is that steamer bound?" asked Mr. Lowington of the pilot, who had not yet left the ship, and was really waiting to be invited to supper.

"To Christiania, sir," replied the pilot, who, like all of his class on the coast of Norway, spoke a little English.

"Where does she stop next?"

"At Lillesand."

"How far is that?"

"About two miles."

"Two miles! Why, it is farther than that to the sea," exclaimed Mr. Lowington.

"He means Norwegian miles," suggested one of the instructors, who was listening with interest to the conversation.

"True; I did not think of that. A Norwegian mile is about seven English miles. It is fourteen miles, then, to Lillesand."

With the assistance of Professor Badois, who acted as interpreter, the pilot explained that the steamer which had just left was several hours late, and would go that night to Frederiksværn, where the steamers from Bergen and Christiania made connections with the boat for Gottenburg and Copenhagen. The Christiania steamer would reach Christiansand the next evening, and the boys who had been carried away could return in her.

"Why did she carry them off? It would not have taken five minutes to land them," added the principal.

"She was very late, and her passengers for Gottenburg and Copenhagen would lose the steamer at Frederiksværn if she does not arrive in season," the pilot explained through Professor Badois.

But Mr. Lowington was so grateful that the crew of the second cutter had all escaped with their lives, that he was not disposed to be very critical over the conduct of the Norwegian steamer. The boys were safe, and would return the next night at farthest. The accident was talked about, during the rest of the day, on board of all the vessels of the squadron. The officers and seamen on board of the ship had witnessed the accident, and had seen all the crew of the second cutter go over the bows of the steamer. They had not observed, in the excitement of the moment, that ten, instead of nine, had left the wrecked boat; and as Ole Amundsen was dressed precisely like the crew, his presence in the cutter was not even suspected.

The first cutter was sent to the town for Dr. Winstock and Mr. Mapps, and in an hour or two the excitement had entirely subsided. The routine of the ship went on as before, and as there was little work to be done, the absentees were hardly missed.

At half past eight the next morning, the signal, "All hands, attend lecture," was flying on board of the

Young America. The boats from the Josephine and the Tritonia came alongside the ship, bringing all the officers and crews of those vessels. Paul Kendall and lady, and their friends, were brought off from the shore; Shuffles and his wife also appeared, and a further delegation from each of the yachts asked admission to the ship to hear the lecture, or rather to attend the exercise in geography and history, for the occasion was even less formal than on the first cruise of the ship. The steerage was crowded, after the boatswain had piped the call, and Mr. Mapps was doubtless duly flattered by the number of his audience. On the foremast hung a large map of Sweden and Norway.

"If you please, young gentlemen, we will begin with Scandinavia," said the professor, taking his place near the foremast, with the pointer in his hand. What was Scandinavia?"

"The ancient name of Norway, Sweden, and Denmark," replied one of the students.

"The barbarous tribes from the northern part of Europe at different times invaded the southern sections, conquering various other tribes, occupying their territory, and thus mingling with all the people from whom originated the present nations of Europe. Thus, in remote ages, the Scandinavians, among others, by their conquests and their emigration, have contributed largely to the modern elements of society. With this explanation we will look at Scandinavia in detail, beginning with Norway. Between what degrees of latitude does it lie?"

"Between forty and ninety," replied an enthusiastic youth.

"True — quite right; and a safe answer. If you had said between one and ninety, the answer would have been just as good for any other country as for Norway. I would like to have the jacket fit a little closer."

"Between fifty-eight and seventy-one, north," answered one who was better posted.

"Exactly right; about the same latitude as Greenland, and our newly-acquired Alaska. Our ship is anchored in the same parallel as the northern part of Labrador, and one degree south of the southern point of Greenland. But it is not as ' cold as Greenland, here,' the temperature being some twelve degrees milder, because the warm waters of the Gulf Stream are discharged upon its shores. You know its boundaries. It is one thousand and eighty miles from the Naze to the North Cape, and varies from forty to two hundred and seventy miles in width. How many square miles has it?"

"One hundred and twenty-three thousand square miles."

"Or a little larger than the six New England States, New York, and New Jersey united. The country is mountainous, and abounds in picturesque scenery. Precipices, cataracts, and rushing torrents are very numerous in the central and northern parts. The Vöringfos is a waterfall, and the Rjukanfos, near the central part, are cataracts of about nine hundred feet perpendicular descent; but of course the volume of water is not very large. The highest mountains are between eight and nine thousand feet high. Norway has an abundance of rivers, but none of them are very long. The coast, as you have seen, is fringed with islands, which, with the numerous indentations, form a vast number of bays, straits, channels, and sounds, which are called *fjords* here. One of the principal of these is Christiania Fjord, which you will ascend in a few days. The country also abounds in lakes, which, as in most mountainous regions, are very narrow, being simply the widenings of the rivers. The largest of these is Miösen Lake, fifty-five miles long, and from one to twelve wide.

"The soil is not very good, and the Norwegians are not progressive farmers. They cling to the methods of their sires, and modern improvements find but little favor among them. The winter is long, and the summer short; but by a provision of provident nature, the crops mature more rapidly than in some of the southern climes, as grain has been reaped six weeks after it was sowed. The principal crops are the grains; but the supply is not equal to the demand, and considerable importations are received from Denmark and Russia. In the south the farmers devote themselves to stock-raising, while in the north the Lapps derive nearly all the comforts of life from the reindeer, the care of which is their chief industry.

"The extensive product of pine and fir have created a vast trade in lumber, which constitutes three fourths of the exports to the United Kingdom, and a considerable portion of the inhabitants in the wooded districts are employed in cutting, sawing, and sending to market the wealth of the forests. Next in importance to this are the fisheries, which yield about five million dollars a year. Cod, haddock, and herring are cured for exportation, and are an important source of revenue. Besides these, the roe of the cod is sent to France, Italy, and Spain, as bait for sardines. Norway supplies London with lobsters. Norway iron, as well as Swedish, is very celebrated; but the mines are poorly managed, as are those of copper and silver.

"The kingdom of Norway is divided into eighteen provinces, which are called Amts. Its population, in 1865, was one million seven hundred thousand, showing an increase of about two hundred thousand in ten years. The government is a constitutional monarchy."

"I thought it was a part of Sweden," said one of the students.

"Not at all. The King of Sweden is also the King of Norway; but each country has its own independent and separate government. Each has its own legislature, makes its own laws, and raises and expends its own revenues. The king exercises his functions as ruler over both kingdoms through a council of state, composed of an equal number of Swedes and Norwegians, whose duty it is to advise the sovereign, and, in accordance with a peculiar feature of monarchy, to take the responsibility when any blunder is made; for "the king can do no wrong." If anything is wrong, some one else did it. Having the same king, who rules over each nation separately, is the only connection between Norway and Sweden. The former pays about one hundred and twenty thousand dollars of his civil list, and he is obliged to reside in Norway during a small portion of each year.

"The constitution of Norway is one of the most democratic in Europe. The legislative and part of the executive power is vested in the Storthing, which means the 'great court,' composed of the representatives of the people. The king has but little power, though he has a limited veto upon the acts passed by the legislative body. He can create no order of nobility, or grant any titles or dignities. The members of the Storthing are elected indirectly by the people; and when they assemble, they divide themselves into two houses, corresponding to our Senate and House of Representatives. All acts must pass both chambers, and in case of disagreement, the two bodies come together, and discuss the subject.

"The religion of Norway is Lutheran, and few of any other sect are to be found; formerly, no other was tolerated, but now religious freedom prevails, though Jesuits and monks of any order are sternly excluded. The clergy, who are generally very well educated, have an average income of about a thousand dollars a year, and I think are better paid than even in our own country. The people are well instructed, and one who cannot read and write is seldom found.

"The early history of Norway is that of most of the countries of Europe — a powerful chief subjugated his neighbors, and united the tribes into a nation. Harold the Fair-haired, whose father had conquered the southern part of the country, fell in love with Gyda, the daughter of a petty king, who refused to wed him till he had absolute sway over the entire country. Pleased with the lady's spirit, he vowed never to cut or comb his hair till all Norway lay at his feet. It appears that he eventually had occasion for his barber's services, and wedded the lady. This was in the ninth century; and the victories of Harold drove many of the Norsemen, or Northmen, to seek their fortunes in other lands. They discovered and colonized Greenland and Iceland, and even established settlements on the continental portion of North America. Traces of them have been found on the Gulf of St. Lawrence, and some claim that they founded settlements farther south. They figure largely in the early history of England and Scotland, and even carried their piratical arms into Russia, Flanders, France, Italy, and other territories.

"A son of Harold, who had been educated in England, brought Christianity into Norway; but it was three centuries before the new faith had established itself. Like the Hindoos, Greeks, and Romans, the ancient Scandinavians had a mythology, upon which their religion was based. They believed that in the beginning all was chaos, in which was a fountain that sent forth twelve rivers. These streams flowed so far from their source that the waters froze, and the ice, defying the modern law of nature, sank till the fathomless deep was filled up. Far south of the world of mist, in which this miracle was wrought, was a world of fire and light, whence proceeded a hot wind that melted the ice, from the drops of which came the ice-giant, whose name was Ymir, and from whom proceeded a race of ice-giants. From the wedding of the ice and heat of the two extremes of the world came a cow, from which ran four streams of milk, the food of the ice-giants. While this wonderful beast was licking the salt stones in the ice, which formed her diet, a quantity of human hair grew out of them, and the next day a human head was developed, and then appeared a whole man. Bör, the son of this man, married a daughter of one of the ice-giants, and they had three children, the oldest of whom was Odin, who became the rulers of heaven and earth, because they were all good, while the children of Ymir, the ice-giant, were evil. Then, as now, the Good and the Evil were at war. Finally the ice-giant was slain, and being thrown into space, the world was created from his body; his blood forming the sea and the rivers; his flesh the earth; his hair the grass; his bones the rocks; his teeth and broken jaws the stones; and of his head the heavens, at the four ends of which were placed four dwarfs, called North, South, East, and West. Of this giant's brains, thrown into the air, they formed the clouds, while of the sparks from the land of fire were made the stars.

"As the sons of Bör, who, you must remember, were the gods of heaven and earth, were walking on the shore of the sea, they discovered two blocks, whereof they created a man and a woman. Odin gave them life and souls, while his brothers endowed them with other human faculties and powers. Odin was the Jupiter, the chief, of the northern gods. He is the god of song and of war, and was the inventor of the Runic characters, or alphabet. He was the ruler of Valhalla, the home of heroes slain in battle. There is much more that is curious and interesting in the mythology of the Scandinavians, which I must ask you to read for yourselves.

"Olaf II. propagated Christianity with fire and sword. He demolished the temples of paganism, and founded Trondhjem, or Drontheim, as it is called on our maps. His successor, St. Olaf, followed his example, till his cruelty excited a rebellion, and Canute the Great, of Denmark, landing in Norway, was elected king. Olaf fled into Sweden, where he organized an army, and attempted to recover his throne; but he was defeated and slain in a battle near Trondhjem. His body was found, a few years later, in a perfect state of preservation, which was regarded as a miracle, and Olaf was canonized as a saint. His remains are said to have wrought many miracles, and up to the time of the Reformation, thousands of pilgrims annually visited his shrine at Trondhjem. Even in London churches were dedicated to this saint.

"Canute gave Norway to his son Sweyn, who, upon the death of his father, was dispossessed of the throne by Magnus I., the son of St. Olaf. He was succeeded by Harold III., a great warrior, who founded Osloe, now Christiania. After Olaf III. and Magnus III. came Sigurd, who, in 1107, made a pilgrimage of four years to Jerusalem, with a fleet of sixty vessels, and distinguished himself in the holy wars. His death was followed by civil dissensions, until Hako IV. obtained the throne. He lost his life in an attempt to retain the Hebrides Islands, claimed by Scotland. Then war with Denmark, the monopoly of trade by the Hanse towns, and a fearful plague, which depopulated whole sections, produced a decline in the national prosperity of Norway. Hako VI., who died in 1380, had married the daughter of the King of Denmark, and the crown of Norway descended to his son, Olaf III., of Denmark, in whom the sovereignties of Norway and Denmark were united. Olaf was succeeded by his mother Margaret, celebrated in history as 'the Semiramis of the North.' She conquered Sweden, and annexed it to her own dominions. By the 'Union of Calmar,' signed by the principal nobles and prelates of the three Scandinavian kingdoms, the three crowns were united in one person, the subjects of each to have equal rights. This compact was disregarded, and Norway was hopelessly oppressed by the ruler. The Union, however, continued till 1623; but Norway was subject to Denmark till 1814.

"When the allied powers of Europe, which were engaged in putting down the first Napoleon, rearranged the map of Europe, the destiny of Norway was changed. Russia wanted Finland, and she offered Norway in compensation for it to Sweden, with the further condition that Bernadotte should join the allies. He accepted the terms, and the King of Denmark was compelled, by force of arms, to cede Norway to Sweden. The Norwegians would not submit to the change, and declared their independence. Prince Christian, of Denmark, who was then governor general of Norway, called a convention of the people at Eidsvold, and a new constitution was framed, and the prince elected King of Norway. Bernadotte invaded Norway with a Swedish army, while the allies blockaded the coast. Resistance was hopeless, and as Sweden offered favorable terms, Christian abdicated, and an arrangement was immediately effected. The constitution was accepted by the king, and Norway became an independent nation, united to Sweden under one king. Bernadotte became King of Sweden and Norway under the title of Charles XIV., John. He refused the Norwegians a separate national flag; but when he attempted to alter the constitution to suit his own views, the Storthing resolutely and successfully resisted his interference. This body abolished titles of nobility — an act which the king vetoed; but three successive Storthings passed the law, and thus, by the constitution, made it valid in spite of the veto. The Norwegians were not to be intimidated even by the appearance of a military force, and have ever been jealous to the last degree of their rights and privileges as a nation.

"Bernadotte was succeeded by his son Oscar I., who gave the Norwegians a separate national flag; and he flattered the vanity of the people by allowing himself to be styled the 'King of Norway and Sweden' in all public acts relating to Norway, instead of 'Sweden and Norway.' In 1859, Oscar was succeeded by his son Charles XV., who is now the King of Sweden and Norway. In the history of Denmark and Sweden, more will be said of this kingdom.

"In French, Norway is *Norvège;* in German, *Norwegen;* in Spanish, *Noruega;* and *Norge* in the Scandinavian languages. Now, I dare say you would like to visit the shore."

The professor closed his remarks, and the several boatswains piped away their crews.

CHAPTER V.

MR. CLYDE BLACKLOCK AND MOTHER.

BELONGING to the squadron were fourteen boats, ranging from the twelve-oar barge down to the four-oar cutter. In the waters of Brockway harbor, rowing had been the principal exercise of the students, though the daily evolutions in seamanship were well calculated to develop the muscles and harden the frame. They had been carefully trained in the art, and, enjoying the amusement which it afforded, they were apt scholars. As the safety of the squadron and the saving of life at sea might often depend upon the skill with which the boats were handled, the principal devoted a great deal of attention to this branch of nautical education. To give an additional zest to the exercise, he had occasionally offered prizes at the boat-races which the students were encouraged to pull; and the first cutter was now in possession of a beautiful silk flag, won by the power of the crew in rowing.

Every boy in the squadron was a swimmer. In the summer season this accomplishment had been taught as an art, an hour being devoted to the lesson every day, if the weather was suitable. Cleats, the adult boatswain of the Josephine, was the "professor" of the art, having been selected for the responsible position on account of his remarkable skill as a swimmer. The boys were trained in diving, floating, swimming under water, and taught to perform various evolutions. Not alone in the tranquil bay were they educated to the life of the fishes, but also in the surf, and among the great waves. They were taught to get into a boat from the water in a heavy sea. A worn-out old longboat had done duty during the preceding summer as a wreck, in order to familiarize the students with the possibilities of their future experience. It was so prepared that a portion of its planking could be suddenly knocked out, and the boat almost instantly filled with water; and the problem was, to meet this emergency in the best manner. Other boats were at hand in case of a real accident, or if any naturally timid fellow lost his presence of mind. While the "wreck," as the practice boat was called, was moving along over the waves, pulled by half a dozen boys, Cleats, without warning or notice of his intention, opened the aperture near her keel. Sometimes she was loaded with stones, so that she went to the bottom like a rock, though this part of the programme was always carried out on a beach, where the receding tide would enable the professor to recover the boat. The crew were then to save themselves by swimming ashore, or to another boat. Sometimes, also, the "wreck" was loaded with broken spars, pieces of board, and bits of rope; and the problem was for the crew to construct a raft in the water, often in a rough sea. All these exercises, and many others, were heartily enjoyed by the boys, and a ringing cheer always announced the safety of a crew, either on the shore, in a boat, or on the raft.

Many persons, and even those who are tolerable swimmers, have been drowned simply by the loss of their presence of mind. The dashing of the waves, or the great distance of the land or other place of safety, intimidates them, and they are unable to use their powers. But the students of the squadron were gradually and carefully accustomed to the water, so that they could swim a reasonable distance without wearing themselves out, could rest their limbs by floating, and were taught to avail themselves of any expedient to secure their safety. If a boat was stove on the rocks in a surf, or was run down by a vessel, the fact of being in the water did not frighten them out of their wits, for they had been trained to feel quite at home, as in their native element. They were actually drilled to confront danger in every imaginable form. But a gentle and timid boy was not pitched into the water, even after he had learned to swim. His constitutional shrinking was slowly and skilfully overcome, so that even the most delicate — though but few such ever found their way into the ranks of the squadron — took to the water as a pastime. Of course the degree of proficiency in the art of swimming, and of the acquired ability to meet danger in the water, differed very widely in different boys; but all were accustomed to the waves, and, in a measure, to leading the life of a duck or a fish.

The crews of the several boats piped over the side, and took their places, the rest of the students being distributed in the barges and cutters, till only the adult officers remained in the ship. Each one, as it was loaded, pulled off, and took its station in the order in which the boat squadron usually moved. The com modore's barge and the ship's first cutter, each twelve oars, led the van, while the other boats came in four ranks of three each. All the boats carried the American flag at the stern, and each one had its number at the bow. All the Young America's boats had their numbers on a white, the Josephine's on a green, and the Tritonia's on a blue flag.

The tactics of the boat squadron were many and various, which had been adopted more to give interest to the exercise than for any inherent utility. These movements were regulated by signals from the commodore's barge. Mr. Lowington had decided to make an excursion among the islands in the Fjord before dinner, and visit the town in the afternoon. A pilot was put in the commodore's barge, and Captain Cumberland, as acting flag officer, was in command of the squadron. The principal and Professor Badois were passengers in his barge.

The cutters were formed in their usual array, and the two boats from the yachts brought up the rear. The signal officer, who was a quartermaster from the ship, at the order of the captain, elevated the white flag crossed with red, with which all the signals were made. The coxswains of the several boats could see this flag, while the oarsmen could not, being back to the barge, and not allowed to look behind them.

"Oars!" said each coxswain, as soon as the signal appeared.

At this command the several crews, who had been laying on their oars, prepared for the stroke. The signal officer dropped the flag to the port side of the barge.

"Give way!" added each coxswain; and the boat squadron moved off.

In order to keep the lines full, the larger quarter boat of the Grace had been borrowed and manned, and now took the place of the second cutter, which had been stove, and upon which the three carpenters of the squadron were now at work, making the necessary repairs. The fleet made a splendid appearance, with the flags flying, and with the officers and crews in their best uniforms. The people on the shore, and on board of the various vessels in the harbor, gathered to see the brilliant array. The crew of an English steamer cheered lustily, and the lady passengers waved their handkerchiefs. Suddenly the signal on the commodore's barge went up again.

"Stand by to toss!" said the several coxswains, as the fleet of boats came abreast of the steamer, which was the Orlando, bound from Hull to Christiania.

The signal went down to the port side.

"Toss!" continued the coxswains, only loud enough to be heard by the crews, for they had been taught that the unnecessary screaming of orders makes an officer seem ridiculous, and injures the effect of the manœuvre.

At the word every oar went up, and was held perpendicularly in the air with the left hand. A bugle blast from the barge at this moment brought every student to his feet, with his right hand to his cap.

"One!" said the coxswain of each boat, at a dip of the signal flag.

A rousing cheer, accompanied by a swing of the cap, followed, and was twice repeated, making up the complement of the three cheers, in return for the salutations of the steamer's people. Her crew returned the compliment in like manner. At another blast of the bugle, the crews were seated with their oars still up. Again the signal in the barge was elevated.

"Stand by!" said the coxswains, which was only a warning to be ready.

The flag dropped to port.

"Let fall!" added the coxswain; and all the oars dropped into the water together, while the flag was again elevated. "Give way!" and the stroke was resumed.

The passengers of the Orlando clapped their hands vigorously, as they witnessed the perfection of the movements. The fleet proceeded up the bay towards the west front of the town, where a considerable collection of people had assembled to witness the novel parade. The barge led the way to the extreme west of the bay, where the signal flag was again exhibited, and then swung first to the port and then to the starboard. This was the signal for coming into single line, and the coxswain of each boat gave the orders necessary to bring it into range. It was so managed that each boat came into the new order as it turned to pass in front of the town; so that they proceeded in a single line before the people, but not more than twenty feet apart. Once more the signal flag appeared, with a double motion upwards.

"Stand by to lay on your oars!" said the coxswains. "Oars!" they continued, as the flag swung down to starboard. "Hold water!".

These orders soon brought the boats to a stand. The signal flag moved in a horizontal circle.

"Pull, starboard; back, port. Give way!" continued the coxswains; and the effect of this evolution was to turn the boats as on a pivot. "Oars!" and the crew ceased pulling, with their oars all on a level, and the blades feathered.

The boats had been turned half round, and each coxswain aligned his own by the barge on the right. In this position three cheers were given in compliment to the people on the shore, though the Norwegians seemed to be too dull and heavy to comprehend the nature of the movement. The boats swung again, and continued on their way, in single line, through the narrow passage between Odderö and the main land. Under the direction of the native pilot, the barge led the way among the islands, affording the students an opportunity to see the shores. When the fleet came into the broad channel, the order was resumed, as at first, and after various manœuvres, it was dismissed, each boat returning to the vessel to which it belonged.

The appearance of the fleet, including the two beautiful yachts, and the evolutions of the boats, had created a decided sensation on board of the Orlando, which was crowded with passengers, most of them tourists on their way to the interior of Norway. The crews of the several vessels piped to dinner as soon as they returned from the excursion; but the meal was hardly finished before visitors from the steamer began to arrive, and the boatmen in the harbor made a good harvest on the occasion. Among those who came to the ship was an elegantly dressed lady, with her son and daughter, attended by a servant man in livery. Mrs. Garberry Blacklock was duly presented to the principal by one of the gentlemen who had introduced himself. She was evidently a very fine lady; for she was "distinguished" in her manners as well as in her dress. And her son, Clyde Blacklock, was as evidently a very fine young gentleman, though he was only fourteen years of age. It is doubtful whether Miss Celia Blacklock could be regarded as a very fine young lady, for she appeared to be very pretty, and very modest and retiring, with but a very moderate estimate of her own importance.

For the tenth time Mr. Lowington briefly explained the nature of the institution over which he presided; and the fine lady listened with languishing *ennui*.

"But it is a very rough life for young gentlemen," suggested Mrs. Blacklock. "I should fancy they would become very, *very* rude."

"Not necessarily," replied the principal. "We intend that the students shall behave like gentlemen, and we think the discipline of the ship has a tendency to promote good manners."

"They must live like sailors, and sailors are very, *very* rude."

"Not necessarily, madam. There is nothing in the occupation itself that — "

"But I wish to know what the fellows do," interposed Mr. Clyde Blacklock.

"There is nothing in the occupation itself that begets rudeness," added Mr. Lowington, giving no attention to the young gentleman, who had so impolitely broken in upon the conversation of his elders. "I see no reason why a young man cannot be a gentleman in a ship as well as on shore."

"I dare say you have sailors to do the dirty work."

"No, madam; our students do all the work."

"Do they put their own fingers into the pitch and the tar?" inquired the lady, with a curl of the lip which indicated her horror.

"Certainly; but we think pitch and tar are not half so defiling as evil thoughts and bad manners."

"They are very, *very* disagreeable. The odor of tar and pitch is intolerable."

"We do not find it so, for —"

"I say, I wish to know what the fellows do."

"We are accustomed to the odor of them," continued the principal. "To some people the scent of musk, and even otto of roses, is not pleasant; and, for my part, I rather enjoy that of tar and pitch."

"That is very, *very* singular. But Clyde desires to know what the young gentlemen do," added the lady, glancing at her son, behind whom stood the man in livery, as though he were the boy's exclusive property."

"They have a regular routine of study," replied Mr. Lowington, addressing the lady, and declining even to glance at the original inquirer, for the rudeness of Mr. Clyde in interrupting the conversation seemed to merit a rebuke. "They attend to the studies usually pursued in the highest class of academies, including the modern languages and navigation, the latter being a speciality in the course."

"I don't care what they study," said Clyde. "What do they do in the ship?"

"We prepare boys for college, and beyond that pursue a regular college course, so far as our facilities will permit. Our students have the advantage of travel; for, in the present cruise, we shall visit all the principal nations of Europe."

"What do they do in the ship?"

"Clyde desires to know what the boys do in the ship," added the lady.

"They learn good manners, for the first thing, madam. There are fifteen officers in this vessel, and nine in each of the others. They are all students, who take their rank according to their merit. The best scholar in each is the captain, and so on."

"Does the captain manage the ship?" asked Clyde.

"Certainly."

"I should like to be the captain," exclaimed the young gentleman.

"Do you think you could manage the ship?" asked his mother, with a smile which expressed the pride she felt in the towering ambition of her son.

"I could, if any fellow could."

"Clyde is very fond of the sea; indeed, he worries me sadly by his adventurous spirit," said his mother.

"I think it would do him good to go to sea," added the principal, rather dryly.

"The students made a beautiful appearance in their boats to-day," continued Mrs. Blacklock. "It was really very, *very* wonderful."

"They handle the boats very well indeed, but their skill was only acquired by long and careful training. As we have a considerable number of visitors on board, madam, we will show you a little seamanship.

Captain Cumberland," he added, turning to the young commander, who had been making himself agreeable to Miss Celia Blacklock.

The captain asked the young lady to excuse him, and stepping up to the principal, bowed gracefully, and raised his cap.

"He's a regular swell," said Clyde to his man.

"He's a young gentleman as is highly polished, which these naval officers is generally," replied Jeems.

Mr. Lowington directed the captain to call all hands, and go through the evolutions of loosing and furling, for the gratification of the guests of the ship. Captain Cumberland bowed and raised his cap again as he retired, and the principal hoped that Clyde would take a lesson in good manners from him.

"Will you walk to the quarter-deck, Miss Blacklock," said the captain, touching his cap to the young lady, to whom he had been formally introduced by the principal. "We are going to loose and furl, and you can see better there than here."

"With pleasure," replied Miss Celia. "But what did you say you were going to do?"

"Loose and furl the sails," replied the captain, as he conducted the fair miss to the quarter-deck, where they were followed by Mr. Lowington and the rest of the party.

"Mr. Judson," said the commander.

"Here, sir," replied the first lieutenant.

"Call all hands to loose and furl."

"All hands, sir," responded Judson, touching his cap to his superior, as all on board were required to do.

"They are all swells," said Clyde to his man.

"All hands, loose sails!" shouted the boatswain, as he blew the proper blast on his whistle.

In a few moments every officer and seaman was at his station for the manœuvre indicated by the call. The students, aware that they were simply to "show off," were fully determined to astonish the wondering crowd on the decks.

"Stand by to lay aloft, the ready-men!" shouted the first lieutenant, as he received the order from the captain.

It was repeated by the second lieutenant on the forecastle, the third in the waist, and the fourth on the quarter-deck.

"All ready, sir!" reported the several officers.

"Lay aloft!"

At the command those whose duty it was to prepare the sails and rigging for the manœuvre sprang up the rigging, and in three minutes the midshipman aloft reported that all was ready.

"Lay aloft, sail-loosers!" continued the first lieutenant.

The seamen, who were arranged in proper order on deck, the royal yard men first, then those who belonged on the top-gallant yards, the topsail, and the lower yards, placed in succession, so that each could reach his station without passing others, leaped into the rigging, and went up like so many cats.

"Man the boom tricing-lines!"

These are ropes by which the studding-sail booms, which lie on the yards, are hauled up out of the way.

"Trice up!"

The studding-sail booms were drawn up.

"Lay out! Loose sails!"

The hands jumped upon the foot-ropes, and worked themselves out to their places on the yards, where they loosed the sails, overhauled the rigging, and made everything ready for the final evolution. The midshipman in the tops reported to the officers on deck when the preparations were completed, and the lieutenants on deck, in their turn, reported to the first lieutenant.

"Let fall!" said the executive officer; and all, as one, the sails dropped from the yards.

The precision of the movement called forth a demonstration of applause from the visitors. Mr. Clyde Blacklock stood with his mouth open, looking up at the students on the yards, but occasionally glancing at the "swellish" first lieutenant, who seemed to be the master-spirit of the occasion, because he spoke in a loud voice, while the captain, who really controlled the evolutions, could hardly be heard, except by the executive officer, to whom alone his order was given.

"Lay in! Lay down from aloft!" said the first lieutenant; and in a moment more all hands were on deck again.

"Do you ever man the yards, sir?" asked a gentleman of the principal.

"Occasionally, sir — not often. You are aware that it requires some preparation, for we are obliged to extend life-lines over the yards," replied Mr. Lowington. "We are not in condition to do it now. If we should happen to be visited by the king at Copenhagen or Stockholm, and had previous notice, we should certainly do it."

The crew were then required to go through the manœuvre of furling sails, which was performed with the same precision as the first evolution, and to the great satisfaction of the guests, who were then invited to visit the cabins and steerage of the ship.

" Mother, I like this thing," said Mr. Clyde Blacklock.

" It's all very, *very* fine, Clyde," replied the tender mother.

" And the ship's going up the Baltic, and then up the Mediterranean."

" Yes, Clyde."

" And I want to go in her."

" You, Clyde!"

" Yes, that's what I say."

" And be a sailor?"

" I always told you I wanted to be a sailor. Didn't that head master, or whatever he is, say it would do me good to go to sea?"

" Perhaps he did, but I can't go with you, my dear."

" I don't want you to go with me. I'm not a baby!" protested the indignant youth.

" But you are my only son, dear."

" If you had forty only sons, it would be all the same to me. I say I want to go in this ship, and be a sailor."

Mrs. Blacklock was appalled, and was sorely disturbed by the announcement of her son. The young gentleman insisted that he should be entered at once as a member of the ship's company. He suggested to his anxious mother that she could travel by land while he went by sea, and that she could see him every time the ship went into port. The lady appeared to see no alternative, but evidently felt compelled to yield to her son's demand. It was plain enough, even to a casual observer, that Clyde was the head of the family. Mrs. Blacklock promised to speak to the principal, but she hoped he would not be able to take her son. Before she had an opportunity to make the application, the Orlando's bell rang for her passengers to return. The sound seemed to be a relief to the lady; but Mr. Clyde put his foot down just there, and upset all her hopes.

"Come, Clyde; the Orlando is ready to go," said she.

"Let her go," replied the hopeful son.

"But we must go on board."

"You may go. I'm off to sea in this ship."

"Not now, my dear," pleaded Mrs. Blacklock.

"Now's the time. If you don't speak to that head master yourself, I shall do so."

"Not now, my dearest boy. This ship is going to Christiania, and we will speak to the gentleman on the subject when she arrives. Come, Clyde; the boat is waiting for us, and all the other passengers have gone."

"You can't fool me, mother. I'm going to sea now. I like this ship, and I rather like those swells of officers."

Clyde positively refused to leave the ship, though his mother, almost in tears, begged him to accompany her.

"My son won't go with me," said she, as Mr. Lowington came towards her to ascertain the cause of their delay.

"If you desire, madam, the boatswain will put him into the boat for you," replied the principal.

"Put me into the boat!" exclaimed the indignant youth. "I should be glad to see him do it!"

"Should you? Peaks!"

"On deck, sir," replied the big boatswain, touching his cap to the principal.

"Pray, don't, sir — don't!" begged the lady. "Clyde wants to go to sea in your ship."

"O, does he, indeed!" exclaimed the principal. "We have a vacant place, and he can be accommodated."

The fond mother's heart sank at this announcement. Mr. Lowington, though his experience with students of this description had been far from satisfactory, felt that his duty to humanity required him to take this boy, who was evidently on the high road to ruin through the weak indulgence of his mother.

CHAPTER VI.

A DAY AT CHRISTIANSAND.

"BUT, madam, your steamer seems to be on the point of starting," suggested Mr. Lowington, as the Orlando rang her bell, and whistled violently.

"I cannot help it," replied the lady, apparently taking no notice of the steamer. "I came over here on a pleasure excursion, and now I feel as though I had lost my son."

"Lost him, madam! We intend to save him," laughed Mr. Lowington. "But we have no claim upon him. If you desire to leave in the steamer, the boatswain shall put the boy on board whether he is willing or not."

"No, no; that would be very, *very* harsh. Let the steamer go. This matter is of vastly more consequence than going to Christiania. James," she added, turning to the man in livery, "you will take the boat, get our baggage from the steamer, and take it to the hotel on shore."

"Yes, mem," replied James, as he very deliberately went over the side into the boat.

"This will be a sad day to me, sir," continued Mrs. Blacklock, as she glanced at her son, who was whistling an air from the last opera, as indifferent as though his mother had been at peace in her own drawing-room.

"I beg to repeat, madam, that I have not the slightest wish to take your son into this institution."

"But Clyde insists upon joining the ship, and what can I do?"

"You can say no, if you please."

"You had better not say it, mother; if you do, I will run away, and go to sea in a merchant ship," added Clyde, shaking his head.

"You hear, sir, what he says," replied Mrs. Blacklock, with a long and deep sigh.

"That would be the very best thing in the world for a boy troubled with his complaint," answered Mr. Lowington.

"I have no complaint; I'm not sick," growled Clyde.

"I'm afraid you are, my boy, though you don't know it. The most dangerous maladies often make great progress even before their existence is suspected."

"Nothing ails me," added Clyde.

"This seems to be a very nice ship, and you say the students are all gentlemen," continued the lady, glancing around her at the ship and the crew. "If Clyde must go to sea—"

"I must, mother," interposed the young gentleman, very decidedly.

"If he must go to sea, he had better go with you, sir."

"If you will walk into the cabin, madam, I will show you our regulations," said the principal, leading the way down the steps.

Clyde followed, apparently unwilling that a word should be said which he could not hear.

"I want to speak with your mother alone," interposed Mr. Lowington,

"I'm going too," persisted Clyde, after Mrs. Blacklock had descended the stairs.

"I prefer to see your mother alone," added the principal, firmly.

"You are going to talk about me, and I want to hear what is said," replied the youth, rudely.

"Peaks, remain here," said the principal to the big boatswain, who had followed them to the companion-way.

Mr. Lowington descended the steps, and Peaks slipped in behind him, fully understanding his duty without any explanations. Clyde attempted to follow, but the entrance was effectually blockaded by the stalwart forward officer.

"Get out of my way; I want to go down there," said Clyde, in no gentle tones.

"It can't be done, my hearty," replied Peaks.

"I'm going down, any way."

"I think not, my little gentleman."

"Yes, I am! Get out of my way."

"Ease off, my hearty. Don't get up a squall."

"I want to see my mother," growled Clyde.

"You were not invited to the cabin, and your mother was," answered Peaks, very mildly.

"I don't care if I wasn't; I'm going down."

"So you said before;" and the boatswain tried to pacify the youngster, and to induce him to be reasonable; but Clyde had always had his own way, and was ready to fight for it now, even though he had nothing to gain by it.

Captain Cumberland was still walking with Miss Celia, explaining to her the nature of the discipline on board, and giving her an account of the voyage across the Atlantic. A group of the officers had collected on the quarter-deck, and, much amused at the scene, were observing the conduct of Clyde. As he became more violent, his sister tried to quiet him, and induce him to behave like a gentleman; but he replied to her in a tone and with words which made the captain's cheeks tinge with indignation.

Finally, when he found that abuse had no effect upon the stout boatswain, he drew back, and made a desperate plunge at his heavy opponent. Peaks caught him by the shoulders, and lifted him off his feet like a baby. Taking him in his arms, with one hand over his mouth, to smother his cries, he bore him to the waist, where his yells could not be heard by his mother.

"Be quiet, little one," said Peaks, as he seated himself on the main-hatch, and twined his long legs around those of the prisoner, so that he was held as fast as though he had been in the folds of an anaconda. "Hold still, now, and I'll spin you a sea-yarn. Once on a time there was a little boy that wanted to go to sea—"

"Let me go, or I'll kill you!" sputtered Clyde; but the boatswain covered his mouth again, and silenced him.

"Kill me! That would be wicked. But I'm not a mosquito, to be cracked in the fingers of such a dear little boy as you are. But you snapped off my yarn; and if you don't hold still, I can't spin it ship-shape."

Clyde had well nigh exhausted his breath in his fruitless struggle, and before his sister went far enough forward to see him, he was tolerably calm, because he had no more strength to resist. Then the boatswain told his story of a boy that wanted to go to sea, but found that he could not have his own way on board the ship.

In the cabin, Mrs. Blacklock told a pitiful story of the wilfulness of her son; that she was obliged to do just as he said, and if he wanted anything, however absurd it might be, she was obliged to give it to him, or he made the house too "hot" for her. Her husband had died when the children were small, and the whole care of them had devolved on her. Clyde had made her miserable for several years. She had sent him to several celebrated schools; but he had got into trouble immediately, and she had been compelled to take him away, to prevent him from killing himself and her, as she expressed it. Her husband had left her a handsome property, but she was afraid her son would spend it all, or compel her to do so, before he became of age.

Mr. Lowington repeated only what most of her friends had told her before — that her weak indulgence would be the ruin of the boy; that he needed a strong arm. He was willing to take him into the Academy ship, but he must obey all the rules and follow all the regulations. The perplexed mother realized the truth of all he said.

"You will take him as an officer — won't you, sir?"

she asked, when she had in a measure reconciled herself to the discipline proposed.

"Certainly not, madam," replied the principal. "If he ever becomes an officer, he must work himself up to that position, as the other students do."

"But you could let him have one of the rooms in the cabin. I am willing to pay extra for his tuition."

"No, madam; he must go with the other students, and do precisely as they do."

"Where will his servant lodge?"

"His servant?"

"Yes, James. He will want a servant, for I don't know that he ever dressed himself alone."

"He can have no servant, except those of the ship."

"That's very, *very* hard."

"Perhaps it is, but if the boy can't dress himself alone, he must lie in his berth till he acquires the art by hard thinking. I wish you to understand the matter thoroughly before you leave him, madam."

Mrs. Blacklock struggled with the hard terms; but even to her the case seemed like a desperate one, and she was willing at last to try the experiment, though she intended to follow the ship wherever she went, to save him from suicide when his situation became absolutely hopeless. The terms arranged, she followed Mr. Lowington on deck, where Clyde was discovered in the loving embrace of the big boatswain, who released him as soon as he saw the lady.

"Now, Clyde, my dear, we have arranged it all," said Mrs. Blacklock; and it ought to be added that such a result would have been utterly impossible if the subject of the negotiations had been present.

"I don't care if you have," replied Clyde, bestowing a fiery glance upon the boatswain, who was smiling as blandly as though earth had no naughty boys.

"Why, what's the matter, Clyde!" demanded the anxious mother.

"I've had enough of this ship," howled the little gentleman, as he glanced again at the stout forward officer.

The complacent face of Peaks maddened him, and Clyde felt that, perhaps for the first time in his life, he had lost a battle. He could not bear the sight of the boatswain's placid features, unruffled by anything like anger or malice. He felt that he had not even provoked his powerful adversary. He howled in his anger, and then he cried in his desperation. Suddenly he seized a wooden belaying-pin from the rail, and shied it at the boatswain's head. Peaks caught it in his hand, as though he had been playing toss-ball with his victim; but the next instant his anaconda fold encircled the youth again. Mrs. Blacklock screamed with terror.

"There is no harm done, madam," interposed the principal. "We don't allow boys to throw things here."

"You are very, *very* harsh with the poor boy."

"And the poor boy is very, very harsh with us. He throws belaying-pins at our heads."

"He did not mean any harm."

"Perhaps not; but that's an unpleasant way of manifesting his regard."

"I've had enough of this ship! I won't go in her!" howled Clyde, struggling to escape from the grasp of the officer.

"Do you hear that, sir? Poor boy!"

"He will soon learn better than to behave in this violent manner. We can cure him in ten minutes after you have left the ship."

"What! whip him?" exclaimed the mother, with horror.

"No, madam; we never strike a student under any circumstances, unless it be in self-defence; but if a boy won't go when ordered, we carry him. We always have force enough to do this without injury to the person."

"But see the poor boy struggle!"

"It will do him no harm."

"He says now that he will not go in the ship."

"If I were his parent, it would be as I said, not as he said, after he had ceased to be reasonable. I would consult the wishes and opinions of a boy of mine, as long as he behaved properly — no longer. You have only to leave him, and I assure you he shall be treated as kindly as he will permit us to treat him. I do not wish to influence you, but I am confident that ruin lies in that boy's path, unless he is reformed."

Mrs. Blacklock actually wept. She loved the boy with a blind affection in spite of the disrespect and even abuse that he heaped upon her. It was a terrible struggle to her, but she finally decided to leave him on board of the ship, perhaps satisfied that nothing else could ever save him from himself, and her from the misery his reckless conduct constantly occasioned her.

"You wished to go to sea, Clyde, and I have decided to leave you in this ship," said the poor mother, trembling with emotion.

"But I tell you I won't stay in this ship," roared Clyde, as Peaks, at a signal from the principal, released his prisoner.

"I can do nothing with you, my dear boy. You won't obey me, and I must leave you to those who can control you. I am going on shore now, but I shall see you again at Christiania."

"I won't stay!" howled Clyde.

"Good by, Clyde," said Mrs. Blacklock, desperately, as she folded her son in her arms, and kissed him on both cheeks.

"I tell you I won't stay!" cried the angry youth, breaking away from his mother's embrace.

"Make it short, madam," suggested Mr. Lowington.

"Do try to be good, Clyde, and then you can come home very, *very* soon," added Mrs. Blacklock, as the principal conducted her to the accommodation ladder, where the first cutter had been manned to put her on shore.

"I tell you again, I won't stay! If you leave me, I'll jump overboard."

"O!" groaned the weak mother.

"If you do, young man, we will pick you up with the greatest pleasure," said Mr. Lowington, as he hurried the lady to the side.

"O, if he should!" gasped she.

"There is not a particle of danger, madam; Mr. Peaks will take excellent care of him," replied her comforter.

The boatswain, at a nod from Mr. Lowington, again embraced Clyde, but did not injure him, nor permit him to injure himself. The lady was handed into the boat, and Captain Cumberland politely performed this service for Miss Blacklock. Of course the poor mother was in an agony of doubt and anxiety, but the students in the cutter seemed to be so cheerful, contented and gentlemanly, that she hoped for the best.

Clyde was appalled at the situation, and one of the stern realities of life seemed suddenly to dawn upon him. As soon as his mother disappeared over the side, he ceased to struggle, for he gained nothing by it, and the students appeared to be amused by his sufferings. Peaks released him, and the victim of wholesome discipline looked about him with a wondering stare; but there was no mother to cajole or intimidate, and he was thrown entirely upon his own resources for the means of resistance, if he purposed to resist. He appeared to be stupefied by the situation, and Mr. Lowington, taking advantage of his bewilderment, invited him into the main cabin, where he kindly but firmly "laid down the law" to him. Clyde was by no means conquered, but was rather considering how he should escape from this trying position. At the close of the interview, the principal handed the patient over to one of the stewards, and requested him to see the new comer clothed in the uniform of the ship. Peaks was directed to keep an eye on the victim while the crew were on shore.

All hands were soon seated in the boats, and in half an hour all the students in the squadron were turned loose in the streets of Christiansand. Though the instructors were of the party, they were not required to exercise any particular supervision over their pupils.

There was hardly anything to be seen, and as a large number of the students had never crossed the Atlantic before, they wanted to know if they had come so far to see such a town. Most of the houses were of wood, but they were neat and well kept. As the capital of the province of Christiansand, the town was the residence of the Stift Amtmand, or governor, and of the bishop of the diocese. It was founded in 1641, and having an excellent harbor, it is a place of considerable commercial importance, having a population of about ten thousand.

The boys visited the cathedral, which is a fine building of gray stone, and being the first which most of them had seen, it had a considerable interest to them. They observed the people, and their manners and customs, so far as they could, with more interest than the buildings, which differed in no important respect from those in the United States. Passing across the water front of the town, they came to the Torrisdal River, over which there is an excellent bridge. They crossed the stream, and walked to an antiquated church. Some of the houses on the way were very neat, pretty structures, not unlike the one-story dwellings seen all over New England.

"Here's a Runic stone," said Dr. Winstock, as the captain and several of the officers followed him into the burying-ground connected with the ancient church.

"What is a Runic stone?" asked Lincoln, the third lieutenant.

"A stone with Runic characters upon it."

"I haven't the least idea what the word means, though Poe sings, in the 'Bells,' —

'Keeping time, time, time,
In a sort of Runic rhyme!'

Runic is derived from a word which means secret; and a Runic stone is any memorial, table, or column, on which Runic characters are inscribed, as a tombstone, a boundary mark. There are sixteen of these characters, forming an alphabet, which were used by the ancient Scandinavians, and were thought by them to possess magical properties, and willow wands inscribed with them were used by the pagans of the north in their magic rites. Sticks were used as almanacs, to keep the account of the days and months, and also constituted the day-books and ledgers of the ancients. In Germany, in modern times, the baker, for example, and the purchaser of bread, each had a stick, and the number of loaves delivered was notched upon both. Scarcely less primitive was the custom of some of our American farmers, who kept their accounts on the barn door; and I have heard a story of one who, when required to produce his books in court at a lawsuit, carried in the barn door, and held it up before the judge and jury. In Denmark and Sweden you will see more Runic writings, especially in the museum at Copenhagen."

"They seem to bury people here, in about the same manner as with us," said Captain Cumberland.

"There is not half so much difference between things here and those at home as I expected to find," added Judson.

"The houses are almost the same, and so are the people," continued Norwood.

"People coming to Europe are often disappointed

because they find almost everything so near like what they have been accustomed to," replied the doctor. "You will find Norway and Sweden more like New England than any other countries on the continent. But I think you will find differences enough to excite your interest and attention before you return."

The students walked back to Christiansand, and having exhausted the town, went on board the vessels of the squadron, ready and even anxious to continue the voyage. The pilots were on deck, Paul Kendall and lady had returned to the Grace, and the principal only waited the arrival of the steamer Moss, from Frederiksværn, to give the order to get under way. The boats were all hoisted up except the first cutter, which was to bring off the unfortunate crew of the professor's barge, as soon as they arrived.

At eight o'clock the steamer came in, and the first cutter, with the principal on board, hastened to her landing-place, to meet Sanford and his companions. To his great astonishment and regret, they were not on board of the Moss. The captain, who spoke English very well, knew nothing about the absentees, and was quite confident they were not on board of the Foldin, the boat which had picked them up. Captain Hoell had said nothing to him about the accident, but then the Foldin had arrived only that morning, instead of the night before, when she was due, and their interview had been very hurried. "Did any person in the Moss know anything about the unfortunates?" the captain was kind enough to inquire; and a passenger was found who heard some one say that a party of young men had been landed by the Foldin at Lillesand. But the Moss had left Lillesand at six o'clock, and her captain had not seen or heard of the persons described. Mr. Lowington was very anxious about the fate of the second cutter's crew, and feared that some of them had been injured by the collision, so that they were unable to take the steamer back to Christiansand. He returned to the cutter and pulled off to the Tritonia, and directed Mr. Tompion, the second vice-principal, in charge of her, to run into Lillesand, and ascertain what had become of the absentees. Without waiting for the signal, the Tritonia got under way, and under full sail, with a fresh breeze, stood out of the harbor. The other vessels followed her soon after, the principal intending to lay off and on till the Tritonia reported.

The ship had been searched from keel to truck for Ole Amundsen on the day before. Of course he was not found, and the conclusion was that he had dropped into the water and swam ashore, though it was difficult to understand how he had accomplished the feat without detection. Inquiries in regard to him were made on shore, but if any one knew him, application was not made to the right persons.

Mr. Clyde Blacklock had not yet jumped overboard, and during the busy scene of getting under way, he stood with his mouth agape, watching the proceedings with wondering interest. He was not quite sure, after his anger had subsided, that he had made a bad bargain. There was something rather pleasant in the motion of the ship, and the zeal and precision with which the students worked, showed that they enjoyed their occupation. No one noticed Clyde, or even seemed to be aware of his presence. Before, when he behaved in an extravagant and unreasonable manner, the boys only laughed at him. They did not beg him to be pacified, as his mother and James always did; on the contrary they seemed to enjoy his chagrin.

As soon as the ship was under way, the new student was informed that he belonged to the port watch, second part, and the silver star, which designated his watch, was affixed to his left arm. He was told that he would be called with the others to take his turn on deck during the night.

"What am I to do?" he asked, rather blankly.

"Just the same as the others do?" replied De Forrest, the fourth lieutenant, who had the deck with the second part of the port watch. "I have your station bill."

"What's that?"

"It is a card on which all your duties are explained. Here it is," added De Forrest, producing the station bill. "You are No. 71; all the even numbers belong to the starboard watch, and all the odd numbers to the port."

These cards were all printed; for among the various amusements provided for the students, a couple of octavo Novelty presses, with a sufficient supply of type and other printing material had been furnished. All the blanks for use in the ship were printed on board, and the Oceanic Enterprise, a weekly Journal, had been regularly issued during the voyage across the Atlantic, though a gale of wind, which disturbed the equilibrium of the press and the printers, had delayed its publication a couple of days on one occasion.

Clyde read the station bill which was handed to him by the officer, but it would have been just as intelligible to him if it had been in Runic character.

"'Reefing, main-topsail, and main-topsail halyards,'" said Clyde, reading from the card. "What does all that mean?"

"You mind only what you have to do yourself, and not trouble your head about orders that have nothing to do with your work; for the orders come as thick as snow flakes at Christmas. When all hands are called to reef topsails, you are one of them, of course. When any thing is said about topsails, or topsail-halyards, you are the man."

"Good; I understand that, and I shall make a sailor, I know," added Clyde.

"I hope you will. The order will come to 'settle away the topsail halyards.' Be ready to help then."

"But I don't know the topsail halyards from a pint of soup."

"Here they are," added the lieutenant, conducting his pupil to the rail, and pointing out the main-topsail halyards. "Then, when the officer says, 'Aloft, topmen,' you will run up the main rigging here, and the midshipman in the top will tell you what to do. At the word, you will lay out on the yard, and do as the others do. At the words, 'Lay down from aloft,' you will come on deck, and hoist up the main-topsail. Nearly all your duty is connected with the main-topsail. In tacking, you will go to the clew-garnets."

"What are they?"

"These ropes, by which the corners of the mainsail are hauled up," answered De Forrest, pointing out the clew-garnets. "You will also let go the main tack. In getting under way, you will help loose the main-topsail. In anchoring, you are at the main clew-lines, and the main brace. Here they are. In loosing and furling you are on the main-topsail. In boat service, you are attached to the third cutter. You sleep in berth No. 71, your ship's number, and eat with mess No. 6."

De Forrest, as instructed by the principal, carefully explained the duties of the new comer, indicating every rope as he mentioned it, and describing its use. He was prudent in his manner, and tried to give the proud youth no offence by making him feel the superiority of an officer. The lieutenant then conducted him to his mess room, and pointed out his berth.

The wind was still from the southward, and quite fresh; and though the squadron went under short sail, it was off Lillesand in a couple of hours. The Tritonia, which was a fast vessel, did not detain her consorts more than a couple of hours. Mr. Tompion boarded the ship, and reported that the crew of the second cutter had landed at Lillesand, and fearing that they should miss the ship if they returned to Christiansand, had taken carioles, and left early in the morning for Christiania. There were ten of the party, and one of them was a Norwegian, though he was dressed like the others. Mr. Lowington could not imagine who the Norwegian was that wore the Academy's uniform, for it did not occur to him that Ole could have joined them. He was glad to hear that all of them were well, and able to travel; and had no doubt they would arrive in safety at Christiania. He was aware that the crew of the second cutter were rather wild boys; but as there were no large towns in the interior, he had no fear that they would be led astray among the simple Norwegians.

The fleet filled away again, and at eight bells the following morning was off Frederiksværn.

CHAPTER VII.

UP THE CHRISTIANIA FJORD.

"I SHOULD like to know where this place is," said Ryder, the second master, as he appeared upon the quarter-deck of the ship, with one of the forty bound volumes of Harper's Magazine, which were contained in the library.

"What place?" asked Lincoln, the third lieutenant, as he glanced at the volume.

"That's more than I know; but here is a picture of a steamer between two high bluffs of rock, and under it, she is said to be entering the fjord."

"We are just at the mouth of the fjord now, and if there are any such rocks as those here, I should like to see them. Why, you see they rise above the steamer's main-topmast."

Lincoln took the book, and read the description; but he was none the wiser for his labor, for the narrow strait through which the steamer in the picture was passing was not particularly described. The book was shown to the pilot, who did not know just where the place was; but after he had been told that the steamer came from Gottenberg, and was on her way to Christiania, he thought that the bold rocks must be in the vicinity of Frederiksværn. He offered to take the ship through the pass, as the wind was fair, and Mr. Lowington consented that he should do so, for in order to enable the students to see the fine scenery on the fjord, the studies were to be laid aside for the day.

"I don't see where there can be anything like this," said Ryder, as he surveyed the shores.

"There are plenty of islands here, but certainly none of them rise to any such heights as those in the picture," replied Lincoln. "They are bare rocks out at sea, but some of them are a little green farther in. It don't begin to be so wild as I supposed it was in these parts. Why, I have read and heard so much about the Christiania Fjord, that I supposed it was the grandest scenery in the world."

"It don't look much like the picture — does it?" laughed Ryder.

In a short time the ship was approaching the narrow pass. The cliffs on each side were very bold and rugged, and if the students had not been feasting themselves with grand anticipations, they would have appreciated the scenery much better. Ryder and Lincoln laughed when they compared the reality with the pictures they had. The scenery could not be called grand, though it was certainly very fine. The strait was very narrow, and on each side of it rings were fastened in the rocks, which were painted white around them, for the convenience of vessels warping out in a calm or against the wind. On the high rock, — it could not have been a hundred feet high, — at the right, was a small fort, which looked grim and terrible in its way, but which any well-ordered man of war, with modern ordnance, could have battered down in half an hour.

Passing through the strait, the ship came in sight of the small village of Frederiksværn, which is a naval station, where a number of gunboats are housed in a series of uniform buildings. The town itself is only a hamlet, but as the vessels proceeded, those on board saw Laurvig at the head of the bay, which is a place of considerable importance.

"Little Fœrder," said the pilot, an hour later, as he pointed to a tall, red light-house, at the entrance of the fjord.

"Then the land we see beyond must be Sweden," added Ryder.

"*Sverige*," nodded the pilot.

"I suppose that is Sweden, but I don't see the use of having half a dozen names to a country."

"And this is *Norge*," added the second master, pointing to the other side.

"Yes, *Norge*," answered the pilot, pleased to hear the young officer apply the Norwegian name.

On the port hand of the ship was a vast sea of rocky islands, of all shapes and sizes. Those farthest from the mainland were entirely destitute of soil or verdure; but in the distance a few pines, and the fresh tints of the early grass, could be seen.

"Keep her north-north-east," said the pilot.

"Man the weather and stand by the lee braces!" shouted the first lieutenant.

Clyde Blacklock took out his station card, and looked to see whether the order applied to him.

"You are on the main brace," said Scott, a good-natured young tar, who happened to be near the new student. " There you are, on the weather side."

" Who spoke to you?" demanded Clyde, dropping his card, and looking Scott in the face.

" I haven't been introduced to you, I know; but I thought you wanted to know your duty," laughed Scott.

" You take care of yourself, and I'll mind my own duty," growled Clyde.

" All right, my lad," replied the good-natured student, whose station was at the weather fore brace.

Clyde walked aft, and placed himself in the line of those who were to haul on the weather main brace.

" Slack the lee, and haul on the weather braces," said the first lieutenant, and the other officers repeated the order.

" Walk away with it!" shouted the fourth lieutenant to those at the main brace.

Clyde took hold, and tugged with all his might; but the brace would not come away. To tell the exact truth, there was a disposition among the students to haze the new comer, and the main brace men had agreed among themselves to let him do the whole of the work. They pretended to haul, but not one of them bore a pound upon the brace.

" Pull!" shouted Clyde, at the top of his lungs, as he strained at the rope. " Why don't you pull, boys?"

" Silence on the quarter-deck!" cried the executive officer — for all work was required to be performed in silence. " Walk away with the main brace."

"Come, boys, why don't you pull?" roared Clyde, who was blest with a pair of hearty lungs.

"Silence, Blacklock! You mustn't hollo like that when you are on duty," interposed De Forrest.

"Who says I mustn't?" demanded Clyde, dropping his hold upon the brace, and walking up to the officer who had dared to give him these words of counsel, which were uttered in a mild and pleading tone, rather than in those of authority.

"Starboard the helm," said the executive officer.

"Starboard, sir," repeated the quartermaster at the wheel.

"Walk away with that main brace!" added the first lieutenant.

The main brace men, finding that Clyde was at issue with the fourth lieutenant, applied themselves to their work, and the main yard swung round.

"Steady!" said the executive officer.

"Steady, sir."

"Avast hauling! Belay, all."

By these manœuvres the ship had been kept away, and was now headed directly up the fjord.

"I don't allow any fellow to speak to me like that," blustered Clyde. "I want you to understand that I am a gentleman."

"Go forward, Blacklock, and don't make a row on the quarter-deck," replied De Forrest, mildly.

"I'll not go forward!"

"Then I must report you to the first lieutenant."

"I'm willing to do my work, but I won't be fagged by any nob in gold lace."

"You are making a mistake, Blacklock," said De

Forrest, in a low tone, as he walked towards the angry Briton, with the intention of reasoning with him upon the absurdity of his conduct.

Mr. Lowington had cautioned him and other officers to be very prudent in dealing with the new student till he had become accustomed to his duty, and certainly De Forrest was prudent in the extreme. Perhaps Clyde misunderstood the purpose of this officer when approaching him, and suspected that he intended to use violence, for, drawing back, he made a pass at De Forrest with his fist. But the latter detected the nature of the demonstration in season to ward off the blow, and, still in the exercise of the extreme prudence which had before characterized his conduct, retreated to the other side of the quarter-deck.

"Enough of that," said Judson, the first lieutenant, as he stepped between Clyde and De Forrest.

Clyde was very angry. Though he had made up his mind to perform his duty in the beginning, he fancied that no one had the right to command him to be silent. In his wrath he pulled off his blue jacket, tossed it upon the deck with a flourish, and intimated that if the first lieutenant wanted to fight, he was ready for him. Happily the first lieutenant did not wish to fight, though he was fully prepared to defend himself. At this crisis, the principal observed the hostile attitude of the young Briton, and quietly ordered Peaks to interfere.

"Go forward, Blacklock," said Judson, calmly.

"I won't go forward! I have been insulted, and I'll break the sconce of the fellow that did it," added Clyde, glancing at the fourth lieutenant.

"Come, my hearty, let us go forward, as we are ordered," interposed Peaks, as he picked up Clyde in his arms, and in spite of his struggles, carried him into the waist.

It was useless to resist the big boatswain, and the pressure of Peaks's arms soon crushed out Clyde's anger, and like a little child, he was set down upon the deck, amid the laughter of his companions. He felt that he was not getting ahead at all; and though he reserved the expression of his anger, he determined at the first convenient opportunity to thrash both Judson and De Forrest. He had also decided to run away at the first chance, even if he had to camp on a desolate island in doing so. He regarded Peaks as a horrible ogre, whose only mission in the ship was to persecute and circumvent him.

"I'll have it out with those nobs yet," said Clyde, as Peaks left him, restored to his senses, so far as outward appearances were concerned.

"Have it out! Have what out?" asked Scott, the good-natured.

"I'll whip that nob who told me to be silent."

"Don't you do it, my jolly Briton," laughed Scott.

"I can do it."

"Do you mean the first lieutenant?"

"Yes, that I do; and I'll teach him better manners."

"I wouldn't hurt him; Judson's a good fellow."

"I don't care if he is; he'll catch it; and De Forrest, too. They insulted me."

"I dare say they didn't mean to."

"If they didn't, I'll give them a chance to apologize," added Clyde, a little mollified by the mild words of his companion.

"That's very kind of you; but officers don't often apologize to seamen for telling them of it when they disobey the rules of the ship."

"Rules or not, I'll hammer them both if they don't apologize."

"Don't be cruel with them," laughed Scott.

"And that big boatswain — I'll be even with him yet," blustered Clyde, as he shook his head menacingly.

"Are you going to thrash him too?" asked Scott, opening his eyes.

"I'll take care of him. He don't toss me round in that way without suffering for it."

"Well, don't hurt him," suggested the good-natured seaman.

"He'll get a broken head before he grows much older," added Clyde, drawing out a belaying-pin from the fife-rail. "I shall not be in this ship a great while longer; but I mean to stay long enough to settle my accounts with the big boatswain and the two nobs on the quarter-deck."

"How are you going to do it, my dear Albion?"

"Leave that to me. No man can insult me without suffering for it."

"Perhaps the officers will apologize, but I don't believe Peaks will. He's an obstinate fellow, and would do just what the principal told him to do, even if it was to swallow you and me, and half a dozen other fellows. You don't mean to lick the principal too — do you?"

"I haven't had any trouble with him."

"But he is at the bottom of it all. He told Peaks to persecute you. I'm not sure that the principal isn't more to blame than all the others put together."

"No matter for him; he has done very well."

"Then you mean to let him off?"

"I say I've nothing against the head master."

"Don't be too hard on Peaks," added Scott, as he climbed upon the rail to see the scenery of the fjord.

"I suppose all these islands, points, bays, and channels have names, just as they do on the other side of the ocean," said Laybold, at whose side the good-natured tar seated himself.

"Of course," nodded Scott.

"I wonder what they are."

"Don't you know?"

"Certainly not — how should I?"

"I didn't know but you might have seen the chart," added Scott, gravely.

"There's a town!" exclaimed the enthusiastic Laybold, as the progress of the ship opened a channel, at the head of which was a village, with a church.

"I see; that's Bossenboggenberg," said Scott.

"O, is it? Is that a river?"

"Not at all. That's only a channel, called the Hoppenboggen, which extends around the Island of Toppenboggen. That channel is navigable for small vessels."

"Where did you learn all those names?" demanded Laybold, amazed at the astonishing words which his companion rolled off so glibly.

"My father had to send me to sea to keep me from

learning too much. My hair all fell off, and the schoolmasters were afraid of me."

"There's another town ahead on the port hand," said Laybold, a little later.

"That is Aggerhousenboggen, I think. Let me see; here's Cape Tingumboggen, and that must be the opening to the Stoppenboggen Fjord. Yes, that must be Aggerhousenboggen."

"Where did you learn to pronounce Norwegian so well, Scott?"

"O, I learned Norwegian when I was an infant. I could speak it first rate before I learned to utter my mother tongue."

"Go 'way!" protested Laybold. "Do you know what island that is on the starboard hand."

"To be sure I do. Do you think my education has been neglected to that extent? That's Steppenfetchenboggen. A very fine island it is, too," continued Scott, rattling off the long names so that they had a decidedly foreign ring.

"I don't see how you can pronounce those words," added Laybold. "They would choke me to death."

"I don't believe they would," laughed Scott.

The squadron passed through several narrow passages, and then came to a broad expanse of water at the mouth of the Drammen River. The students were perched on the rail and in the rigging of the various vessels, observing with great interest the development of the panorama, which seemed to be unrolled before them.

"It is rather fine scenery," said Lincoln, who still carried the book in his hand, and occasionally glanced at the pictures; "but I think the artist here must have multiplied the height of the cliffs by two, and divided the height of houses, men, and masts by the same number."

"It certainly looks like an exaggeration," replied Ryder.

"Look at this," added Lincoln, pointing to a scene on the coast of Norway. "There's a large steamer carrying a top-gallant yard on the foremast. That mast is probably a hundred and fifty feet high, and there are hills and bluffs beyond it — which would lose by the perspective — five times as high."

"Still it is very fine scenery."

"So it is; but no finer than we have on the coast of Maine. You remember last summer we went through the Reach, down by Machias? That was something like this, and quite as pleasant."

"We mustn't be too critical, Lincoln," laughed Ryder.

"I don't intend to be critical; but I had an idea, from the pictures I have seen, that Christiania Fjord was something like the Saguenay River, where the cliffs rise perpendicularly four or five hundred feet high. These pictures would certainly lead one to expect such sights."

"Horton," said the pilot, pointing to a town which now came into view, as the vessel passed beyond a point of land.

It was a small place, in appearance not unlike a New England village. At the wharf were a couple of small steamers, one of which had come down the Drammen, and the entire population of the town seemed to have turned out on the occasion, for the shore was covered with people. They were all neatly dressed. On the opposite side of the fjord was the town of Moss, where the convention by which Norway and Sweden were united was drawn up and agreed upon.

The fleet sailed rapidly before the fresh breeze across the broad expanse, and then entered a narrow passage. There was a gentle declivity on each side of the fjord, which was covered, as far as the eye could see, with pines. Dröbak, on the right, is a village of one street, on the side of the hill. The houses are mostly of one story, painted yellow, with roofs covered with red tile. Before noon the passage began to widen, and the fleet entered another broad expanse of water, filled with rocky islands, at the head of which stood the city of Christiania. Some of the islets were pretty and picturesque, in some instances having a single cottage upon them, with a little garden. The rocks were often of curious formation, and the shore of one island was as regular and smooth as though it had been a piece of masonry. After rounding a point of rocks, the fleet came into full view of Christiania. The city and its environs are spread out on the southern slope of a series of hills, and presents a beautiful landscape to the eye. On the left the country was covered with villas, prominent among which was Oscarshal, a summer palace of the late king. On the right was the castle of Agershuus, rising abruptly from the water. At a little distance trom the town was a kind of hotel, built on a picturesque island, with its pretty landing-place, not unlike some similar establishments near the head of Narragansett Bay. At the wharf in front of the city, and lying in the bay, was a considerable number of steamers, some of them quite large. The fleet ran up to the front of the city and anchored.

"This is the end of my voyage," said Clyde Blacklock, when everything had been put in order on board of the ship.

"You are not going yet — are you?" laughed Scott.

"Very soon."

"I thought you were going to stop, and whip Peaks and the two lieutenants."

"Time enough for that. I suppose the ship will stay here two or three days — won't she?"

"Perhaps a week. I suppose we shall go on shore this afternoon, and see the sights."

"I say, Scott, if you tell those officers what I've been saying to you, I'll serve you in the same way," added Clyde, as for the first time it occurred to him that he had been imprudent in developing his plans to another.

"No! You won't lick me, too — will you?"

"Not if you behave like a man, and don't peach," answered Clyde, in a patronizing tone.

"I will try to be a good boy, then," laughed Scott.

"I only want to catch them on shore, where I can have fair play. I'm not to be fagged by any fellow that ever was born."

Clyde walked uneasily about the deck till the crew were piped to dinner, evidently thinking how he should carry his big intentions into execution. To one less moved by fancied insults and indignities the case would have looked hopeless. He devoured his dinner in a much shorter period than is usually allotted by well-bred Englishmen to that pleasing diversion, and hastened on deck again. Peaks was there, acting as ship-keeper, while the carpenter was painting the second cutter, the repairs upon which had been completed. · The big boatswain was seated on one of the cat-heads, where he could see the entire deck of the ship, and observe every craft that approached her. The new student observed his position, and thought he was seated in a very careless manner. A very wicked thought took possession of the Briton's mind, and he ascended to the top-gallant forecastle. The boatswain sat very composedly on the cat-head, with his feet hanging over the water, and was just then studying the beauties of the landscape. A very slight exercise of force would displace him, and drop him into the water.

"Well, my hearty, you stowed your grub in a hurry," said Peaks, when he discovered the new pupil.

"I was not very hungry, and thought I would take another look at the town," replied Clyde. "What's that big building off there, near the hills?"

"That may be the county jail, the court-house, or the lunatic asylum. I haven't the least idea what it is," answered Peaks, indifferently. "The professors can tell you all about those things."

"I wonder where that ship came from?" added Clyde, pointing to a vessel which was standing in ahead of the Young America.

"That isn't a ship," replied Peaks, as he turned partly round, so that he could see the craft. "That's a 'mofferdite brig; or, as bookish people would say, an hermaphrodite brig — half brig and half schooner. You must call things, especially vessels, by their right names, or you will fall in the opinion of—"

At that instant the big boatswain dropped into the deep waters of the fjord.

"And you will fall, in my opinion," said Clyde, as, taking advantage of his antagonist's attention to the brig, he gave him a smart push, which displaced him from the cat-head.

But Peaks, who was half man and half fish, was as much at home in the water as on the deck, and struck out for the cable, by which the ship was anchored, as the nearest point of support. Clyde walked along the rail till he came to the swinging-boom, where the boats which had been lowered for use after dinner were fastened. Climbing out on the boom, he dropped down by the painter into the third cutter, one of the four-oar boats. Bitts, the carpenter, who had been the only person on board except the boatswain, was in the waist busily at work upon the boat, and did not observe that anything unusual had transpired. Clyde had practised gymnastics a great deal, and was an active, agile fellow. Casting off the painter of the third cutter, he worked her astern, so as to avoid Peaks. Then, shipping a pair of oars, he pulled for the shore.

In the mean time, the boatswain, disdaining to call for assistance, and not having observed the movements of Clyde, climbed up the cable to the hawse-hole, and then, by the bowsprit guys, made his way to the topgallant forecastle, where he discovered the Briton in the cutter, pulling with all his might for the shore.

Shaking the water from his clothes, he hastened to the main cabin, and informed the principal that the new scholar had left the ship.

"Left the ship!" exclaimed Mr. Lowington. "Were you not on deck while the students were at dinner?"

"Yes, sir, most of the time; but just at the moment when the young sculpin left the ship, I happened to be in the water," answered Peaks, shrugging his shoulders like a Frenchman, and glancing at his wet garments.

"How came you in the water?"

"The little Britisher pushed me overboard, when I was sitting on the cat-head."

"I see," added the principal. "We must get him back before his mother arrives."

By this time most of the students had come up from the steerage, and the order was given to pipe away the first cutter. Peaks was directed to change his clothes, and go in her. He was ready by the time the crew were in their seats, for, as he was not a fashionable man, his toilet was soon made. The boats from the other vessels of the fleet, including those of the yachts, were already on their way to the town. The first cutter pulled to the shore; but Clyde had already landed, and disappeared in the city.

As at Christiansand, Paul Kendall and lady decided to remain on shore during the stay of the fleet. They had several pieces of baggage, and the custom-house officers on the wharf were obliged to examine them, after which they followed a porter to the Victoria Hotel, which was said to be the best in the place. Peaks found a man who could speak English, and immediately applied himself to the business of finding the runaway. Clyde had been seen going up one of the streets, but no one knew anything about him.

The fugitive felt that he had achieved a victory. He had "paid off" the big boatswain, and no fellow on board of the ship could believe that he had not kept his word. He walked up the street till he came to Dronningensgaden. People looked at him as though he were a stranger, and he became aware that his uniform was exciting attention. In the Kirkegade he found a clothing store, in which the shop-keeper spoke English. In changing his dress on board of the ship, he had retained the contents of his pockets, including a well-filled purse. He selected a suit of clothes which pleased him, and immediately put it on. At another store he bought a hat, and then he appeared like a new being. With the bundle containing his uniform, he walked till he found a carriage, in which he seated himself, and ordered the driver to leave him at the Victoria Hotel. He thought it would only be necessary for him to keep out of sight till evening, when his mother would probably arrive in the Foldin, and he was confident he could induce her to withdraw him from the Academy. He would stay in his room the rest of the day, and by that time the search for him, if any was made, would be ended.

"I want a nice room for myself, another for my mother and sister, who will arrive this evening, and a place for the man," said Clyde, as the porter of the hotel touched his cap, and helped him out of the carriage.

The young man was evidently a person of some importance. The porter, the clerk, and the head waiter, who came out to receive him, bowed low. A man took his bundle, and he was ushered to a room on the ground floor. As he crossed the court, he discovered several of the Orlando's passengers in the reading-room. He had not entered his chamber before there was another arrival, — Paul Kendall and lady, — who were assigned to the next room.

CHAPTER VIII.

THE SIGHTS OF CHRISTIANIA AND OTHER MATTERS.

AS there was in Christiania much to be seen that needed explanation, the students were required to keep together, and several guides from the hotel were obtained, to conduct the party to the various objects of interest in the city. A walk through some of the principal streets brought them to the new Parliament house, which is called the *Storthingsbyggningen*. It is a fine building, but with nothing remarkable about it. In the lower house, the students seated themselves in the chairs of the members, and Mr. Mapps took the speaker's desk.

"Christiania was founded in 1624, on the site of the ancient city of Osloe, which was destroyed by fire. It is the residence of the king during his sojourn in Norway, and the new palace, which you saw on the hill, was completed for his use in 1848. The city, as you have seen, is regularly laid out, and the buildings are either of brick or stone. Formerly the dwellings were of wood, but the frequent fires caused the adoption of a law that no more wooden buildings should be erected within the precincts of the city. The place has considerable commerce, and now contains nearly sixty thousand inhabitants.

"A street here is called a *gade*, and you observe that the street and its name form one word, as Carl-Johansgade, or Charles John Street; Kongensgade, or King Street; Kirkegaden, or Church Street. The same word is used in German.

"The money of Norway is different from that of Sweden or Denmark. The specie dollar, which is generally called a 'specie,' is the unit, and contains five marks of twenty-four skillings each. A specie, or *specie-daler*, as it is written, is worth about one dollar and eight cents of our money. It is near enough for our purpose to say that a mark is twenty-two cents, and a skilling one cent. The coins in circulation are the mark, the two, the four, and the twelve skilling piece. Species and half species are coined, but paper money is generally used for large sums, each denomination being printed on a particular colored paper.

"It is probable that the French system of weights and measures will soon be introduced in Sweden and Norway; but now a Norwegian *pund* is one and one tenth pounds avoirdupois; a *fod* is twelve and two hundredths inches; and a *kande* is three and three tenths pints."

Mr. Mapps descended from the rostrum, and after the party had looked at the chamber of the upper house, and other apartments, they walked to the king's palace — the first royal dwelling which most of the students ever saw. They passed through the throne room, the court saloon, the dining room, and other rooms, and some of them concluded that royalty was not half so splendid as they had supposed. But Norway is a poor country compared with many others in Europe, and it is a pity that she ever thought it necessary to spend a million and a half of dollars in a weak attempt to imitate the grandeur of other realms. There was nothing in the palace to astonish even our young republicans, though the rooms of the queen, on the first floor, were pretty and prettily furnished. The building, which is a great, overgrown structure, without symmetry or elegance, is in a beautiful situation, and surrounded by pleasant grounds, well laid out, from which a fine view of the city and fjord is obtained.

Connected with the university are several museums and cabinets, which are open to the public, and well worth a visit, though they do not compare with those of the great cities of Europe. The party walked through all these rooms, one of which contained a small collection of northern antiquities. From the university the students went to a kind of garden, which is a weak imitation of "Tivoli," in Copenhagen, containing promenades, concert room, a small opera house, and a drinking saloon. The castle of Agershuus, on a hill at the southern side of the city, was next visited. Its guns command the harbor, and it is regarded as a place of great strength, for it has successfully resisted several sieges. Climbing a long flight of steps, the party reached the ramparts, which are laid out in walks, and are much resorted to by the citizens, as they command a lovely view of the fjord and the surrounding country. A portion of the castle is used as a prison, and the convicts work in gangs about the premises.

"This was Robin Hood's prison — wasn't it, Mr.

Mapps?" asked Lincoln, who had an inquiring mind, after he had enjoyed the prospect from the ramparts for a while.

"I think not," replied the instructor. "Höyland, sometimes called the Robin Hood, but, I think, more properly the Baron Trenck, of Norway, was sentenced to imprisonment for life in this castle."

"What for?" inquired Norwood.

"For robbery and other crimes. Like Robin Hood and Mike Martin, he robbed the rich and gave to the poor, which none of you should believe makes the crime any less wicked; especially as he did not scruple to use violence in accomplishing his purpose. For some small theft he was shut up in this prison; but while the overseer was at church, Höyland broke into his room, stole some of his clothes, and quietly walked out of the castle and out of the town. He was recaptured, but repeatedly made his escape. Though he was heavily ironed, this precaution was found to be useless, and he was placed in solitary confinement in the lowest room of the citadel, where he was kept securely for several years. One evening his jailer told him that he could never get out of this room, and that he might as well promise not to attempt such an impossible feat; but Höyland replied that it was the turnkey's duty to keep him in prison if he could, and his to get out if it were possible. The next day the prisoner was missing, and the means of his escape were not at first apparent; but on further examination it was found that he had cut through the thick plank flooring of his cell, under the bed, and tunnelled under the wall into the yard of the prison.

He had replaced the planks when he left, and passing over the ramparts without difficulty, dropped into the ditch, and departed without bidding any one good by. All attempts to find him were unsuccessful, and it was believed that he had left the country.

"A year afterwards the National Bank of Norway was robbed of sixty thousand *specie-dalers*, in the most adroit and skilful manner, even without leaving any marks of violence on the iron box in which the money was kept. Not long after this occurrence, in the person of a prisoner who had been committed to the castle for a petty theft, the officers recognized Höyland. He was considerate enough to inform the authorities that his late escape had been effected, after three years of patient labor, with no other tool than a nail, while others slept. As a portion of his ill-gotten wealth was concealed in the mountains, he had the means of making friends in Christiania, where he had hidden himself. Making the acquaintance of the bank watchman, he cunningly obtained wax impressions of the key-holes of the locks on the money-chest, by which he made keys, opened the box, took the money, and locked it after him. But, like all other evil-doers, he came to grief at last. Though he was a skilful carver in wood and stone, he was not allowed to have tools, of which he made a bad use, and he was compelled to amuse himself by knitting socks on wooden pins. Unable to escape again, and not having the patience to exist without something to do, in utter despair he committed suicide in his prison."

After the visit to the fortress, the boys were allowed to walk about the city at their own pleasure; and a few of the officers went with Mr. Lowington and the doctor to the establishment of Mr. Bennett, an Englishman, who fitted out travellers intending to journey in the interior with carioles and all the other requisites. His rooms were stored with books and Norwegian curiosities and antiquities. In the court-yard of the house was a large number of second-hand carioles, which are the sole vehicles used for crossing the country. A traveller, wishing to go to Trondhjem or Bergen, would purchase the cariole in Christiania, and when he had done with it, dispose of it at the other end of his route, horses between being supplied according to law at the post stations on the road. Travellers coming from Trondhjem or Bergen sell their vehicles to Mr. Bennett. In his rooms are miniature models of the cariole for sale, which visitors purchase as a memento of their tour; as those who climb Pilatus and Rhigi, in Switzerland, buy an alpenstock on which are printed the names of the mountains they have ascended with its help.

The principal and his companions walked up to the Victoria Hotel, and inquired for Captain Kendall. He had just returned from a ride, and while the waiter was taking Mr. Lowington's card to him, Peaks presented himself in the court-yard.

"Can't find him, sir," said the boatswain, touching his hat.

"He must be somewhere in the city."

"This man has toted me all over the town, but we can't hear a word of him. He wore the uniform of the ship, and people can't tell one student from another."

"I am confident he has not left the city."

"Perhaps he has," replied Peaks, as the servant returned, followed by Captain Kendall.

"Have you lost anything or anybody?" asked Paul, laughing, after he had saluted the principal.

"Yes, we have lost a student; an English boy we shipped at Christiansand. Have you seen him?"

"Yes, sir; his room is No. 32 — next to mine," replied Paul, still laughing, as though he were much amused.

He was much amused; and that others may sympathize with him, let the reader return to Clyde Blacklock, who had shut himself up in his room to await the arrival of his mother. He had not been in the house ten minutes before he began to be impatient and disgusted with his self-imposed confinement. He examined himself carefully in the looking-glass, and was satisfied that his new clothes disguised him from his late shipmates, and also from those whom he had met on board of the Orlando. Certainly they had wrought a very great change in his appearance, and with the round-top hat on, which was entirely different from anything he had worn before, even his mother would not recognize him, unless they came near enough together to enable her to scrutinize his features. Of course none of the people from the squadron would come to the hotel, and he had not yet been called upon to register his name.

He unlocked his door, and went into the long entry which opened into the court-yard. It was stupid to stay alone in his chamber. It was some relief even to promenade the hall, for one so nervous as he was at this time. If any of the Orlando's passengers came near him, he could retreat into his room. He walked up and down several times, but this soon became stale amusement.

"Who's in the next room to mine?" he asked, as one of the waiters passed him in his promenade.

"Gentleman and lady from America, sir," replied the man; "an uncommon handsome young woman, sir."

Before the waiter could further express his opinion of the guests in No. 31, Paul Kendall came out of the room, and, seeing the servant, ordered a carriage to be ready in half an hour.

"Is there much to see in this place, sir?" asked Clyde, politely.

"Not much, I think," replied Paul.

"I dare say you are going into the interior, sir."

"Not far."

"There is fine fishing there," persisted Clyde.

"So I am told; but I haven't much time to spend in such sport, and I am afraid my wife would not enjoy it as well as I should. Do you go to the interior?"

"Yes, sir; I intend to do so when my mother and sister arrive. My mother goes a-fishing with me."

"Does she, indeed? You are from England, I suppose," added Paul, who suspected that the young man was one of those lonesome travellers eager to make a friend, and actually suffering from the want of one.

"Yes; Mockhill Manor, New Forest, Hampshire."

"Are you travelling alone?" asked Paul, who was

full of sympathy for the apparent loneliness of the young man.

"I am alone just now, but I expect my mother and sister from Christiansand to-night," replied Clyde.

"Can I do anything for you?" inquired Paul, who, after this explanation, did not regard the young gentleman's situation as so hopeless.

In his own travels he had himself experienced that sense of loneliness which is a decided misery, and had met others afflicted with it. From the manner of Clyde, he concluded he had an attack of it, and he desired to alleviate his sufferings; but if the young man's friends were coming that night, his case could not be desperate.

"No, sir; I don't know that you can. I thought, as your room is next to mine, we might make it jolly for each other. You are an American, sir, the waiter says."

"Yes, I am," laughed Paul.

"But you don't talk through the nose."

"Don't I? Well, I don't perceive that you do, either."

"I'm not a Jonathan," protested Clyde. "I dare say you are a fine gentleman, but I can't say that of all the Americans."

"Can't you? Well, I'm sorry for them. Can you say it of all the Englishmen?"

"Yes, sir; I think I can of all we meet travelling. The Americans are big bullies. I settled accounts with one of them this very day," chuckled Clyde.

"Ah! did you, indeed?"

"I think some of them know what it is to bully and

insult an Englishman by this time," added Clyde, rubbing his hands, as he thought of poor Peaks, floundering in the waters of the Fjord. "Perhaps you've heard of that American Academy ship that came into Christiania to-day."

"Yes, I have heard of her," answered Paul, curiously.

"I saw her first at Christiansand, and went on board of her with my mother and sister. I liked the looks of her, and fancied the young chaps on board of her were having a nice time. I wanted to ship in her, and I did so; but I was never among such a set of tyrants in the whole course of my life."

"Then you joined the ship," replied Paul, who had heard of the new addition to the Young America's crew, but had not seen him.

"I'm blamed if I didn't; but before my mother left the ship, a big bully of a boatswain insulted me, and I changed my mind. Yet the head master persuaded my mother to let him keep me in the ship, and I'm blamed if she didn't leave me there."

"Left you there," added Paul, when Clyde paused, apparently to give his auditor the opportunity to express his sympathy for his unfortunate situation.

"Yes, sir; she left me there, and she won't hear the last of it for one year," replied Clyde, shaking his head. "It was a mean trick, and I'll pay her for it."

"Probably she did it for the best," suggested Paul, disgusted with the assurance, and especially with the want of respect for his mother which the youth manifested, though he was anxious to hear the conclusion of his story.

"I don't care what she did it for; it was a scurvy trick. I told her I wouldn't stay in the ship, any how, and she permitted the big boatswain to hold me while she went ashore in a boat. But I knew myself, if my mother didn't know me, and I determined not to stay in her three days; and I didn't," chuckled Clyde, as he thought of what he called his own cleverness.

"What did you do?" asked Paul, deeply interested.

"I was willing to bide my time, and so I hauled sheets, and luffed, and tacked, and all that sort of thing, till we got to Christiania. When I was pulling the main boom, or something of that kind, — I don't just know what it was now, — one of the fellows in gold bands insulted me."

"What did he say to you?"

"He ordered me to be silent, and another nob did the same thing. I offered to fight them both, and I would have liked to show them what an English boy's fist is made of; but the cowards set the boatswain on me again. I would have licked him if he had fought fair; but he caught me foul, and I could do nothing. I meant to be even with that big boatswain, and I think I am," said Clyde, rubbing his hands again with delight, and laughing heartily when he thought of his brilliant achievement."

"Well, what did you do?"

"I just waited till the ship got to Christiania; and then, when all the students were at dinner, I found the big boatswain sitting on a beam that runs out over the water — I forget what they call the beam, but it's at the bow of the ship."

"The bowsprit," suggested Paul.

"No; I know the bowsprit. It wasn't that. There was another beam like it on the other side."

"O, the cat-head!"

"That's just it. Well, I went up to the big boatswain, and asked him to look at a ship, — or a 'mofferdite brig, he called it. He looked, and I just gave him a push, which dropped him off the cat's head into the bay," continued Clyde, who told his story with many a chuckle and many a laugh, seeming to enjoy it hugely himself, in spite of the want of sympathy on the part of his listener.

"You pushed him overboard!" exclaimed Paul.

"That I did, and did it handsomely, too. He never knew what hurt him till he struck the water. He swam for the bow, and I dropped into a boat, and came ashore. I saw him climb up to the deck, but I was out of his way then. Wasn't that cleverly done?"

"Rather," replied Paul, concealing his indignation.

"I think it was very cleverly done," added Clyde, annoyed at the coolness of his companion. "You couldn't have done it better yourself, sir."

"I don't think I could," replied Paul, dryly. "And you expect your mother this evening."

"Yes; and she shall take my name off the books of the ship."

"Perhaps she will not."

"O, but she will. Then the two nobs that insulted me on the ship shall hear from me."

"What do you intend to do with them?"

"I'll whip them both; if I don't my name isn't Clyde Blacklock!"

"But they will take you back to the ship before your mother arrives."

"I dare say they will, if they see me; but I don't intend to go out of the hotel till my mother comes. I shall stay in my room, or near it, the rest of the day."

The conversation was interrupted by the appearance of Mrs. Kendall, who had been preparing for a ride about the city. Paul conducted her to the carriage, satisfied that the new scholar could be found when wanted. During their excursion he told his wife the adventures of Clyde.

"But what a simpleton he was to tell you these things!" added Grace.

"He did not suspect me of knowing anything about the ship. He is one of those fellows, who, having done what he regards as a good thing, cannot help boasting of it. He considers himself a first-class hero."

When Paul returned from the ride, he found Clyde still walking about the hall, as uneasy as a fish out of water.

"Did you see anything of the Academy ship, sir?" asked he, after Mrs. Kendall had gone to her room.

"I saw her at anchor in the harbor, and all her people are walking about the town," replied Paul.

"I've kept clear of them so far; but I want to catch the two fellows with the gold bands."

"Perhaps some of them will catch you."

"Not they! I'm too cunning for clumsy fellows like them."

"I see you are," laughed Paul, amused at the assurance of the young Briton.

"If I see them, I'll settle the Alabama claims with

them on my own account. But you ought to have seen the big boatswain floundering in the water, sir."

"No doubt it was very funny."

"It was, indeed," added Clyde, as the waiter appeared, and handed a card to Captain Kendall.

"In the court yard, sir," said the servant; and Paul followed the man to the place where the visitors were waiting.

Peaks, as dry, clean, and good-natured as ever, was talking to Mr. Lowington. Paul could not help laughing as he thought of the confidence which Clyde had reposed in him, and that the fugitive had voluntarily, and without any precautions, told his adventures to one who really belonged to the fleet.

"He has told me all about it," said Paul.

"Told you?" exclaimed Mr. Lowington.

"Yes, sir; how he pushed Peaks overboard, and then ran away," laughed Paul. "I don't often wear my uniform on shore, for my wife thinks it attracts too much attention; so that he did not suspect me of any connection with the fleet."

"But where is he now?" asked the principal.

"I left him in the hall only a moment since."

"Show me his room, my hearty," said Peaks to the waiter.

"Call a carriage," added Mr. Lowington. "He will make a disturbance in the streets."

The servant led the way to the room of Clyde, followed by the rest of the party. All were rather anxious to see the clever Briton, who had done such wonders of valor and cunning, captured.

But Clyde had a pair of eyes, and, withal, a pair of

ears. From the hall where he promenaded were several doors opening into the court-yard. Perhaps the youth had a Yankee's curiosity to see who called upon his new acquaintance, and he went to one of these doors. He saw Paul walk up to the principal, and shake hands with him. There was the big boatswain too, and there were two of the nobs with the gold bands. It was evident enough to Clyde, then, that he had made a blunder in relating his exploits to a stranger. But the battle was not lost yet. His chamber was on the ground floor, and had a window which opened into Dronningensgaden. Without losing another instant, he opened the window, and dropped out into the street. He did not even wait to take the bundle which contained his ship's uniform.

When Peaks entered the chamber, the bird had flown, and the open window indicated the means by which he had escaped; but Clyde had several minutes the start of his pursuers, and had made good use of his time. The boatswain dropped out of the window, followed by Norwood and Lincoln, while the principal and the doctor went round by the doors as the more dignified means of egress. Peaks went one way, and the two lieutenants the other way.

Clyde, fearful that haste might look suspicious, walked a short distance, till he came to a building on which was a sign, *Hôtel du Nord*, and which appeared to be under repairs. He stepped in at the open door, and went up stairs. Men were at work in some of the rooms; but he avoided them, and appeared to be looking over the building. At last he came to an open window on the street from which he had entered. He looked out, and in the distance saw his pursuers running rapidly in opposite directions. After he had remained in the hotel about an hour, he ventured to leave, and walked very cautiously up the street. Feeling the need of an overcoat, he entered a store, and purchased one, which still further disguised him, so that if he met any of his late shipmates, they would be still less likely to recognize him. He walked till he came to a carriage stand; where, entering a vehicle, he pointed in the direction he wished to go, which was towards the king's palace. When the driver stopped at the gate, he pointed towards the hills in the rear of the city. The Norwegian looked astonished, and could not understand him.

"I want to go out of town."

The driver drove his horse to the other side of the street, and hailed a short, stout man, who was passing at the time.

"Do you want a guide, sir?" asked the stranger.

"Yes," promptly replied Clyde.

"Where do wish to go?"

"Over there," replied Clyde, pointing again in the direction he wished to go.

"To Sandviken?"

"Yes; that's the place," added the youth, who did not care where he went, if he could only get out of the city.

"It is more than eight miles," suggested the guide.

"I don't care if it is eighty; that's where I want to go. Are you a *commissionaire?*"

"Yes. I belong to the Victoria Hotel."

"All right; jump in."

The man made a bargain with the driver, and in a few moments Clyde was on his way to Sandviken, confident that he had escaped any further pursuit. He had already come to the conclusion not to see his mother until after the Young America had left Christiania.

In the mean time, Peaks had given up the chase. Paul assured the principal that Clyde would come back as soon as his mother arrived. Mr. Lowington did not care to have the new scholar see his mother again if he was to be a student in the Academy; but as Clyde could not be found, there appeared to be no alternative.

In a couple of hours, the fugitive reached Sandviken, where he informed his astonished guide that he intended to proceed to Christiansand by land. His courier was willing to go with him so long as he was paid; and as Clyde had plenty of money, and disbursed it freely, there was no difficulty. Though the next day was Sunday, the young traveller continued his journey, and on Monday afternoon arrived at Apalstö, at the head of one of the inland lakes, where he intended to sleep; but the station-house was full. Clyde was tired, and did not feel like going any farther. While he was sending his courier to look up a bed for him, about a dozen boys wearing the uniform of the Academy ship flashed upon his view. He was astonished and alarmed. He suspected that this party had been sent to the interior to head him off. He was determined not to be an easy victim.

One of the party had a good-sized salmon in his hand, which indicated that they had been a-fishing.

They took no notice of him, though they could not help seeing him, and Clyde took courage from this circumstance.

The fishing squad was composed of the crew of the second cutter — the unfortunates who had been run down by the steamer.

CHAPTER IX.

THE EXCURSION WITHOUT RUNNING AWAY.

THE second cutter was a wreck on the water, and the crew saved themselves by climbing up the bow of the steamer which had run down the boat. They received prompt assistance from those on board, and, as the cutter did not sink, and would not have done so, having no ballast, even if she had been cut in two, the crew were so well trained that not one of them was guilty of the absurdity of jumping overboard, and therefore no one was even very wet.

It appeared to be one of those cases where both parties had struggled to avoid the catastrophe, but the more they struggled the worse was the situation. If the cutter, on the one hand, had continued on her course, she would have escaped. If the steamer, on the other hand, had not changed her course when the calamity was threatened, the boat could have avoided her. The change of purpose in each had confused the other, and rendered unavailing the attempt to avoid the collision. The boat would have gone clear of the steamer if the latter had not put her helm to starboard. But the catastrophe was accomplished so quickly that there was not much time to philosophize; and as nothing worse than a stove boat had resulted from it, there was not much reason to complain. We are not aware that any one did complain; and we only state the appearances, not the facts.

The steamer started her wheels again after the cutter had been secured and made fast astern. The captain spoke only a few words of English, and Sanford found it quite impossible to hold a conversation with him. But Ole Amundson was at hand in this emergency.

"Tell him he needn't stop for us, Ole," said the coxswain.

"Don't you want to return to the ship?" asked the astonished waif.

"No, no," replied Sanford, in a low tone, so that some of the doubtful members of his crew might not hear him. "Where is the steamer going, Ole?"

"To Christiania, stopping at all the ports on the coast," answered Ole, when he had obtained the information from the captain.

"All right; we will go to the first place where she stops," added Sanford. "Don't say a word to the rest of the fellows, Ole."

"The first port she stops at is Lillesand," said Ole.

"Very well; we will go there."

Ole explained to the captain that the boys he had picked up wished to go to Lillesand, where they could join their ship. This plan exactly suited the young Norwegian, for he did not like the idea of being landed at Christiansand, or taken back to the ship.

"Where are we going? Why don't he put us on shore, or on board of the ship?" demanded Burchmore.

"It's a mail steamer; she is very late," replied Ole.

"But is she going to carry us off, because she is in a hurry?"

"Only to a port up here a little ways. We can come right back in another steamer," Ole explained; and Burchmore was satisfied.

Now, the captain had certainly declared that he was in a great hurry, and was not willing to wait for the boat which had put off from the ship; but he proposed to hail a boat which was passing, and send his involuntary passengers to the town in her. Ole assured him his companions wished to go to Lillesand, and he was too glad to avoid any delay. As the first cutter followed the steamer, it was decided, after consultation with the captain, to turn the stove boat adrift, so that it could be towed back to the ship by the first cutters. Sanford cast off the painter, and the pliant master of the steamer was glad to get rid of this check upon the speed of his boat. The boys watched the water-logged craft till it was picked up by the first cutter, and then passing behind an island, the squadron was out of view.

"How came you here, Ole?" asked Rodman.

"Came in the boat; but I didn't think you were going to smash her. I thought I was killed that time, sure," laughed the waif.

"But how came you in the boat?" inquired Wilde.

"I got in, of course; nobody put me in."

"When?"

"When it hung at the davits in the ship, just before the pilot came on board."

"What do you get in there for?"

"My education has been neglected, and I have to

do a great deal of thinking to make up for it. I don't like to be disturbed when I'm thinking; so I got into the boat, and covered myself with the sail."

"Tell that to the fishes," snuffed Wilde.

"You can, if you wish; I don't speak their language," laughed Ole.

"But really, Norway, what did you get into the second cutter for?" said Sanford.

"The pilot was a first cousin of mine, and I was afraid he would whip me for making faces at him when I was a baby. He never forgets anything."

"Nonsense!"

"Well, if you know better than I, don't ask me any more about it."

Ole was no more inclined to explain how he came in the second cutter than he had been to solve the mystery of being in a water-logged bateau, out of sight of land. It only appeared that while the students covered the rail and crowded the rigging to see the land, he had put himself into the boat. When the hands were called to man the braces, he, having no duty to perform, had not answered the call, and was left alone in the cutter. At sea, every precaution was taken to provide for the safety of the crew in case of any calamity. Each boat was provided with a sail, a mast, a compass, and several breakers of water, and a quantity of provisions was ready to be put in when needed. Ole stowed himself beneath the sail, which lay under the middle board, extending fore and aft. Before De Forrest took his place in the stern-sheets, Stockwell had discovered the absentee, and communicated the fact of his presence to those near him. The crew of the second cutter were entirely willing to keep his secret, as they were that of any one who needed their help. Among such boys it was regarded as dishonorable in the highest degree to betray any one; and, indeed, the principal discountenanced anything like "tale-bearing," to which the students gave a very liberal construction. Sanford had proposed that De Forrest should take a walk on shore, in order to give Ole an opportunity to escape from his confinement, which, on account of the singular obstinacy and suspicion of that officer, had threatened to be indefinitely continued, till the collision came to his aid.

"How's this?" said Stockwell, as he seated himself by the side of the coxswain, on one of the settees on the quarter-deck of the steamer.

"How's what?" asked Sanford.

"It seems to me that we are clear of the ship, and without running away."

"Don't say a word. We got spilled out the boat, and it was not our doing. We obeyed De Forrest's orders to the very letter, so that no fault can be found with us."

"Of course not."

"If De Forrest had not ordered me to shove off, I shouldn't have done so."

"Then the boat might have been ground up on the rocks."

"Do you see anything green in my eye?" replied Sanford, suggestively.

"You don't mean to say that you smashed the boat on purpose?"

"Certainly I don't mean to *say* anything of the

sort. I obey orders if I break owners, or boats either, for that matter."

"What are you going to do next?"

"I don't know. The programme is to go back in the steamer that returns to Christiansand to-morrow night."

"O, then you mean to go back."

"Your head's as thick as the broadside of an iron-clad. Of course I mean to go back."

"Immediately?"

"In the next boat."

Stockwell did not exactly like the sharp way with which Sanford dealt with his innocence. Certainly the coxswain and himself had talked about an excursion to the interior of Norway without running away; but now, though the circumstances favored the plan, his friend plainly announced his intention to return to Christiansand and join the ship. But it could be said of the coxswain that his ways were dark, and Stockwell was more inclined to wait than to question him. In two hours the steamer arrived at Lillesand, and the party went on shore. The place was only a small village, but they found accommodations for the night.

"What time does the steamer for Christiansand leave this place?" asked Sanford, as the party gathered at the station-house, which is the hotel, post-office, and establishment for furnishing horses to travellers.

"To-morrow evening," replied Ole.

"To-morrow evening!" exclaimed the coxswain. "That will never do! What time?"

"About eight o'clock," answered the waif, whose

devotion to the truth did not prevent him from stating the time two hours later than the fact warranted. "She may be two or three hours later."

"The squadron sails for Christiania to-morrow afternoon," added Sanford. "The ship will be gone before we can get there."

"She will not go without us," suggested Burchmore.

"Yes, she will," said Stockwell, who was beginning to fathom the dark ways of the coxswain. "The principal will suppose we have gone on to Christiania."

"That's so."

"But what are we to do?" demanded Tinckner.

"That's the question," added Sanford, with a blank look, as though he considered the situation as utterly hopeless.

"We are not so badly off as we might be," said Boyden.

"I don't see how it could be any worse," replied Sanford. "But I don't know that it is our fault. The captain of the steamer would not stop, after he had picked us up; at least, I don't know anything about it; but Ole said he wouldn't stop."

"He could not stop," protested the waif, vehemently. "He had only just time enough to reach Frederiksværn in season for the other steamer. If he lost her, he would be turned off. He wouldn't stop for love or money."

"No matter for that; here we are, and what are we going to do? It's no use to cry for spilled milk," continued Stockwell. "The ship will go to Christiania, and won't come near this place. Mr. Lowington will expect to find us there when he arrives, and all we have to do is to make good his calculation. We have plenty of money, and we can get there somehow or other."

Involuntarily, every fellow put his hands into his pocket; and then, if not before, they recalled the suggestion of the coxswain, made before they took their places in the cutter, that they should bring their money and their pea-jackets; but then, it seemed simply absurd that the boat had been smashed by his contrivance.

"Was it for this, Sanford, that you told us to bring our money?" said Burchmore.

"I should say a fellow ought always to carry his money with him. No one can tell what will happen to him when he goes away from the ship," replied the coxswain. "You can see that it's lucky you have it with you. We might have to spend the summer here if we had no money. When will a steamer go from here to Christiania, Norway?"

"Next Friday — just a week from to-day," replied the Norwegian, very seriously.

"A week!" exclaimed Burchmore.

"That is not long; a week is soon gone."

"But we can't stay here a week," protested Tinckner.

"I don't want to do it," added Sanford; "but if we have to do it, I suppose I can stand it as well as the rest of you."

"We can't any of us stand it," said Wilde. "Who's going to stay a week in such a place as this? I'm not, for one. I'll swim up to Christiansand first."

"Can't we hire a boat, and go back to Christiansand?" Burchmore proposed. "It is not more than twenty miles, and it would be a fine sail among these beautiful islands."

"All right; look up a boat, Norway," replied Sanford, as though entirely willing to adopt this plan.

Ole walked about the place for half an hour, accompanied by three of the boys. Perhaps he was careful not to find what he wanted; at any rate, no boat seemed to be available for the purpose desired, and when the excursionists met again, it was reported that no boat suitable for the accommodation of the party could be found.

"Then can't we engage horses, and go round to Christiansand by land?" inquired Burchmore.

"In carioles?" queried Ole, with an odd smile.

"Carioles or wagons; anything we can find."

"You can, but it will take you a day and a half," replied Ole.

"A day and a half to go twenty miles."

"About seventy miles by land," added Ole. "You must go almost up to the north pole before you can cross the river."

"O, nonsense!" exclaimed Burchmore, who could not help feeling that Ole was not altogether reliable on his figures and facts.

"If you don't believe it, go and ask the postmaster, or any one in the town," continued the waif.

"That's all very well to talk about asking any one, when no one speaks a syllable of English."

"I will do the talking for you."

"Of course you will; you have done it all thus far."

"I don't mean to say that you must really double the north pole, or that it is just seventy miles by land; but it's a long distance," Ole explained.

"No matter how far it is; we will go," added the pliant coxswain. "I'm willing to do whatever the fellows wish. It shall not be said that I was mulish."

"But if it is seventy miles, or anything like it, we couldn't get to Christiansand before the ship left."

"That's just what I was thinking," answered Sanford, with a puzzled expression on his face. "Ole says it is a long way, and I have been told that these Norwegians are very honest, and will not lie; so I suppose he has told the truth."

It was barely possible that the waif had learned to lie in England, where he had acquired his English.

"I suppose we must give up the idea of going in a boat, or going by land. We can only wait till the steamer comes," continued Burchmore, putting on a very long face.

"We can't stand that," protested Wilde.

"Well, what are you going to do?" demanded Burchmore.

"Can't you tell us, Norway?" said Tinckner.

"I know what I should do if I were in your situation, and wanted to make a sure thing of it."

"Well, what?" asked Burchmore, gathering a hope from the words of the waif.

"I should go to Christiania."

"But how?"

"By land, of course."

"It's up by the north pole."

"It is about a hundred and fifty miles from here by

water, and it can't be any more by land," said Sanford. "But I don't care what you do; I will do as the others say."

"I like the idea," added Stockwell. "It is the only safe thing we can do. "If we go back to Christiansand, we shall be too late for the ship. If we wait for a steamer to Christiania, she will be gone when we get there."

"How much will it cost to go to Christiania in this way?" inquired Wilde, who did not feel quite sure that his funds would stand such a drain.

"Here are the prices in the post-house," said Ole, as he led the way to a partition on which the posting was put up. "For one mile, one mark six skillings."

"We know all about it now," laughed Rodman. "What's a mark, and what's a skilling?"

"Twenty-four skillings make a mark, and a skilling is about a halfpenny English," Ole explained.

"About a cent of our money," continued Rodman. "One mark and six skillings would be thirty skillings, or about thirty cents."

"That will never do," interposed Wilde, shaking his head. "One hundred and fifty miles, at thirty cents a mile, would be forty-five dollars; and I suppose we have to pay for our grub besides."

"It would come to ten or twelve pounds, and Wilde has only ten pounds," added Rodman.

"No, no; you are are all wrong. That means a Norwegian mile — about seven of ours. It would be only four and two sevenths cents a mile; say, six or seven dollars to Christiania; and the grub would cost as much more," said Stockwell. "Three pounds will cover the whole expense, and that won't break any body."

After considerable discussion, it was agreed to adopt the plan proposed, and Ole was instructed to make the necessary arrangements with the station-master. The party went out to the stable to examine the carioles. They were a kind of gig, without any hood or top, with a small board behind, on which stands or sits the boy who drives the team back to the station after it has left the passenger. Tourists generally purchase the carioles in which they ride, and are not bothered with the boys. The students were not very nice about their accommodations; and finding that when two persons went in the same vehicle only half a fare extra was charged, they decided to engage but five carioles. As the law did not require the station-master to keep this number of horses in waiting, it was necessary to send "forbud" before the party started. This was an order to all the stations on the road to have five horses ready, and may be forwarded by mail or by special messenger, the expense of which was paid by the young tourists.

It was solemnly agreed that the expense should be equally divided, and Burchmore was elected cashier and paymaster. With the assistance of Ole, he changed twelve pounds into Norwegian money, and found himself heavily loaded with the small coins of the country, which would be needed in making change at the stations. After all this important business had been disposed of, the party walked all over the town and its suburbs, and were duly stared at by the astonished people.

"We ought to write a letter to Mr. Lowington, and tell him how we are situated," suggested Churchill, as they were returning to the station.

"Exactly so; and carry it to him ourselves," replied Stockwell. "I move you that Burchmore be appointed bearer of despatches."

"I mean to have the letter sent by mail," added Churchill.

"We shall be in Christiania as soon as any mail, if there is no steamer for a week," said Sanford.

"True; I didn't think of that," continued the proposer of this precaution. "The principal will be worried about us."

"Let him worry," replied the coxswain; "that is, we can't do anything to relieve his mind."

"I don't see that we can," added Churchill.

For the want of something better to do, the students turned in at an early hour in the evening, and turned out at an early hour in the morning. They all slept in the same room, some of them in beds, and the rest on the floor; but those who slept on the floor were just as well satisfied as those who slept in the beds. After a breakfast consisting mainly of fish, they piled into the carioles. They were all in exceedingly jolly humor, and seated themselves in and on the vehicles in various uncouth postures. One boy in each cariole was to drive the horse, and he was carefully instructed to do nothing but simply hold the reins, and let the well-informed animal have his own way. The horses were rather small, and very shaggy beasts; but they went off at a lively pace. At the first hill they insisted upon walking up, and most of the boys followed their example. Behind three of the carioles were the small boys who were to bring the teams back. These juvenile Norwegians were as sober and dignified as though they had been members of the Storthing, refusing to laugh at any of the wild tantrums of the crazy students.

At the first station, where the road from Lillesand joins that from Christiansand to the north, the horses ordered by "forbud" were in readiness, and the party had only to pass from one set of carioles to another. The grim post-boys did smile faintly when they received their perquisites, and others, just as immovable, took their places for the next post. The road now lay along the banks of a considerable river, and the scenery was rather interesting, though by no means grand. They passed an occasional farm; but generally the buildings were of the rudest and shabbiest description, though occasionally there was a neat residence, painted white or yellow, with roof of red tile. The boys walked up all the hills, leaving the sagacious horses to take care of themselves. All the students voted that it was jolly to travel in this manner, and there was no end to the sky-larking and racing on the road. At noon, they stopped long enough to dine, and at night found themselves at Tvetsund, at the foot of Nisser Lake, where they lodged. As this was as far as they had sent their "forbud," they decided to proceed by boat through the lake, a distance of about twenty miles.

The next day was Sunday, which was always observed with great strictness on board of the ship, no play and no unnecessary work being permitted.

There was a little church in the village, but none but Ole could understand a word of the preacher's prayer or sermon; so that the students voted it would be useless for them to go there. Four of the party, still controlled by the influences which prevailed on board of the ship, did not wish to travel on Sunday; but when it was represented that the ship might leave Christiania before the party arrived, they yielded to the wishes of the other five, and procuring boats, they proceeded on their way. At the head of the lake they took the road, and walked about seven miles to Apalstö.

"We are stuck here," said Sanford, after they had taken supper at the station-house. "This posting is a first-class fraud."

"Why, what's the matter?" demanded Burchmore, alarmed by the manner of the coxswain.

"No horses to be had till Tuesday morning."

"That's a fraud."

"Well, it can't be helped," added Sanford, philosophically. "I'm willing to walk, if the rest of the fellows say so."

"We can't walk to Christiania."

"That's so; and we should not find any more horses at the next station than here. Norway says we didn't send 'forbud,' which must be done when more than three horses are wanted."

"Why didn't Ole send 'forbud,' then?"

"He said we had better go by boat part of the way; it would be easier. But part of us can take the three horses that are ready, and go on with them."

"I don't believe in separating."

"We are only a day and a half from Christiania, and we shall arrive by Wednesday noon. The ship won't leave before that time."

So Burchmore was persuaded to submit to his fate like a philosopher, which, however, was not considered very hard, when it was announced that there was excellent fishing in the vicinity. It is to be feared that Ole and the coxswain had created this hinderance themselves, for the law of the country allows only three hours' delay in the furnishing of horses. The farmers are compelled to supply them, and doubtless twenty could have been provided in the time allowed, though the young tourists were able to give twelve hours' notice. This, however, did not suit the coxswain's purposes, and as he and Ole had occupied the same cariole, there was no want of concert in their words and actions. On Monday the students went a-fishing, paying a small sum for a license to do so, though this is not necessary in all parts of Norway. The united catch of the whole party was one salmon, taken by Burchmore, and weighing about eight pounds. It was voted by the party, before this result was reached, in the middle of the afternoon, that fishing in Norway was "a first-class fraud." We heard of a party of three, who fished two weeks, and caught eight salmon, though this want of luck is the exception, rather than the rule, in the north.

As the party returned from their excursion, bearing the single trophy of their patience, Clyde Blacklock discovered them. He was alarmed at first, but when he recognized no one among them whom he had seen on board of the ship, he concluded they did not belong to her.

"Good evening, sir," said he, addressing Sanford, who seemed to be the chief of the excursionists. "You have been a-fishing?"

"Yes; and ten of us have one fish to show for a whole day's work," laughed the coxswain.

"Poor luck; but you seem to be sailors," continued the Briton.

"We belong to the ship Young America."

"Ah, indeed!"

"That's so."

In half an hour Clyde and Sanford were on excellent terms. The former, when he learned that his new acquaintance had not been sent after him, was quite communicative, and even told the story of his experience on board of the ship, and of his escape from bondage. Sanford laughed, and seemed to enjoy the narrative; but straightway the coxswain began to tremble when he learned that Clyde had with him a Norwegian who spoke English. It was necessary to get rid of so dangerous a person without any delay. The Briton liked Sanford so well that he was not willing to leave him; and, indeed, the whole party were so jolly that he desired to join his fortunes with theirs. Sanford wrote a brief letter to Mr. Lowington, stating the misfortunes of the party, and that they expected to arrive in Christiania on Wednesday or Thursday.

"Now, Mr. ——. I don't know your name," said Sanford, when he found Clyde, after he had written the epistle.

"Blacklock," replied the Briton — "Clyde Blacklock."

"Well, Blacklock, if you want an up-and-down good time, come with us."

"Where? To Christiania? into the lion's den?"

"Not yet, but — don't open your mouth; don't let on for the world," whispered the coxswain, glancing at his companions.

"Not a word," added Clyde, satisfied he had found the right friend.

"We are going to the Rjukanfos to-morrow, but only one or two of us know it yet. Your man will spoil all. Send him back to Christiania this very afternoon. Here's a blind for him; let him take this letter."

Clyde liked plotting and mischief, and as soon as his guide had eaten his supper, he was started for his home in the capital, glad enough to go, for he had been paid for all the time agreed upon; and Sanford ceased to tremble lest he should expose to his companions the mistake in regard to horses, or another blunder which was to be made the next morning.

CHAPTER X.

GOTTENBURG AND FINKEL.

ON Saturday night, as Clyde had anticipated, his mother arrived at Christiania; and the people at the Victoria informed her of the disappearance of her son. The next morning she hastened on board of the ship, and heard the principal's story. Mrs. Blacklock wept bitterly, and was fearful that her darling boy was forever lost; but Mr. Lowington assured her that no serious harm could befall him. He spoke very plainly to her in regard to Clyde's character and his ungovernable passions, assuring her that he must certainly come to an evil end within a few years, if he was not restrained and controlled. The poor mother felt the truth of all he said, and was willing that he should continue the beneficent work upon which he had commenced. She spent the forenoon on board, and was introduced to Kendall and Shuffles and their ladies. The principal illustrated what he had said about Clyde by relating the history of the present captain and owner of the Feodora, and Mrs. Blacklock went away even hopeful that her boy might yet be saved to her.

On Monday, the first secular day of the month, the new list of officers was announced in each vessel of the squadron. The changes on board of the ship were not very violent, though the third lieutenant became captain, while Cumberland became the commodore.

"I congratulate you, Captain Lincoln," said Dr. Winstock to the new commander, when he appeared in the uniform of his new rank.

"Thank you, sir," replied Lincoln.

"I have been satisfied for some time that you would attain this position."

"I am only sorry to be promoted over Judson and Norwood, for they have always been good friends of mine."

"If they are good and true friends they will rejoice at your success, though it places you over them. You have worked very hard, and you are fully entitled to your rank."

"Thank you, sir. I have tried to do my duty," replied Lincoln, modestly.

"When I see a young gentleman use the library as freely as you do, I am always tolerably confident that he will attain a high rank. We go on shore this forenoon, I believe."

"I heard we were to make an excursion to-day, and another to-morrow."

"You will see something of the interior of Norway, after all, though it is not quite possible to transport two hundred boys over a country where the facilities for travel are so meagre," added the surgeon.

"For my part, I should like to walk, even a hundred miles."

"That is not practicable. How could such a crowd be lodged and fed, in some of the small villages where you would be compelled to pass the night?"

"I suppose it would not be possible, and I shall be satisfied with whatever the principal thinks best," replied the captain.

The students were called to muster, and Mr. Lowington explained that he proposed to spend the day, in picnic style, at Frogner Sæter, and that the party would walk. The boats were then prepared, and the crews of the several vessels went on shore. Captains Kendall and Shuffles procured carriages, for the ladies were not able to walk so far. Passing out of the more densely settled portions of the city, the excursionists came to a delightful region, abounding in pleasant residences, some of which were grand and lofty. For a time the landscape was covered with small cottages, painted white or yellow; but as they proceeded they came to a country very sparsely settled, and very similar to that of New England. The road lay through woods of pine and fir, and had been constructed by Mr. Heftye, a public-spirited citizen, who owned a large estate at the summit of the hill.

"This looks just like Maine," said Captain Lincoln, who walked at the side of Dr. Winstock.

"Exactly like it. There is a house, however, which is hardly so good as those you see in Maine," replied the doctor.

"It isn't any better than a shanty, and the barn is as good as the house. I wonder what that is for;" and Lincoln pointed to a bunch of straw, on the top of a pole, at the entrance of the barn. "I have seen two or three of those here, and near Christiansand."

"It was grain placed there for the birds during the winter."

"That's very kind of the people, I must say."

"They are very kind to all their animals."

Near the summit of the hill, the party came to the summer-house of Mr. Heftye, a very neat structure of wood, with a piazza, from which is obtained a beautiful view of the surrounding country. Another half hour brought them to the top of the hill, where the proprietor had erected a wooden tower, or observatory. It was some sixty or seventy feet high, and was stayed with rope guys, extending to the trees on four sides, to prevent it from being blown over. Only twenty of the boys were permitted to go up at one time, for the wind was tolerably fresh, and the structure swayed to and fro like the mast of a ship in a sea. From the top, mountains fifty miles distant could be seen. Christiania Fjord lay like a panorama in the distance, stretching as far as the eye could reach. To the west the country looked wild and desolate, and was covered with wood-crowned mountains, though none of any considerable height could be seen. It was a magnificent view, and some of the most enthusiastic of the students declared that it was worth a voyage to Norway; but boys are proverbially extravagant.

A couple of hours were spent on the hill, the lunch was eaten, and the boys declared that they were well rested. The return walk was not so pleasant, for the novelties of the region had been exhausted. The road passed through private property, where there were at least a dozen gates across it in different places; and as the party approached, a woman, a boy, or a girl appeared, to open them. Kendall or Shuffles rewarded each of them with a few skillings for the service. When their two and four skilling pieces were exhausted, they were obliged to use larger coins, rather than be mean; but it was observed that the Norwegians themselves, though able to ride in a carriage, never gave anything. It was amusing to see the astonishment of the boys and girls when they received an eight skilling piece, and the haste with which they ran to their parents to exhibit the prize.

The party reached the vessels at five o'clock, and after supper the boats were again in demand for a visit to Oscarshal, the white summer palace, which could be seen from the ship. Mr. Bennett had provided the necessary tickets, and made the arrangements for the excursion. It is certainly a very pretty place, but there are a hundred country residences in the vicinity of New York, Boston, or any other large city of the United States, which excel it in beauty and elegance, as well as in the expense lavished upon them. Before returning to the anchorage, the boat squadron pulled about for a couple of hours among the beautiful islands, and when the students returned to the fleet, they felt that they had about exhausted Christiania and its environs.

The next day they went by the railroad train to Eidsvold, and there embarked in the steamer Kong Oscar for a voyage of sixty-five miles up the Mjosen Lake to Lillehammer, where they arrived at half past five in the afternoon. The scenery of the lake is pleasant, but not grand, the slope of the hills being covered with farms. Near the upper end, the hills are higher, and the aspect is more picturesque. Some of the western boys thought it looked like the shores of the Ohio River, others compared it with the Delaware, and a New Hampshire youth considered it more like Lake Winnipiseogee.

Lillehammer is a small town of seventeen hundred inhabitants. M. Hammer's and Madame Ormsrud's hotel were not large enough to accommodate the party, and they began to experience some of the difficulties of travelling in such large numbers; but Mr. Bennett had done his work well, and sleeping-rooms were provided in other houses for the rest. The tourists rambled all over the town and its vicinity, looked into the saw-mills, visited the farms, and compared the agriculture with that of their own country; and it must be added that Norway suffered very much in the comparison, for the people are slow to adopt innovations upon the methods of their fathers.

Early in the morning — for steamers in Norway and Sweden have a villanous practice of starting at unseemly hours — the students embarked for Eidsvold, and were on board the vessels long before the late sunset. On the quarter, waiting for the principal, was Clyde's courier, who had arrived that morning, after the departure of the excursionists. He evidently had not hurried his journey, though he had been told to do so. He delivered Sanford's brief note, which was written in pencil, and Mr. Lowington read it. The absentees were safe and well, and would arrive by Thursday. He was glad to hear of their safety, but as the squadron was now ready to sail, he regretted the delay.

"Where did you leave the boys?" asked the principal of the courier.

"At Apalstö," replied the guide, whose name was Poulsen.

"Do you belong there?"

"No, sir; I live in Christiania. I went down there with a young gentleman last Saturday."

"Who was he?"

"Mr. Blacklock, sir; a young English gentleman."

"Ah! did you? And where is Mr. Blacklock now?"

"I left him at Apalstö with a party of young gentlemen who were dressed like the people here; and he sent me back with this letter," replied Poulsen, who proceeded to explain that Clyde had engaged him as courier for Christiansand, but had changed his mind when he met the party belonging to the ship, and had concluded to return to Christiania with them.

This was precisely what he had been told to say by the young Briton, and probably he believed that it was a correct statement. The principal saw no reason to doubt the truth of it, for Clyde must be satisfied that his mother was in Christiania by this time, and would naturally wish to join her. Anxious to console Mrs. Blacklock, Mr. Lowington called for a boat, and hastened on shore to see her. He found her, her daughter, and Paul Kendall and lady, in the reading-room at the Victoria — a unique apartment, with a fountain in the centre, a glass gallery over the courtyard, and lighted with many-colored lamps. The principal communicated the intelligence he had received of her son to Mrs. Blacklock, whose face lighted up at the news.

"Then you have heard from the absentees, Mr. Lowington," said Paul Kendall.

"Yes; they are on their way to Christiania, and Sanford says they will arrive to-morrow, at farthest; but they may be delayed," replied the principal.

"No one need worry about them if they are safe and well," added Paul, glancing at Clyde's mother.

"They are safe and well, but I intended to sail for Gottenburg to-morrow morning. I have almost concluded to do so, and leave some one to accompany the boys to Gottenburg in the steamer. I do not like to delay the whole fleet for them."

"It would take a long time to beat out of the fjord against a head wind," added Paul.

"If the wind is fair to-morrow morning, I shall sail, whether they arrive or not."

"A steamer leaves for Gottenburg on Saturday morning, and she may arrive as soon as your ship," added Paul.

"Very true. I think I will leave Peaks to look out for the absentees. Are you sure the steamer goes on Saturday?"

"Yes, sir; here is the time table," replied Paul, producing a paper he had obtained at Mr. Bennett's. "Dampskibet Kronprindsesse Louise."

"That's Norwegian, Paul. Can you read it?" laughed Mr. Lowington.

"A little. 'Hver Löverday;' that means on Saturday; 'at 6 fm.,' which is early in the morning. She arrives at Gottenburg about midnight."

"That will answer our purpose very well. We shall get under way early in the morning, Paul."

"Then I will go on board of the yacht to-night, sir; but you need not wait for me, for I think I can catch you if you should get two or three hours the start of me. I haven't used my balloon jib yet, and am rather anxious to do so."

"I shall not wait for you, then, Paul."

After a long conversation with Mrs. Blacklock, in which he assured her again that nothing but firmness on her part could save her son from ruin, the principal left the hotel, and returned to the ship. In the evening Mr. and Mrs. Kendall went on board of the Grace. On the following morning, the wind being a little north of west, the signal for sailing was displayed on board of the Young America, and at six o'clock the fleet were under way. The weather was beautiful, and the fresh breeze enabled all the vessels to log eight knots an hour, which brought them fairly into the Skager Rack early in the afternoon.

"I suppose we are off the coast of Sweden now," said Norwood, as he glanced at the distant hills on the left.

"The pilot said Frederikshald was in this direction," replied Captain Lincoln, pointing to the shore. "It is at the head of a small fjord, and is near the line between Norway and Sweden."

"Charles XII. was killed there — wasn't he?"

"That's the place. The fortress of Frederiksteen is there, on a perpendicular rock four hundred feet high."

"I wish we went nearer to the Swedish coast," added Norwood.

"We shall see enough of it before we leave the Baltic," said Lincoln.

"Probably we shall not care to see it after we have been looking at it a week."

"According to the chart, this part of the coast is fringed with islands, but they don't look so bare and desolate as those of Norway. I had an idea that everything on this side of the ocean was entirely different from what we see on our side," added the captain.

"That was just my idea."

"But it isn't so. It ·is almost the same thing here as the coast of Maine. The shore here is hilly, and through the glass it looks as though it was covered with pine forests."

"I expect to see something different before we return."

"Not in the Baltic; for I fancy most of the southern coast looks like that of our Middle and Southern States."

"Up here, even the houses look just as they do at home."

"I don't believe we shall find it so in Denmark."

As there was little to be seen, the regular routine of the squadron was followed, and those who were in the steerage, attending to their recitations, did not feel that they were losing anything. Later in the day, the wind was light, and the vessels made very little progress, though the course brought them nearer to the coast, where on the port bow appeared a high promontory, extending far out into the sea. The wind died out entirely just before sunset, and the sails hung motionless from the spars; for there was no swell to make them thrash about, as at sea. It was utter silence, and it was hard to believe that very ugly storms often made sad havoc in this channel.

When the sun rose the next morning it brought with it a light breeze from the west, and the fleet again skimmed merrily along over the water. Its course was near the town of Marstrand, a noted Swedish watering-place, situated on an island. Soon after, pilots were taken, and the vessels stood into the harbor of Gottenburg, which is formed by the mouth of Göta River. Along the sides of the channel were posts set in the water, for the convenience of vessels hauling in or out of the harbor. The fleet came to anchor in a convenient part of the port, and those on board proceeded to take a leisurely survey of the city. The portion of the town nearest to them was built on low, flat land, and they could see the entrances of various canals. Farther back was a series of rugged hills, which were covered with pleasant residences and beautiful gardens. After dinner the students were mustered on deck, to listen to a few particulars in regard to the city, though it was understood that the general lecture on Sweden would be reserved until the arrival of the squadron at Stockholm."

"What city is this?" asked Mr. Mapps.

"Gottenburg," replied a hundred of the students.

"That is plain English. What do the Swedes call it?"

"G-ö-t-e-b-o-r-g," answered Captain Lincoln, spelling the word.

"Perhaps I had better call on Professor Badois to pronounce it for you."

"Yāt-a-borg," said the instructor in languages, repeating the pronunciation several times, which, however, cannot be very accurately expressed with English characters. "And the river here is Ya-tah."

"The French call the city *Gothembourg*. It is five miles from the sea, and is connected with Stockholm by the Göta Canal, which is a wonderful piece of engineering. Steamboats ply regularly between Gottenburg and the capital through this canal, the voyage occupying three or four days."

"I intend to make a trip up this canal as far as the Wenern Lake, with the students," said Mr. Lowington.

A cheer greeted this announcement, and then the professor described the canal minutely.

"The principal street of Gottenburg," he continued, "is on the canal, extending through the centre of the city. There are no remarkable buildings, however, for the city is a commercial place. It was founded by Gustavus Adolphus, and, like many other cities of the north, being built of wood, it has several times been nearly destroyed by fire. The buildings now are mostly of stone, or of brick covered with plaster. The environs of the city, as you may see from the ship, are very pleasant. Now a word about the money of Sweden. The government has adopted a decimal system, of which the unit is the *riksdaler*, containing one hundred *öre*. The currency in circulation is almost entirely paper, though no bills smaller than one riksdaler are issued. The silver coins in use are the half and the quarter riksdaler, and the ten-öre piece; the latter being a very small coin. On the coppers, the value in öre is marked. A riksdaler is worth about twenty-seven cents of our money. Sweden is a cheap country."

The signal was made for embarking in the boats,

and in a few moments the Gottenburgers, as well as the people on board of the foreign vessels in the harbor, were astonished by the evolutions of the squadron. The students landed, and dividing into parties, explored the city. Their first care was to examine the canal, and the various craft that floated upon it; but the latter, consisting mainly of schooners, were not different from those they saw at home. They visited the exchange, the cathedral, the residence of the governor of the province, and other principal edifices.

"How do you feel, Scott?" asked Laybold, after they had walked till they were tired out, and it was nearly time to go to the landing-place.

"Tired and hungry," replied the wag. "I wonder if these Swedishers have anything to eat."

"Probably they do; here's a place which looks like a restaurant."

"I feel as though I hadn't tasted food for four months. Let's go in."

They entered the store, which was near the *Bourse*. A neatly-dressed waiter bowed to them, and Scott intimated that they wanted a lunch. The man, who understood English, conducted them to a table, on which a variety of eatables was displayed, some of which had a familiar look, and others were utterly new and strange. The waiter filled a couple of wine-glasses from a decanter containing a light-colored fluid, and placed them before the boys.

"What's that?" asked Scott, glancing suspiciously at the wine-glass.

"*Finkel*," replied the man.

"Exactly so; that's what I thought it was," replied

Scott, who had never heard of the stuff before. "Is it strong?"

"No," answered the waiter, shaking his head with a laugh. "Everybody drinks it in Sweden."

"Then we must, Laybold, for we are somebody."

Scott raised the glass. The fluid had the odor of anise-seed, and was not at all disagreeable. The taste, too, was rather pleasant at first, and Scott drank it off. Laybold followed his example. We must do them the justice to say that neither of them knew what " finkel " was. Something like strangulation followed the swallowing of the fluid.

"That's not bad," said Scott, trying to make the best of it.

"No, not bad, Scott; but what are you crying about?" replied the other, when he recovered the use of his tongue.

"I happened to think of an old aunt of mine, who died and left me all her money," added Scott, wiping his eyes. "But you needn't cry; she didn't leave any of the money to you."

"What are you going to eat?"

"I generally eat victuals," replied Scott, picking up a slice of bread on which was laid a very thin slice of smoked salmon. "That's not bad."

The waiter passed to Laybold a small plate of sandwiches, filled with a kind of fish-spawn, black and shining. The student took a huge bite of one of them, but a moment elapsed before he realized the taste of the interior of the sandwich; then, with the ugliest face a boy could assume, he rushed to the door, and violently ejected the contents of his mouth into the street.

"What's the matter?" demanded the waiter, struggling to keep from laughing.

"What abominably nasty stuff!" exclaimed Laybold. "It's just like fish slime."

"Don't you like it, Laybold?" asked Scott, coolly.

"Like it? I don't like it."

"Everybody in Sweden eats it," said the waiter.

"What's the matter with it? Is it like defunct cat?" asked Scott.

"More like defunct fish. Try it."

"I will, my lad," added Scott, taking a liberal bite of one of the sandwiches.

"How is it?" inquired Laybold.

"First rate; that's the diet for me."

"Very good," said the waiter.

"You don't mean to say you like that stuff, Scott."

"The proof of the pudding is the eating of the bag. I do like it, even better than 'finkel.'"

"I don't believe it. No one with a Christian stomach could eat such stuff."

"You judge by your own experience. I say it is good. Yours isn't a Christian stomach, and that's the reason you don't like it."

"You are a heathen, Scott."

"Heathen enough to know what's good."

"Some more finkel, sir?" suggested the waiter.

"No more finkel for me," replied Scott, whose head was beginning to whirl like a top.

"Better take some more," laughed Laybold, who was in the same condition.

"I can't stop to take any more; I'm hungry," replied Scott, who continued to devour the various viands on the table, till his companion's patience was exhausted.

"Come, Scott, we shall be late at the landing."

"We won't go home till morning," chanted the boozy student.

"I will go now;" and Laybold stood up, and tried to walk to the door — a feat which he accomplished with no little difficulty.

"Don't be in a hurry, my boy. Come and take some finkel."

"I don't want any finkel."

"Then come and pay the bill. I shall clean out this concern if I stay any longer."

"How much, waiter?" stammered Laybold.

"One riksdaler."

"Cheap enough. I should have been broken if they charged by the pound for what I ate."

"That's so," added Laybold, as he gave the waiter an English sovereign, and received his change in paper.

"Now, my boy, we'll go to sea again," said Scott, as he staggered towards the door. "See here, Laybold."

"Well, what do you want?" snarled the latter.

"I'll tell you something, if you won't say anything about it to any one."

"I won't."

"Don't tell the principal."

"No."

"Well, then, we're drunk," added Scott, with a tipsy grin.

" You are."

" I am, my boy; I don't know a bobstay from a bowling hitch. And you are as drunk as I am, Laybold."

" I know what I am about."

" So do I know what you are about. You are making a fool of yourself. Hold on a minute," added Scott, as he seated himself on a bench before a shop.

" Come along, Scott."

" Not for Joseph."

" We shall be left."

" That's just what I want. I'm not going to present myself before the principal in this condition — not if I know it."

Laybold, finding that it was not convenient to stand, seated himself by the side of his companion. Presently they discovered a party of officers on their way to the boats, and they staggered into a lane to escape observation. The two students, utterly vanquished by "finkel," did not appear at the landing, and the boats left without them.

CHAPTER XI.

ON THE WAY TO THE RJUKANFOS.

"WHAT may the Rjukanfos be?" asked Clyde Blacklock, after his courier had started on his return to Christiania.

"O, it's a big thing," replied Sanford. "You can bet high on it."

"Doubtless I can; but is it a mountain, a river, or a lake?"

"'Pon my word, I don't know. Here, Norway!" he shouted to Ole, who was with the rest of the party.

"I'm here, Mr. Coxswain," replied the waif.

"What's the Rjukanfos? You told me we ought to go there; but I'll be hanged if I know whether it's a lake or a river."

"Neither a lake nor a river," replied Ole. "It's a big waterfall. *Fos*, on the end of a word, always makes a waterfall of it. There's another, the Vöring-fos; but that's too far away."

"How far is it?"

"I don't know; but it's a long distance," added Ole. "All the other fellows think we are going to Christiania in the morning."

"All but Stockwell and Rodman," answered Sanford, who had told Ole about the new recruit.

"So you are going to play it upon them — are you?" laughed Clyde.

"Just a little. We don't want to leave Norway without seeing something of the country, and the rest of the fellows won't go. So we are going to take them along with us."

"Excellent! That will be a magnificent joke," exclaimed Clyde. "I'm with you. I suppose you all ran away from the ship when you found the tyranny was too much for you."

"O, no! We didn't run away. We wouldn't do that. Somehow, by an accident, our boat was stove, and we were carried off by a steamer. Then we couldn't get back to Christiansand before the ship sailed, and we were obliged to come across the country to Christiania, you see."

"I see," replied Clyde, knowingly. "But you don't mean to go back to the ship — do you?"

"Certainly we do," protested Sanford.

"Then you are bigger spoonies than I thought you were."

"But we are afraid the ship will be gone before we can reach Christiania."

"O, you are afraid of it."

"Very much afraid of it."

"You wouldn't cry if you found she had gone — would you?"

"Well, perhaps we should not cry, for we think we ought to be manly, and not be babies; but, of course, we should feel very bad about it."

"O, you would!"

"Certainly we should; for if we were caught running away, staying away longer than is necessary, or anything of that sort, our liberty would be stopped, and we should not be allowed to go on shore with the rest of the fellows."

"You are a deep one, Mr. Coxswain," added Clyde.

"O, no! I'm only a simple-minded young man, that always strives to do his duty as well as he knows how."

"I dare say you think it is your duty to visit the — what-ye-call-it? — the waterfall."

"You see it is just as near to go that way as the other."

"Is it?"

"Well, if it isn't, we shall not know the fact till after we have been there."

"I think I understand you perfectly, Mr. Coxswain; but I don't intend to return to the ship under any circumstances."

"You can do as you please, but if we should happen to miss the ship, why, we shall be obliged to travel till we find her."

"Exactly so," laughed Clyde.

"But don't understand me that we mean to run away, or to keep away from the ship any longer than is absolutely necessary; for we are all good boys, and always mean to obey our officers."

"I don't mean to do any such thing. After I hear that the ship has left Christiania, I shall go there, find my mother, and travel where I please."

The next morning the party started on their journey, and by the middle of the afternoon arrived at a station between Lysthus and Tinoset, where the road to the Rjukanfos branched off from that to the capital. They were compelled to wait an hour here for a change of horses. Rogues rarely believe that they are suspected, and Sanford was confident that his companions, with the exception of Rodman and Stockwell, had no idea of his intentions. Burchmore had not failed to notice the repeated conferences between those who were plotting the mischief. He was not quite satisfied with the delay which had enabled the party to catch that solitary salmon at Apalstö. He was one of the first to enter the station-house where the carioles stopped. On the table he found "The Hand-book of Norway," which contained a large map. He was anxious to possess this book.

"*Hvor?*" said he, using a word he had learned of Ole, which meant "how much." at the same time holding up the book, and exhibiting his money.

"*Tre*," replied the woman in the room; by which he understood her to mean three marks, for at the same time she laughingly held up three fingers.

Burchmore paid the money, and put the book into his pocket. Retreating behind the stable with Churchill, who rode in the cariole with him, he produced the volume, and spread out the map. Without much difficulty he found the road by which the party had come. Everything was right so far, and he was satisfied that they should arrive at Kongsberg that night.

"Can you make out what's up, Burchmore?" asked Churchill, with whom the former had discussed his doubts and fears.

"No; everything is right. Here we are, at the

branching off of these two roads," replied Burchmore, indicating the locality with the point of his knife.

"But Sanford is up to something. He, and Ole, and Stockwell are whispering together half the time. Perhaps they mean to leave us somewhere on the road."

"They can, if they like," added Burchmore. "I am cashier, you know. Each fellow has paid me seven pounds, which I have changed into species and marks. No other one has any Norwegian money, or, at least, not more than a specie or two. They won't leave me."

"They wouldn't make anything by it."

"And Sanford runs with that English fellow, who seems to be a little fast."

"He's a hard one," added Churchill, shaking his head.

"Let them go it; I can keep the run of them now," said Burchmore, as he folded up the map, and put the Hand-book in his pocket. "Don't say anything about this book, Churchy."

"Not a word."

"I know where we are now, and I think I shall know better than to wait a whole day for horses again. That was a sell."

"Do you think so?"

"I thought so at the time, but I didn't want to make a fuss. I changed a sovereign for Ole yesterday, and I believe Sanford has bought him up. Never mind; we take the right hand road here, and as long as we keep moving I haven't a word to say."

In less than an hour the horses were ready, and the

procession of carioles moved off. Ole and Sanford led the way, and turned to the left, instead of the right.

"That's wrong," said Burchmore, very much excited.

"But what do they mean by going this way?" added Churchill.

"I don't know, and I don't care; I only know it is the wrong way. Hallo!" he shouted to Sanford, and stopped his pony, which compelled three others behind him to stop also.

"What's the matter?" called Sanford.

"You are going the wrong way," replied the cashier.

"No, this is right; come along;" and the coxswain started his team again.

But Burchmore refused to follow him, and continued to block the way against those behind him.

"Out of the way!" cried Clyde, who was in the rear.

"This is not the right way to Kongsberg," said Burchmore.

"Out of the way, or I'll smash you!" added the imperious Briton.

The cashier was a peaceable young gentleman, and turned his horse out of the road. The cariole of Sanford was now out of sight.

"Why don't you go ahead?" demanded Tinckner. "How do you know it is the wrong road?"

"I am certain of it. Those fellows are up to some trick."

As a portion of the procession did not follow its leader, Sanford and his companions turned back.

"What's the matter, Burchmore? Why don't you come along?" cried the coxswain, angrily.

"This is not the right road."

"Isn't it, Ole?" added the coxswain, turning to his companion in the cariole.

"Certainly it is."

"I know it isn't," protested the cashier, vehemently. "You are up to some trick."

"What trick?" asked Sanford, mildly, as he put on his look of injured innocence.

"I don't know what; but I know this is not the right road to Kongsberg."

"Who said anything about Kongsberg? We intend to go by the shortest way. Don't we, Ole?"

"To be sure we do," replied the ready waif. "We are not going way round by Kongsberg."

"You can't bluff me."

"Don't want to bluff you. Go whichever way you like; and the one who gets to Christiania first is the best fellow. That's all I have to say."

Sanford turned his pony, and drove off again, followed by Clyde, Stockwell, and Rodman.

"How do you know this isn't the right way?" inquired Tinckner.

"I'll tell you," replied the cashier, jumping out of the cariole, and taking the Hand-book from his pocket.

The others soon joined him, and exhibiting the map, he explained his position to his friends.

"Here's another road to Kongsberg," said Summers, indicating its direction on the map. "They may be going that way."

"It is possible," added Burchmore, puzzled by this discovery. "It is farther that way than by Lysthus."

"Not much; there's hardly any difference. I'm in favor of following Sanford."

So were nearly all of them, and the cashier finally yielded. The tourists resumed their seats, and soon overtook the coxswain, who had evidently expected to be followed. Burchmore was annoyed by the discovery he had made, but as the pony attached to the cariole slowly climbed the hills, he studied the map and the text of the book he had bought.

"We can't go much farther on this tack," said he, as he folded up his map.

"What's to prevent us from keeping on to the north pole?" asked Churchill.

"It is almost night, in the first place, and in the second, we shall come to a lake in the course of an hour, where we must take boats."

"I don't believe anything is wrong about the matter."

"Don't you? Then what are we doing up here?"

"Never mind; we shall soon come to that other road, and then we shall know whether Sanford means to go to Kongsberg or not."

"He has stopped ahead of us. He is waiting for us to come up," added Burchmore.

"Yes; and there is the road which turns off to the right."

"Why don't he go ahead?"

Sanford and those who had arrived with him left the carioles, and gathered at the junction of the two roads. Burchmore followed their example.

"What's the matter? What are you stopping here for?" demanded Clyde Blacklock, rather imperiously.

"Some of the fellows think we are going to play them a trick," said Sanford, with his sweet and innocent smile.

"Who thinks so?" asked Clyde.

"Burchmore."

"Which is Burchmore?"

"That's my name," replied the cashier, rather indifferently.

"Are you the fellow that wants to break up the party?" blustered Clyde.

"No, I'm not. I'm the fellow that wants to go to Christiania. We ought to have kept to the right at the last station."

"I insist on going this way."

"I don't object; you can go whichever way you please," added the cashier, very gently.

"But we mean to keep the party together; and we might as well fight it out here as in any other place."

Clyde threw off his overcoat, as though he intended to give a literal demonstration of his remark.

"I don't consider you as one of the party," added Burchmore.

"Don't you?"

"No, I do not. You don't belong to our ship, and I don't pay your bills."

"No matter for that. If you are not willing to go the way the rest of us wish to go, I'll pound you till you are willing."

"No, no, Old England; we don't want anything

of that sort. Burchmore is a first-rate fellow," interposed the politic Sanford.

"You leave this fellow to me; I'll take care of him. I can whip him out of his boots."

"I shall stick to my boots for the present," replied Burchmore, who did not seem to be intimidated by the sharp conduct of the Briton. "I am willing to listen to reason, but I shall not be bullied into anything."

"What do you mean by bullied? Do you call me a bully?" foamed Clyde.

"You can draw your own inferences."

"Do you call me a bully?" demanded Clyde, doubling his fists, and walking up to the cashier.

"Enough of this," said Sanford, stepping between the Briton and his intended victim. "We shall not allow anybody to lick Burchmore, for he is a good fellow, and always means right."

"I don't allow any fellow to call me a bully," replied Clyde.

"He didn't call you a bully. He only said he would not be bullied into anything."

"It's the same thing."

"No matter if it is, Old England. You volunteered to pound him if he wouldn't go with us; and it strikes me that this is something like bullying," added the coxswain, with a cheerful smile.

"I shall thrash him for his impudence, at any rate."

"It isn't exactly civil to tell a fellow you will pound him if he won't go with us; and who shall thrash you for your impudence, eh, Old England?"

"I mean what I say."

"We shall allow no fight on this question, my gentle Britisher. If you should happen to hit Burchmore, I have no doubt he would wallop you soundly for your impudence."

"I should like to see him do it," cried Clyde, pulling off his coat, and throwing himself into the attitude of the pugilist.

"No, you wouldn't, Albion; and if you would you can't have that pleasure. There will be no fight to-day."

"Yes, there will," shouted Clyde.

"Not much;" and Sanford, Rodman, and Stockwell placed themselves between Burchmore and Clyde.

"Dry up, Great Britain!" added Wilde.

"We have a point to settle here," continued Sanford, taking no further notice of the belligerent Briton. "The right hand road goes to Kongsberg; but there is no hotel in that direction where we could sleep to-night. I propose, therefore, that we go on to — what's the name of the place, Norway?"

"Tinoset," replied Ole.

"To Tinoset, where there is a big hotel."

"How far is it?" asked Churchill.

"Only two or three miles. Then to-morrow we can go on to Kongsberg, unless you prefer to go a better way. I'm always ready to do just what the rest of the fellows say," added Sanford.

The matter was discussed in all its bearings, and even Burchmore thought it better to sleep at Tinoset.

"All right," said Sanford, as he moved off towards his cariole.

"Not yet," interposed Clyde, who still stood with

his coat off. "I haven't settled my affair with this spoony."

Burchmore and Churchill walked leisurely towards their vehicle, while Rodman and Stockwell covered the retreat.

"If you thrash him, you thrash the whole of us, Great Britain," said Rodman.

"What kind of a way is that?" demanded the disgusted Briton.

"We won't have any fight over this matter," added Stockwell. "Jump in, and let us be off."

"We'll settle it when we get to that place," replied Clyde, seeing that this opportunity was lost.

The procession resumed its journey, and in half an hour arrived at Tinoset. As it was early in the season, the hotel was not crowded, as it sometimes is. The town is at the foot of Lake Tins, upon which the little steamer Rjukan made three trips a week each way. The boat was to depart the next morning for Ornæs, which is only a few miles from the Rjukanfos. Sanford declared that the most direct route to Christiania was by steamer through this lake, and then by cariole the rest of the journey. Ole, of course, backed up all he said, and most of the boys wished to go that way. For some reason or other, Burchmore kept still, though he did not assent to the coxswain's plan, and the question was still open when the tourists were called to supper.

"Ole, I want to see you alone," said the cashier, after the meal was finished.

"What for?" asked Ole.

"I have some money for you."

"For me?"

"Come along."

Burchmore led the way to the lake, where they found a retired place.

"What money have you for me?" demanded the astonished Norwegian.

"How much did Sanford give you for humbugging us?"

"For what?"

"For playing this trick on us?"

"I don't know what you mean."

"The coxswain gave you a sovereign for fooling us. I'll give you five species, which is more than a sovereign, if you do what I want."

"I will," replied Ole, promptly.

"In the first place, where are you taking us?"

"To Christiania."

"Nonsense!" exclaimed the cashier, producing his book. "I know all about it. You ought to have gone to Lysthus, instead of taking the left hand road. We are two Norwegian miles out of our way now. Sanford has paid you a sovereign to lead us to some place he wishes to visit. Where is it?"

"I only do what's right," protested Ole.

"Bah! I know better! The story that no horses could be had at Apalstö was a humbug. I'll give you five species if you will do as I tell you."

Ole looked complacent, and held out his hand for the money.

"I don't pay till the work is done; but my word is as good as my bond."

The waif had an "itching palm," and, after considerable discussion, the terms of payment were settled.

"Now, where are we going?" asked the cashier.

"To the Rjukanfos. It is a big waterfall, with high mountains — one of the finest places in Norway."

"Exactly so; but we are not going there," added Burchmore, decidedly. "You will engage the carioles for to-morrow morning, and we must be in Kongsberg by noon, and near Christiania by night."

"Sanford will kill me," replied Ole.

"No, he won't; we will take care of him."

"I can manage it, first rate. I will tell Sanford that we can go up quicker on the other side of the lake, and then cross over."

"Tell him what you please, but my plan must be carried out," answered Burchmore, who, perhaps, believed that he should be justified in fighting the coxswain with his own weapons.

"Here you are; I've been looking for you," said Clyde, presenting himself sooner than he was wanted. "You thought you would keep out of my way — did you?"

"I have not given that subject any attention," replied Burchmore, coolly.

"Yes, you have; you sneaked off here to keep out of my way."

"As you please," replied Burchmore, who began to walk slowly towards the road.

"You don't escape me this time," added Clyde, placing himself in front of the cashier.

"I have no wish to escape you."

"Yes, you have; you are a Yankee coward!"

"Perhaps I am; but I'm not afraid of a British bully."

"Do you call me a bully?"

"Most distinctly I do, and I can prove my words."

Clyde was rather startled by this exhibition of pluck, which he had not expected.

"You call me a bully — do you?"

"I do."

"Then we'll settle it here. Off with your coat," blustered Clyde, as he divested himself.

"I never fight if I can help it; but I always defend myself," replied Burchmore, resuming his walk towards the road.

"Do you mean to run away?" demanded Clyde.

"No; I mean to walk very leisurely back to the station-house."

"No, you don't!" said the Briton, again placing himself before the cashier.

Ole, who did not care, under the circumstances, to be seen with Burchmore by any one of the party, had disappeared by this time; but meeting Sanford near the lake, he had informed him what Clyde was doing. The coxswain hastened to the spot, with Stockwell and two or three others. But they were a little too late; for Clyde, feeling that he had gone too far to recede with honor, had struck Burchmore. When Sanford and the rest of the party reached the place, the belligerent Briton lay on the ground, where, after a sharp set-to and a black eye, he had been thrown by his cool opponent. He picked himself up, and was preparing for another onslaught, when the coxswain stepped between the combatants.

"Enough of that, Albion," said he.

Clyde made a rush towards Burchmore, but the others interfered, and held him back. In vain he struggled in his wrath, but the stout coxswain and his companions threw him upon the ground, and held him there till his anger had in a measure subsided.

"Be off, Burchmore," said Sanford. "We will take care of him."

"I am not afraid of him," replied the cashier.

"Of course you are not; but clear out, and let us have peace."

"He is afraid of me!" roared Clyde.

"Nonsense, Great Britain! He would have mauled you to death if we hadn't interfered. He can whip his weight in wildcats."

Burchmore walked away, and soon disappeared beyond the houses. Clyde foamed in his wrath for a while, but finally consented to be pacified, promising, very faithfully, to whip the cashier the next time he caught him alone.

"Don't you do it, Albion. You never will see your mother again if you attempt it. Wait a few days, and then, if you insist upon it, we will let Burchmore thrash you all you want," replied Sanford, as they walked back to the station-house.

Clyde had a bad-looking eye, and perhaps believed that he had had a narrow escape; but he still maintained his credit as a bully. At the hotel, the question of the route for the next day came up. Burchmore insisted upon going to Christiania by the way of Kongsberg, and Sanford, who had consulted Ole again, assented. The waif had assured him that they could reach the Rjukanfos quicker and better by the road than by the lake.

The next morning the carioles were ready, and the tourists renewed their journey, and went back on the road by which they had come, till they came to that which led to Kongsberg. The "forbud" had been duly forwarded, and there were no delays or interruptions.

"Where's the lake?" asked Sanford, when they had been riding about two hours.

"O, the road don't go near the lake, till we get to the place where we cross," replied Ole, who was carrying out in good faith the arrangement he had made with the cashier.

"How shall we cross the lake?"

"In a steamer which goes at seven o'clock in the morning."

"All right," replied the unsuspecting Sanford.

"We shall come to a large town at noon; and we musn't stop a minute there, or those fellows will find where they are. We can tell them it is Kongsberg, you know," added the wily waif.

"Just so," laughed Sanford; "we'll tell them it is Kongsberg, and they won't know the difference."

"I don't think they will."

At noon, agreeably to the promise of Ole, the travellers arrived at the large town, where they were obliged to change horses.

"This is Kongsberg, Burchmore," said the coxswain.

"Is it, really? or are you playing some trick upon us?" replied the cashier.

" 'Pon my word this is Kongsberg. Isn't it, Ole?"

"Yes, certainly," answered the waif, winking slyly to Burchmore.

"All right, Sanford; if you are satisfied, I am."

"I know it is Kongsberg. I have been here before," added Clyde, wishing to give his testimony in carrying out the deception.

It was quite true that he had been in Kongsberg, but Ole took care that he should not go to the part of the town he had visited before. The road looked familiar to him; but as he rode alone, he had no opportunity to state the fact to others. Before night the party arrived at Drammen, where a regular line of steamers runs to Christiania.

"That's the lake — is it?" said Sanford, pointing to the Drammen River, which, below the town, is nearly two miles wide.

"That's it."

"What does Burchmore say? Does he know where he is?"

"Not yet; I shall tell him this is Drammen, and he will believe me."

"Good! and we will all stick to it that this is Drammen," added Sanford.

"But suppose we should meet some one here who knows about the ship? This is a large town — bigger than that other which we called Kongsberg."

"Whom can we meet?"

"I don't know."

"I should hate to have any one tell the principal that we have been to the Rjukanfos."

"Some of the officers may come up here."

"We must keep out of sight, then."

Others thought this would be good policy in a large town. As they were fatigued, they retired early, and did not come down the next morning till it was nearly time to leave in the steamer. They all went on board, and were soon moving down the river.

"Are we going across the lake, Ole?" asked Sanford.

"This is a kind of arm of the lake, about a dozen miles long. We shall come to the lake in a couple of hours," replied the waif.

"All right; but it must be a very large lake."

"The biggest in Norway."

In a couple of hours the steamer arrived at Holmsbo, on the Christiania Fjord.

"Now you can see that this is a large lake," said Ole.

"But where are we?" demanded Burchmore. "Is this the way to Christiania?"

"Certainly it is," replied Sanford, who did not yet recognize the fjord, though the truth could not be much longer concealed. "Don't you know this water?"

"No, I don't."

"This is Christiania Fjord."

"Is it, really?"

"Yes, it is; you can bet your life upon it."

"I am satisfied then."

In another hour the steamer was fairly in the fjord; Sanford and Stockwell began to rub their eyes; for the scenery looked strangely familiar, though they could not fully identify anything.

"What place is that ahead?" asked Sanford. "I am almost sure I have seen it before."

"So am I," replied Stockwell.

"That place?" added the cashier.

"Yes; what is it?"

"If this is Christiania Fjord, that must be Dröbak. I have a map here," said Burchmore, producing his book, and displaying the map. "Here we are; there's Holmsbo, and this must be Dröback."

"I don't understand it," replied the perplexed coxswain.

"Don't you? Why, I think it is as clear as mud," laughed Burchmore. "We shall be in Christiania in a couple of hours. I thought you were playing some trick upon us, Sanford; but I see now that you were all right. There's the captain; he speaks English."

"What town is that, captain?" asked the coxswain.

"Dröbak; we shall be in Christiania in about two hours," answered the master.

"Where's Ole?" demanded the coxswain, much excited.

"What does it mean?" said Clyde.

"I don't know. Where's Ole?"

The waif evidently considered discretion the better part of valor, for he could not be found; and the coxswain and those in his confidence realized that they had been "sold" in their own coin.

CHAPTER XII.

THE BOATSWAIN AND THE BRITON.

"WHERE'S Ole? I don't understand it," repeated Sanford, after he had made another ineffectual search for the missing waif.

"We have been sold, instead of selling those fellows," added Stockwell.

"That's so; and I should rather like to know how it was done. Ole has sold us out."

"Is this your Rjukanfos?" demanded Clyde Blacklock, who had been looking for some one upon whom to pour out his wrath.

"Not exactly," answered Sanford, indifferently, for he did not particularly enjoy the airs of the Briton.

"But what do you mean by bringing me here?" added Clyde.

"I didn't bring you here. You came of your own free will and accord."

"No, I didn't; you said we were going to the waterfall."

"We thought so ourselves; but we have been deceived. Ole has sold out and made fools of us. You are no worse off than the rest of us."

"To whom did he sell out?" asked Clyde, appeased when he learned that he was not the only sufferer.

"I don't know. I don't understand it at all. We have been cheated out of the Rjukanfos, and brought to Christiania."

"Well, what are you going to do about it?" inquired Stockwell.

"We can't do anything about it. I suppose we shall be on board of the ship in an hour or two, telling the principal how hard we tried to be here before."

"But I'm not going back to Christiania," protested Clyde.

"I don't see how you can help yourself. This boat don't stop again till she arrives there."

"I will not go to the ship again, at any rate," added Clyde.

"Do as you like about that; it isn't our business."

Clyde was much disturbed by the situation. As he always regarded himself as the central figure of the group, he began to suspect that the apparent miscarriage of the plan was a trick to lure him back to the ship; but Sanford seemed to be honest, and to be entirely discomfited by the discovery. Burchmore and Churchill were highly elated at the success attending their scheme, which had, indeed, exceeded their expectations; but they were as much mystified by the disappearance of Ole as the victims of the trick. Being unable to speak the language, they could not inquire for the absentee; but they made a very diligent search for him. They were more successful than Sanford's party had been, for, in going forward, they heard some high words in the quarters of the steamer's crew, in the forecastle. Listening for a moment, they heard the voice of Ole, who appeared to have concealed himself in that part of the vessel, and was properly regarded as an intruder by the rightful occupants thereof.

"Come out here, Ole," shouted Burchmore. "We want you."

Ole turned from the Norwegian sailors, who were scolding at him for taking possession of their quarters, to his friends and allies.

"Where's Sanford?" he asked, rather timidly.

"On deck."

"He'll kill me."

"Nonsense! We will take care of you against any odds," said the cashier, laughing heartily at the fears of the waif. "They have only just ascertained where they are. Come up, Ole."

Thus assured, the young Norwegian climbed up the ladder, much to the satisfaction of the sailors. Burchmore was too well pleased with the trick he had played upon the conspirators to confine the knowledge of it to Churchill and himself, and had explained it to all who were not actually in the confidence of the coxswain. A majority of the party were thus arrayed on his side, though two or three of them would as readily have chosen the other side. The cashier was evidently the safer leader.

"Sanford and that Englishman will pound me for the trick," repeated Ole, as he glanced at the quarter-deck, where his victims were considering the situation.

"No, they won't; we are able and willing to protect you," replied Burchmore. "Come, we will go aft, and hear what they have to say."

The cashier led the way, and the waif reluctantly followed him.

"I believe you wanted to see Ole," said Burchmore, who could hardly look sober, he was so pleased with the result of his operations.

"Yes; I did wish to see him," answered Sanford, rather coldly. "I will see him some other time."

"O, I thought you wanted him now," laughed Burchmore. "I am satisfied that this is really Christiania Fjord."

"So am I," added the coxswain, with a sickly smile.

"And you were quite right, too, in saying that large place was Drammen," chuckled Burchmore.

"Certainly I was."

"Neither were you mistaken in regard to Kongsberg."

"I find that I was not."

"I suppose you remember the Irishman's turtle, that swallowed his own head, Sanford?"

"Of course."

"I don't mean to say that you swallowed your own head; but you found it just where you didn't expect to find it. Isn't that so?"

"We are going to talk the matter over with Ole by and by."

"Do it now. I know all about it. You and Ole arranged the first part of our journey, including the day's fishing we had at Apalstö; and Ole and I arranged the last part of it. It is an even thing now, and if you won't complain of the last part, I won't say a word about the first."

"I don't understand it."

"Don't you! Well, you gave Ole a sovereign to arrange things for you in the beginning, and I gave him five species to arrange them for me afterwards. You can't complain of a fellow, who sells himself at all, for making as much money as he can. Ole only did that."

"He sold us out," growled Sanford.

"Of course he did; if you buy a man, you mustn't grumble when he does a second time what you encouraged him to do in the first instance. But you were going to take us off to the Rjukanfos, fifty or sixty miles out of our way, without our knowledge or consent. I smelt a mice, and turned the tables," laughed the cashier.

"Yes, and you cheated me," interposed Clyde.

"I had nothing whatever to do with you," answered Burchmore, mildly.

"You led me here when I wanted to go another way."

"You went where you pleased, so far as I was concerned. I never invited you to come with me, or even consented to your doing so."

"Did you say the place we came to yesterday was Kongsberg?"

"I did, and so it was. But I think it was Sanford who first proclaimed the fact, and I cheerfully assented to its correctness," chuckled Burchmore.

"But you deceived me, and I'll have it out with you," continued Clyde.

"Just as you please about that; but you had better let that black eye bleach out before you begin again."

"I can whip you!" blustered Clyde. "I'll meet you anywhere."

"No, I thank you. If we meet for any such purpose as you suggest, it will be by accident."

"See here, Great Britain; you needn't make another row," said Sanford.

"I'm going to whip this fellow for what he has done, and for calling me a bully."

"You are a bully," added Sanford.

"That's so," exclaimed Stockwell.

"Now you can lick the whole of us, if you insist upon it," continued the coxswain.

"Perhaps I will," retorted Clyde, shaking his head fiercely. "You have got me into a pretty scrape."

"You are in the same boat as the rest of us."

"The squadron isn't here," shouted Wilde; for the steamer had by this time arrived within sight of the harbor.

"Can the ship have sailed?" asked Sanford, after the party had satisfied themselves that not one of the vessels of the little fleet was there.

"I suppose she has," replied Burchmore. "To-day is Friday, and she didn't intend to lie here all summer."

"Good!" exclaimed Clyde. "That makes everything all right for me. I'm satisfied now."

Indeed, he was so delighted with the discovery that the ship had sailed, as to be even willing to forego the pleasure of thrashing his companions. The steamer went up to the wharf, and the party landed. Sanford and his friends appeared to be willing to take a reasonable view of the situation, and to accept it without grumbling, satisfied that they had been beaten with their own weapons. They were not sorry that the squadron had departed, for this circumstance gave them a new respite from the discipline of the ship, and enabled them to prolong " the trip without running away."

"What are you going to do now?" asked Clyde, as they landed.

"We shall follow the ship, and try to join her," replied Sanford. " That's what we've been trying to do ever since we left Christiansand — isn't it, Burchmore?"

"Certainly it is," replied the cashier; "though we were detained one day at Apalstö, and narrowly escaped being carried by accident to the Rjukanfos."

"Are you going to blow upon us, Burch?" demanded Stockwell, warmly.

"Am I? Did you ever know me to do such a thing?" added Burchmore, earnestly.

"No! no!" replied the whole party.

"I don't think it was just the thing to cheat some of us as you did; but I believe we are about even on that now."

"Of course we all want to get back to the ship as soon as possible," added Sanford, rubbing his chin, significantly.

"Certainly. She has gone to Gottenburg, and all we have to do is to follow her," said Churchill.

"But if you want to go there by the way of the Cape of Good Hope, Sanford, it will be better to have the matter understood so in the beginning," added Burchmore. "I, for one, don't like to be bamboozled."

"I won't try it on again," said Sanford.

"All right, then; if you do, you may fetch up at Cape Horn."

"Where shall we go now?" asked Sanford.

"To the Victoria Hotel. It is the best in the place," replied Clyde.

"That's the very reason why we don't want to go there. We are not made of money, and we may run out before we are able, with our utmost exertions, to reach the ship," added the cashier.

"But my mother is there," continued Clyde.

"Go to your mother, Great Britain, if you like. We shall stay at some cheap hotel," added Sanford.

Clyde protested in vain against this arrangement, and the Americans, with the aid of Ole, found a small hotel, suited to their views of economy. The Briton went with them; but when they were installed in their new quarters, he left them to find his mother, at the Victoria. After dinner, the coxswain and his party wandered all over the city. At the Castle of Agerhaus, they saw an English steamer receiving freight. They ascertained that she was bound to Gottenburg, and would sail at seven o'clock that evening. They immediately decided, as they had seen enough of Christiania, to take passage in her. The arrangement was speedily made, and they went on board, without troubling themselves to inform Clyde of what they intended to do. When the sun went down that evening the party were far down the fjord.

Sanford had ascertained that the ship sailed early on Thursday morning, and the steamer on which they had taken passage could not arrive at Gottenburg till nearly noon on Saturday. It was understood that the squadron would remain but a short time at this port, and it was possible that it would have departed for Copenhagen before the steamer arrived. He hoped this would prove to be the case; but he studied a plan by which the excursion of the party could be prolonged, if the hope should not be realized. He did not wish to return to the ship, because he thought it was pleasanter to travel without the restraints of discipline. Perhaps most of his party sympathized with him, and thought they could have a better time by themselves. Sanford desired to inform Clyde of the intention of the party to leave in the English steamer, and to take him along with them; but his companions overruled him unanimously, for they were too glad to get rid of an impudent, overbearing, and conceited puppy, as he had proved himself to be. The coxswain had no better opinion of him than his friends; but as Clyde was a runaway, according to his own confession, it might smooth their own way, in returning to their duty, if they could deliver him up to the principal. He was even willing to resort to strategy to accomplish this end; but Clyde was so disagreeable that he was saved from this trap.

The ship had gone, and every vessel of the squadron had departed with her. Clyde felt that all his trials were ended, and he had nothing more to fear from the big boatswain. He walked confidently to the Victoria Hotel, where he was sure to find his mother. He had even arranged in his mind the reproaches with which he intended to greet her for delivering him over to the savage discipline of the Young

America, as he regarded it, and as, doubtless, it was for evil-doers. . He passed into the passage-way which led to the court-yard. As he entered the office on the right to inquire for Mrs. Blacklock, he encountered Peaks, who no sooner saw him than he laid violent hands upon him.

"Let me alone!" shouted Clyde, struggling to escape from the grasp of his powerful antagonist.

"Not yet, my beauty," replied the boatswain, as he dragged his victim into his own room, which was near the office. "I've been looking for you."

"I want to see my mother," growled Clyde, when he had exhausted his strength in the fruitless struggle to escape.

"I dare say you do; babies always want to see their mothers."

"I'm not a baby."

"Then behave like a man."

Peaks deposited him on a chair, and permitted him to recover his breath.

"Where is my mother?" demanded Clyde.

"She is safe and well, and you needn't bother your head to know anything more about her," answered Peaks. "She has turned over a new leaf, so far as you are concerned, youngster, and is going to have us make a man of you."

"Where is she?"

"No matter where she is."

"Can't I see her?"

"No, sir."

"I must see her."

"Perhaps you must, my hearty; but I don't think

she wants to see you till you are a decent young gentleman. She told me to be sure and put you on board of the ship, and I'm going to do it."

"Where is the ship?"

"She sailed for Gottenburg yesterday morning; but we shall find her in good time," replied Peaks, taking a bundle from the bureau, which contained the young Briton's uniform. "Now, my bantam, you don't look like a gentleman in that rig you've got on. Here's your gear; put it on, and look like a man again, whether you are one or not. Those long togs don't become you."

The boatswain unfolded the uniform of Clyde, which he had left in his chamber when he leaped out of the window.

"I'm not going to put on those clothes," protested the unhappy youth.

"No?"

"I'm not!"

"Then I'm going to put them on for you."

"I'll cry murder."

"If you cry anything, I shall put a dirty handkerchief in your mouth. Look here, my chicken; don't you know that you are making a fool of yourself? You mean to strain your own timbers for nothing. You'll put this rig on anyhow, and it depends on yourself whether you will do it with or without a broken head."

Clyde looked at the clothes and then at the brawny boatswain. It was foolish to resist, and he yielded to the force of circumstances. He put on the ship's uniform, and threw himself into a chair to await the further pleasure of his tyrant.

"Now you look like a respectable young gentleman, my lad," said Peaks.

"What are you going to do with me?" demanded Clyde, in a surly tone.

"I'm going to keep my eye on you every moment of the time till you are on board of the ship again."

"I want to see my mother before I go."

"It can't be done."

Clyde relapsed into silence. He had never before been subjected to such unheard-of tyranny. It was useless to resist, and the future looked as dark as the present. Probably his mother was in the hotel, but he was not permitted even to see her. Though the boatswain seemed to have it all his own way, he was not at all satisfied with the situation. Mrs. Blacklock and her daughter had gone to ride, but in the course of an hour or two they would return. The waiters would inform her that Clyde had arrived, and she would insist on seeing him. Though she had fully given up the control of him to the ship, the weakness of the mother might induce her to change her mind. Peaks only desired to discharge the duty with which he had been intrusted. The crew of the second cutter had not yet arrived, and he could not depart with his prisoner before they came. He was perplexed; but being a man of expedients, he decided upon his course in a short time. It was absolutely necessary to seek another hotel, where the dangerous proximity of Mrs. Blacklock might be avoided. The boatswain rang his bell, and sent for the *commissionnaire* whom he had employed while prosecuting his search for the runaway. When this man came, he ordered a carriage, and paid his bill.

"Now, youngster, we are going to take a ride," said Peaks to his victim.

"Where are you going?"

"That's my affair. If you make a row in the street, I shall just hand you over to the police, who will lock you up in that stone castle over there. You must understand that you are a deserter from your ship, and will be treated so, if you don't behave like a man. Now come with me."

As a deserter from his ship! The boatswain certainly had the weather-gage of him, and the idea of being thrown into prison was absolutely startling to Clyde. He had no doubt the savage boatswain would do all he threatened, and, almost for the first time in his life, he felt no inclination to bully. He stepped quietly into the carriage with Peaks and the *commissionnaire*. The driver was directed to convey the party to the landing-place. The steamer would sail the next morning; but unless the absent crew of the cutter arrived before that time, he could not go in her. Remaining in Christiania, he feared to encounter Mrs. Blacklock, for the honest tar dreaded a lady's power more than the whole battery of a ship of the line. He was fully resolved, if he passed through fire and water in doing it, to discharge the duty intrusted to him by the principal. The lady was in the city, and the problem was to keep his charge out of sight of her during the rest of his stay. He might meet her; some one at the hotel might, and probably would, inform her of the arrival of Clyde.

After deliberating for some time, he directed his *commissionnaire* to procure a boat, in which he embarked with his prisoner and interpreter. By his order the two oarsmen pulled over to the hotel which was located so picturesquely on the island. Taking a room, he ordered dinner for his little party, and contrived to pass away the afternoon till sunset, when he returned to the city. His man, at his request, conducted him to an obscure hotel, which happened to be the one which Sanford and his friends had just left, to depart by the English steamer. The landlord recognized the uniform which Clyde wore.

"We had more of the young gentleman here," said he, in broken English.

"More of them!" exclaimed Peaks, interested in the intelligence.

"Yes; more as ten of them," added the landlord.

"Arn't they here now?" asked Clyde, who had felt a ray of hope when Peaks brought him to the hotel where he had left his late companions.

"All gone; no more here."

"Where have they gone?" asked the boatswain.

"To Gottenburg. They eat some dinner in my hotel, and at seven o'clock they go in the steamer."

"I saw that steamer go out, but I didn't think the cutter's crew were in her. I'm sorry I didn't know it before," said Peaks, chagrined by this tardy discovery. "How many were there of them?"

"Ten."

"That couldn't be; there were only nine of the crew.

"There was more as ten, but one of them went away."

"I went away," said Clyde.

"You! Were you with them?" demanded Peaks.

"I was."

"Why didn't you say so before?"

"You didn't ask me; and as you were not remarkably civil to me, I didn't feel obliged to tell you the news."

"But there were not ten of them."

"Yes, ten," said Clyde.

"There were only nine when they left the ship."

"I know there were ten with me. One of them was a Norwegian, and a rascal; but he wore the same uniform as the rest of them."

"What was his name?"

"Ole."

"Ole! Why, he's the fellow we picked up out at sea," exclaimed the astonished boatswain. "Where have they been all this time?"

But Clyde suddenly bethought himself that he was altogether too communicative, considering the relations that subsisted between himself and his great enemy and persecutor, and he decided to answer no more questions.

"All right, my hearty," laughed the boatswain, when the Briton declined to answer. "They are on their way to the ship, and you will be very soon."

Peaks was cunning enough to detain his interpreter so that he should not return to the Victoria and inform Mrs. Blacklock where her son was. The way was clear now, for he had no further responsibility in regard to the cutter's crew, and his spirits rose accordingly. He sent his man to engage a "hütte," or stateroom, in the steamer, and then, at a late hour in the evening, paid and discharged him. He compelled Clyde to sleep in the same chamber with him, for it contained three beds, and it is probable that the boatswain kept one eye open during the night, for every time the prisoner moved, his tyrant was on his feet. The Kronprindsesse Louise sailed at six o'clock in the morning, and Peaks and his victim were betimes on board. The boatswain was a happy man when the boat was clear of the wharf, and on her way to Gottenburg. He flattered himself that he had managed the affair very well indeed, for he was not above the vanities of the flesh.

It was midnight when the Kronprindsesse arrived at her destination. Peaks had kept one eye on Clyde all the time, and brought him in safety to his journey's end. Late as was the hour, the first person he saw at the landing was Mr. Blaine, the chief steward of the ship.

"I'm glad to see you, Blaine," shouted the boatswain when he identified his shipmate, and grasped his hand. "Shiver my timbers if I'm not rejoiced to see a man that speaks plain English! Where's the ship?"

"She sailed for Copenhagen this evening."

"No; you don't say so!"

"It's a fact. The students went up the canal as far as the falls, and returned about dark. The squadron got under way at once. I suppose you have the cutter's crew with you, Peaks?"

"No; arn't they on board yet?"

"I haven't seen them."

"But they came down on an English steamer that left Christiania last night."

"An English steamer came in this forenoon, but we haven't seen the cutter's crew."

"That's strange. I shouldn't wonder if those fellows were cutting up a little."

"But we lost two students yesterday, Scott and Laybold. I suppose they ran away."

"There's a screw loose somewhere. These boys have too much money," added Peaks. "But what are you going to do, and what am I to do?"

"I was left here to look out for Scott and Laybold, and meet you when you came. Now, it seems that about a dozen of the rascals are missing."

"I have the Briton here."

"If I were you, Peaks, I should go right on to Copenhagen in this steamer, and you can report the facts to the principal."

The boatswain decided to do this, while the head steward remained to search for the absentees; and in due time Peaks delivered his prisoner on board of the ship in the harbor of Copenhagen.

CHAPTER XIII.

THE MEETING OF THE ABSENTEES.

SCOTT and Laybold, after imbibing a single glass of "finkel" each, which proved to be more than they could carry, retreated into a narrow lane, to escape the observation of a party of officers who were on their way to the landing. Neither of them had any inclination for intoxicating drinks, and had taken the stuff without knowing what it was. But they were conscious that everything was not right with them. They found it quite impossible to walk in a straight line, and even the problem of standing up was not demonstrated to the entire satisfaction of either of them. Talking was not without its difficulties, for their tongues seemed to be double their ordinary thickness, and their lips and other organs of speech were not as manageable as usual. For a time the effects of the potent liquor increased upon them, and as they had taken it in a hungry condition, they realized its full power.

They staggered up the lane, conscious that they were making a ridiculous figure, though the solemn Swedes hardly smiled as they observed the effects of the national beverage. They dreaded an encounter with any of the officers, or others connected with the squadron;

but in this unfrequented lane they were not likely to meet any of their shipmates. As there is more power in four legs than in two, however weak in detail they may be, the tipsy students locked arms, and leaned on each other, one attempting to counteract the obliquities of the other. They wandered along without knowing whither they were going, till they came to a small public house, which had a bench in front of it for the accommodation of the topers who frequented the barroom. By mutual consent, and without argument, the unfortunate couple aimed for this seat as soon as they saw it, for it promised a grateful respite from the perils of locomotion. The "finkel" was now doing its utmost upon them. Their heads were dizzy, and everything was wofully uncertain; still they knew what they were about, and had sense enough left to dread the consequences of their indiscretion. After they had seated themselves, they glanced at each other, as if to ascertain the condition one of the other.

"Lay — bold," said Scott.

"Well, old fellow," replied the other, with a desperate attempt to stiffen his muscles.

"We're zrunk," added Scott, trying to laugh.

"I know that."

"We're very zrunk."

"I'm not zbad zyou."

"I don't zknow."

The conversation extended no further then, for speech required an effort they were incapable of making. Scott gaped violently, and seemed to be sick; but his contortions ended in his falling asleep, with his head tipped back against the wall. Laybold, more nice in the disposition of his helpless body, stretched himself on the bench, and was soon lost to all consciousness of the outer world. The publican who kept the house came out and looked at the juvenile tipplers. Doubtless he had seen too many drunken sailors to misapprehend their condition. He understood the matter perfectly, and being a thrifty Swede, he was disposed to turn their condition to his own emolument. He had sundry vacant chambers in his hotel, whose revenues swelled the sum total of his annual profits, and it hurt his feelings to have them remain unoccupied. Besides, the air was chilly, and the young strangers might take cold, and contract a severe illness by such exposure. But whether he was a publican or a Samaritan in his intentions, he decided to remove the strangers to the rooms beneath his hospitable roof. Summoning the porter to his aid, they jointly bore Laybold to his apartment, and laid him on the bed, which, in spite of the low character of the house, was a model of Swedish neatness. When Scott's turn came, he offered some resistance to the good intentions of the publican; but his head was too thoroughly muddled for successful opposition. Between the effects of sleep and "finkel" he could not obtain a very clear idea of what was going on. He was placed on another bed in the room with his shipmate. They were both comfortably disposed on their clean couches, the pillows nicely adjusted beneath their heads, and their bodies covered with blankets.

The two students were very tired as well as very tipsy, and their slumbers were deep and heavy. It was after nine o'clock, though it was still light in the chamber, and the young tars usually retired, when not on watch, before this seemly hour. "Finkel" and fatigue did the rest, and they slept, without rocking, till long after the early sun broke into the windows of their apartment. We have seen the effect of "finkel" upon one unaccustomed to the use of liquor, and upon boys of fifteen or sixteen it could not but be entirely overpowering. It is a dangerous fluid, and is taken by the Swedes at all times, being the first thing at meals, and especially at the inevitable "snack" that precedes a regular dinner. There is, doubtless, good ground for the fear which has been expressed that the people of Sweden are in danger of becoming "a nation of drunkards."

Scott was the first to open his eyes and come to his senses. He raised himself in the bed, shook off the blanket, and then jumped out upon the floor. He did not comprehend the situation, and was unable, in his own words, to "figure up how he happened to be in that room."

"Laybold, ahoy!" shouted he, after he had examined the apartment, and mentally confessed his inability to solve the problem. "Laybold! All hands on deck!"

"What is the matter?" cried Laybold, springing up, only half awake.

"I'll be muzzled if I know what the matter is, but I believe that the Norway god — what's his name? — Odin, came aboard the ship last night, and turned her into a country tavern," replied Scott, going to the window, and looking down into the lane below.

"How came we here?" asked Laybold, rubbing his eyes.

"That's more than I know; but I think we have been transplanted by the spirits."

"The spirits?" gaped Laybold.

"Yes; I believe they call them 'finkel.' We were tight last night, my boy."

"I remember all about it now. I dreamed that somebody lugged me in here."

"You didn't exactly dream it, for here we are. We are in a pretty scrape."

"That's so," added Laybold, shaking his head. "We didn't mean to run away, but that's just what we have done."

"We didn't run a great way; for, if I remember rightly, running wasn't our *forte* last evening. Who runs may reel, if he can't read, and I reckon we did more reeling than running. But what's to be done?"

"I don't know."

"In the first place, where are we? It's no use to lay out a course till we know the ship's position."

They were utterly unable to determine this question. Each of them had a tolerably vivid recollection of their unfortunate condition on the preceding evening, and even that he had been carried by a couple of men; but they had no idea of time or locality. They washed themselves at the sink in the room, combed their hair with their pocket-combs, and looked then as though nothing had happened. Their heads were a little light, but they did not absolutely ache, and they realized but a small portion of the after effects of a regular "spree." Having made their simple toilet, they decided to explore the premises, and make their way back to the ship. Leaving the chamber, they descended a flight of steps, and, in the hall below, encountered the Samaritan landlord.

"*God morgon*," said the latter, with a jolly smile on his face ; and it was probable that he had taken his morning dose of "finkel." "*Hur star det till?*" (How are you?)

"Nix," replied Scott, shrugging his shoulders.

"You are English," added the landlord, a large portion of whose customers were foreign sailors.

"No; Americans."

"I'm glad to see you."

"I'm glad to see you, too, if you can tell us how we happen to be here."

"Too much 'finkel,' laughed the publican, as he proceeded to explain the situation, and to enlarge upon the fatherly interest which had induced him to take them in for the night.

"All right, my hearty. I see you can keep a hotel," added Scott. "How much have we to pay?"

"Two rigsdalers ; but you want some breakfast."

"I do, for one," replied Scott.

"So do I," said Laybold. "We only had a little lunch last night, and that 'finkel' spoiled my appetite — or the fish spawn. I don't know which."

About five o'clock they sat down to breakfast, which consisted of a great variety of little things, such as the small fishes, herrings, smoked salmon, sausages. The coffee was magnificent, as it generally is in Sweden, even on board of steamers, where, in our own country, it is least expected to be good.

"What is this?" said Scott, taking up half a great brown biscuit.

"That's Swedish bread. We bake it once in six months," replied the landlord.

"Not bad," added Scott, as he tasted the article.

"This is Graham bread, I suppose," said Laybold, as he took a slice of the coarse brown bread. "Bah! it's sour."

It always is; and both the students rejected it, though they ate a hearty meal of white bread, herring, salmon, and sausage.

"Now, how much?" asked Scott, when they were ready to go.

"One rigsdaler and fifty öre each — three rigsdalers in all."

"Cheap enough," said Scott. "Two lodgings and two breakfasts for eighty-one cents."

The students walked through the lane in which they had made their devious way the night before, to the main street on the canal. At the landing-place there were no boats belonging to the squadron, and everything looked exceedingly quiet on board of the ship. Seating themselves on the pier, with their legs hanging over the water, they decided to wait till a boat came to the shore.

"We shall catch it for this," said Laybold.

"No more liberty for a month at least," said Scott, shrugging his shoulders after his fashion.

"I don't think it's fair. We didn't mean to get drunk, and didn't know what 'finkel' was," added Laybold. "I don't half like to go on board again."

"Nor I; but I suppose we must face the music," answered Scott, dubiously. "I'm glad we didn't go on board while we were boozy. The fellows would have laughed at us for a year, if we had."

"That's so; and Lowington would have put us in the brig."

"I don't exactly like to explain the reason why we didn't go on board last night; I always was a bashful fellow."

"You didn't go with the others," said a man, coming up to them at this moment, and speaking in broken English.

"What others? Where?" replied Scott.

"The other students. They took the steamer up the canal at two o'clock this morning."

"Whew!" whistled Scott. "We have lost Göta Canal and the falls."

"They will return to-night by the railroad from Wenersberg," added the man, who was an agent of the canal steamers.

"That's too bad!" exclaimed Laybold, as the man walked away.

"I don't know that it is too bad. Our leave would have been stopped if we had gone on board," laughed Scott, who generally took the most cheerful view of any disagreeable subject. "Why can't we go on our own hook?"

"I like that idea," added Laybold.

But inquiring of the agent, they learned that the canal steamers left only at two o'clock in the morning.

"There's a railroad, or the fellows couldn't come back that way," suggested Laybold.

"That's so; you have more wisdom than a Duxbury clam."

They ascertained that a train left Gottenburg at noon, by which they could reach Wenersberg the same day. They knew nothing of the plan of the principal, which included a special train from the canal to the main line of railway; but they desired to see more of the interior of Sweden, and they were confident they should see the excursionists either at Wenersberg or on the way. It suited them better to make a trip even for a few hours, than to wander about a city which they had already exhausted. But they were obliged to wait some time for the train, and, after a couple of hours of "heavy loafing" about the streets, they returned to the pier. An English steamer had just arrived, and a boat was landing her passengers.

"Who are those fellows?" said Laybold, pointing to the steamer's boat. "They wear the ship's uniform."

"Right; they do, and they came from that steamer," replied Scott.

"There's Sanford! I should know him a mile off. They are the second cutters, or I am a Dutchman."

"Right again," added Scott, as the passengers landed.

The steamer was the one in which Sanford and his companions had taken passage at Christiania the evening before. The absentees, "on a cruise without running away," were sorry to see the ship at anchor in the harbor, for some of them had hoped to be too late for her. When they landed, the first persons they encountered were Scott and Laybold, who gave them a very cordial greeting. Each party had a story to tell of its own adventures, and Scott knew Sanford and his associates too well to think it necessary to conceal from them the fact that he and Laybold had been the sad victims of "finkel."

"But why don't you go on board?" asked Burchmore.

"What's the use? All the fellows have gone up to Wobblewopkins, or some other place, to see the falls, and take an inside view of Sweden," replied Scott. "We intend to go, and do likewise."

"Won't you go with us?" added Laybold.

The intentions of the two were explained to the others, and they all decided to join the party. Sanford was not without a hope that something would occur to prolong the "independent trip without running away."

"How are you off for stamps?" asked Burchmore of the two who were by this arrangement added to his party, for which he had thus far done the financiering.

"We have a little Swedish money, and some sovereigns," replied Scott.

"But how many sovereigns? We may be prevented from joining the ship for a few days, and we want to know where we are in money matters," interposed Sanford.

"We have enough to buy out one or two of these one-horse kingdoms, like Denmark and Sweden. I have twenty sovereigns, and Laybold has about a thousand," answered Scott.

"No I haven't," protested Laybold, laughing at the extravagance of his friend. "I have only twenty-five sovereigns."

"And a letter of credit for a thousand more; so it's the same thing."

"No, no; knock off one cipher, Scott."

"Well, seeing it's you, I'll knock off just one; but not another to please any fellow, even if he were my grandmother's first cousin," added Scott.

"There's some difference between a hundred and a thousand pounds," suggested Sanford.

"A slight difference," said Laybold.

"I don't expect any of us will live long enough to spend a hundred pounds in this country, which is about eighteen hundred of these tricks-bunker dollars, to say nothing of a thousand. Why, we paid only three bunkers for two lodgings and two breakfasts. How's a fellow ever to spend eighteen hundred bunkers? For my part, I think I'm lucky in having less than four hundred of the things to get rid of."

"But you needn't feel under the necessity of spending all your money in this country," laughed the cashier.

"My father promised to send me some more; but I hope he won't do it till I get out of Sweden. If he does I shall be ruined. Here's poor Laybold, with a letter of credit for a hundred pounds, besides twenty-five in cash. I pity the poor fellow. It wouldn't be so bad in London, where it costs a fellow from ten to twenty shillings a day to breathe."

"I think I shall be able to survive," added Laybold.

"I hope so; but you ought to hear him talk about his bankers. Topsails and topping-lifts! His bankers! Messrs. Pitchers Brothers & Co."

"No! Bowles Brothers & Co," interposed Laybold.

"It's all the same thing; there isn't much difference

between bowls and pitchers. One breaks as easy as the other."

"But my bankers don't break."

"His bankers! Do you hear that? Well, I don't believe they'll break, for all my folks, when they travel in Europe, carry the same letter of credit in their trousers pocket. I had to write to my paternal parent all last year, care of Bowles Brothers & Co., 449 Strand, Charing Cross, W. C. London, England. You see I've learned my lesson."

"My letters from home come through the same house," said Laybold, "and so do those of fifty other fellows."

"About the money matters," interposed Burchmore. "Shall I act for the crowd, as I did in Norway?"

"For me, yes; and I hope you'll help Laybold out on the big financial job he has on his hands," said Scott.

"All right," added Laybold.

"I have settled up for the fellows on the Norway trip. Now, each of you give me a couple of sovereigns, which I will change into Swedish money."

This arrangement was made to the satisfaction of all, and the cashier went to an exchange office, where he procured Swedish paper for the gold.

"Scott, I shouldn't wonder if the principal saved you the trouble of spending your twenty pounds before we go much farther," said Sanford.

"I shall thank him with tears in my eyes if he does," replied Scott, with a solemn look.

"I don't believe you will. When the ship came

over before, every fellow had to give up his money, and the purser doled it out to the fellows in shillings or sixpences when they went ashore."

"I'm sure it was very kind of him to take so much trouble."

"You don't think so."

"Of course I do. Only think of poor Laybold, with a letter of credit for a hundred pounds on his hands! I'm thankful I haven't the responsibility of spending so much money on my conscience. I should apply for admission to the first lunatic asylum, if I had to spend so much."

"Nonsense! I made up my mind not to give up my money," said the coxswain. "That rule made plenty of rows on the other cruise, and I expect the fellows on this cruise will be called upon to give up their stamps very soon."

"I was going to say we could get even with the principal by spending it all before we go on board again; but we are in Sweden, and it is quite impossible. They won't let you pay more than seventy-five cents or a dollar for a day's board in this country."

"You went to a sailor's boarding-house, Scott. When you are at a first-class hotel, you will find that they bleed you enough."

"I hope they do better than the landlord where we staid last night; if they don't I shall make money in Sweden. Why, they wouldn't even pick our pockets when we were boozy on 'finkel.' I'm sure they are a great deal more accommodating at sailors' boarding-houses in Boston and New York."

"Come, be serious, Scott. Shall you give up your money when you return to the ship?"

"Cheerfully, for there is no chance to get rid of it in this country."

"But you will want some in Russia, where everything is dear."

"I'm afraid my letter of credit will arrive by that time, and I shall be burdened with new trials."

"Poor fellow!"

The old rule of the ship had not been enforced on the present cruise, and the principal did not intend to renew it until it was absolutely necessary. It had caused much complaint among the wealthy parents of the former students, while it had wonderfully improved the discipline; but Mr. Lowington consented to make the experiment of permitting every boy to manage his own finances.

At noon the party took their places in a second-class compartment of the carriage on the railway, and started for Wenersberg. Ole spoke Swedish as well as Norwegian, and acted as interpreter. Sanford had made peace with the waif, who was now as popular as ever with all the party. Each of them, in turn, had tried to induce Ole to tell how he happened to be in that boat at sea; but he still refused to explain.

The train moved off, and the tourists observed the country through which it passed; but Scott could not help grumbling because the fare was only about a dollar and a quarter for fifty miles, declaring that he should never be able to get rid of his twenty sovereigns at this rate, and that he was threatened with a letter of credit for a hundred more at St. Petersburg. At Herrljunga, the junction of the branch to Wenersberg and the main line, the guard insisted that the tourists should leave the carriage.

"How's this, Ole?" asked Sanford.

"Change for Wenersberg; but the train don't start till five o'clock. We must wait two hours."

"But what time does it get to Wenersberg?"

"About half past eight."

"That's a pretty go!" exclaimed the coxswain. "You made a beautiful arrangement for this trip, Scott."

"What's the matter now?"

"We cannot get to Wenersberg till half past eight; and of course that will be too late to join the ship's company there."

"It isn't necessary to join them there. We shall meet them on the way, and go back with them. They will be at this place some time this afternoon."

"What did we come up here for?" asked Sanford.

"In the first place, to get rid of four or five rix-bunkers; and in the second, to see something of this part of Sweden. We have done both, and ought to be satisfied."

"O, I'm satisfied!"

"You ought to be; you have four and a half bunkers less to spend. We will loaf about this place till the principal comes with the crowd, and when he sees what good boys we have been to look him up, and see that he didn't get lost, he'll forgive Laybold and me for drinking 'finkel.'"

"All right. What time does the train leave for Gottenburg, Ole?" added the coxswain, turning to the interpreter.

"Half past five," replied the waif.

No one took the trouble to examine the time-table in the station-house, which, though in Swedish, was perfectly intelligible so far as it related to hours and towns.

The tourists decided to improve the time they were obliged to wait by taking a walk about the country, examining Swedish houses and investigating Swedish agriculture. Doubtless this was a very interesting amusement; but at quarter past five, the party returned to the station. A long train was just departing in the direction of Gottenburg.

"What train's that?" demanded Sanford.

"I don't know," replied Ole, with a look of alarm.

"Inquire, then," added the excited coxswain.

The party hastened into the little station. It was the regular train for Gottenburg.

"But how's that?" cried Sanford. "You said it left at half past five."

"Yes; I looked at the time-table in Gottenburg, and it said half past five," replied Ole. "Here is one, and I will look again."

"Better wait till morning before you look again," said Scott.

"Here it is; five — "

"That's all, Norway."

"I'm sure it was half past five in Gottenburg," pleaded Ole, whom the coxswain had privately requested to make this blunder.

"What sort of chowder do you call this, son of Odin?" demanded Scott.

"He has made a blunder; that's all," laughed Burchmore, who, though not in the confidence of the coxswain, at once suspected the trick, and, to tell the truth, was not sorry for the mistake.

The mishap was discussed for an hour, and poor Ole was severely blamed, especially by Sanford, for his carelessness; but he bore the censure with becoming meekness.

"What's to be done?" inquired Scott, at last.

"Here's another train at 8.56," replied Ole, pointing to the time-table. "We can return to Gottenburg in that."

"Right, Norway," added Scott.

They found a small hotel in the place, where they obtained a supper, and at the time indicated returned to Gottenburg, where they arrived at about one in the morning. It was too late to go on board of the ship, and they went directly to the little hotel in the lane, where Scott and Laybold had passed the preceding night. It was closed, but they easily roused the landlord.

"So you have again come," said the good-natured host.

"Yes; we have again come. It is too late to go on board of the ship," replied Scott.

"Your ship have sail to-night to Copenhagen."

"No! Impossible!"

"I have seen her sail," persisted the landlord. "I have make no mistake."

"We are dished!" exclaimed Sanford.

"The young gentleman come down at seven o'clock, and the ship have sail at nine o'clock. I know it so well as I know how to speak the English."

"It must be so, then," laughed Scott; "for you have spoke the English more better as nice."

"What shall we do?" continued Sanford, who seemed to be positively distressed at the unfortunate circumstance.

"Do? Go to bed, and go to sleep. What else can we do? You are too big a boy to cry over your misfortunes," replied Scott.

"I don't intend to cry; but I feel very bad about it."

"Dry your tears," said Burchmore. "We may as well take a biscuit, turn in, and call it half a day."

"But when will there be a steamer to Copenhagen?" asked Sanford.

"The Najaden must go Monday afternoon," answered the landlord, who, for some reason best known to himself, did not deem it prudent to mention the fact that the Kronprindsesse Louise would sail within half an hour.

"This will never do," interposed Rodman. "We have been chasing the ship now for a week, and by the time we get to Copenhagen she will be gone. I move we go to Stockholm. We shall be sure to catch her there."

"Good!" exclaimed Wilde.

The proposition was fully discussed, and when a majority favored the movement, the others, among whom was Sanford, yielded an apparently reluctant assent. The Wadstena would start at two o'clock, and there was not a moment to lose. The landlord was astonished at the decision, and his hotel was not filled that night, as he intended it should be. Just as the canal steamer was starting, the young tourists hurried on board, and were soon on their way to Stockholm.

Not a quarter of a mile distant at this moment were Peaks and his prisoner, and Blaine, the head steward, who was on the lookout for them.

CHAPTER XIV.

THROUGH THE SOUND TO COPENHAGEN.

MR. LOWINGTON was almost forced to the conclusion that the experiment of permitting the students to manage their own finances was a failure. If it could be a success anywhere, it must be in the northern countries, where none of the boys spoke the language, and where the lighter intoxicants were not so common as in the more southern portions of Europe. Though he was not aware that any pupils had made an improper use of their money, the non-arrival of the crew of the second cutter, and the disappearance of Scott and Laybold in Gottenburg, seemed to have some relation to the condition of their funds. But he was willing to carry the experiment as far as practicable, and to restore the obnoxious rule only when it was absolutely necessary to do so. Two thirds of the students could be safely trusted to manage their money matters, and it was not pleasant to restrain the whole for the benefit of the minority.

After the boys had walked all over Gottenburg, they were weary enough to retire at eight bells in the evening, especially as they were to turn out at two o'clock the next morning, for the trip up the Göta Canal. At the appointed time, the steamer came alongside the ship, where she took the excursionists on board, the boats of the other vessels conveying their crews to the Young America. As it was still dark, not a few of the boys finished their nap in the little steamer. About eight o'clock, she reached the long series of locks by which the canal passes the Falls of Trollhätten, and the excursionists walked for a couple of hours through the beautiful scenery, and embarking again in the steamer, arrived at Wenersberg, where they obtained a view of the Wenern Lake, and proceeded by special train to Herrljunga, and thence, by regular train, to Gottenburg, where they arrived before eight in the evening. The wind was fair, and the squadron immediately sailed to the southward.

The principal was annoyed by the absence of not less than a dozen of the students; but he had every confidence in the zeal and discretion of Peaks, who was to take charge of the cutter's crew, and he left the head steward at Gottenburg to find Scott and Laybold. He feared that the success of these wanderers would encourage others to follow their example, and increased vigilance seemed to be necessary on the part of the instructors. The next day was Sunday, and it was doubly a season of rest. The breeze was fair, but very light, so that the squadron made only about four knots an hour; but on Monday morning she was fairly in the Sound, which is about three miles in width. On the left was the town of Helsingborg, in Sweden, and on the right Kronberg Castle, with Elsinore, on a kind of land-locked basin, behind it. The vessels continued on their course, keeping within a short distance of the shore, so that those on board could distinctly see the towns and villages. The houses were neat, with red roofs, each one having its little garden. There were plenty of groves and forests, and the trees were oaks and beeches, instead of pines and firs which the voyagers had seen in Norway and Sweden. The country was flat, with nothing like a hill to be seen.

The breeze freshening, the squadron hastened its pace, and in the middle of the forenoon the spires of Copenhagen were in plain sight. Off in the water were several detached forts, built on small islands. The Young America led the way, and soon dropped her anchor off the citadel of Frederikshavn, and near the landing-place, where a crowd of small steamers were lying at the wharf.

"Have you been here before, Dr. Winstock?" asked Captain Lincoln, as he saw the surgeon examining the aspect of the city.

"Yes; several years ago. I have been in every country in Europe."

"Copenhagen don't look just as I expected it would," added the commander. "I thought it must be a very old, black, and musty-looking place."

"You see that it is not, — at least not from the water; but you will find plenty of dismal and gloomy-looking buildings in it. The fact is, Denmark is too small a kingdom to support all the show and expense of royalty: its palaces are too large and costly to be retained as such, and many of them have been permitted to fall into partial decay. But I will not anticipate Mr. Mapp's lecture, for I see the signal is flying."

"She makes a tremendous display of forts and guns," added Lincoln, glancing from the batteries of

Trekroner and Lynetten to the bristling guns of Frederikshavn.

"Doubtless it is a strong place, but the English have twice captured the city. Here are the boats from the other vessels. I suppose we shall go ashore after dinner."

The steerage was soon crowded with students, and Mr. Mapps took his usual position at the foremast, on which appeared the map of Denmark.

"In English this country is called Denmark," said the professor; "but it has this name in no other language. The Danes call it *Danmark*, the adjective of which is *Danske;* and the country is also called the *Danske Stat*, or Danish States. In German it is *Dänemark;* in French, *Danemark;* in Italian, *Danimarca*. It is bounded on the north by the Skager Rack, or Sleeve; on the east by the Cattegat, the Sound, and the Baltic Sea; on the south by the Duchy of Schleswig and the Baltic; and on the west by the North Sea. When this ship was in Europe before, Schleswig-Holstein and Lauenburg belonged to Denmark; but now they belong to Prussia, and Jutland is all that remains of continental Denmark. This peninsula has an area of nine thousand six hundred square miles, or about the size of the State of New Hampshire. With the several islands, the entire area of Denmark is fourteen thousand five hundred square miles. Greenland, Iceland, the Faroe Islands, and several small islands in the West Indies, belong to her. The population is nearly one million eight hundred thousand — about equal to that of Massachusetts and New Hampshire united.

"The country is flat, or gently undulating, and the highest hill is only five hundred and fifty feet high. The soil is sandy on the peninsula, and not very fertile, but very rich on some of the islands. It is indented to a remarkable degree with bays and inlets, and the whole interior is dotted with small lakes, usually connected by a river, like a number of eggs on a string. The Lim Fjord, which you see in the north, formerly only extended to within a short distance of the North Sea; but in 1825 a tempest broke through the narrow neck of land, and opened a passage for small vessels. These inland lakes are full of fish, and salmon was once so plenty that householders were forbidden by law to feed their servants with this food more than once a week.

"The two largest islands are Fünen and Seeland, which are separated by the Great Belt, and the former from the main land by the Little Belt. In winter these are frozen over, as is the Sound in the severer seasons, and have been crossed by armies engaged in military operations. The country is well wooded, and you will find plenty of large oaks and beeches. This morning you passed Elsinore, where Shakespeare locates Hamlet; but you cannot find where 'the morn walks o'er the dew of yon high eastern hill,' for there are no hills there; nor 'the dreadful summit of the cliff, that beetles o'er his base into the sea.' It is a flat region, with only a low cliff to border the sea; certainly with no such tremendous steeps as the poet describes. Besides, Hamlet lived and died in Jutland. But Shakespeare used the poet's license.

"Nearly all of Denmark lies between latitude fifty-five and fifty-eight; but, though the thermometer sometimes falls to twenty-two degrees below zero in winter, the average temperature is mild. The climate does not materially differ from the eastern coast of Massachusetts. The air is so humid that the grass and trees have a livelier green than the countries farther south, and droughts are almost unknown. When France and Germany are parched and dry, Denmark is fresh and green. The people are engaged principally in agriculture and commerce. The chief exports are grain, cattle, and horses.

"The government is a constitutional monarchy. The king is assisted in the executive department by a 'Royal Privy Council' of seven ministers. The legislature is called the Rigsdag, and consists of the Landsthing, or upper house, and the Folkething, or lower house. Of the former, twelve are nominated for life, by the king, from the present or past members of the lower house, and the remaining fifty-four are elected, in four classes, by the largest tax-payers in country districts, in towns, in cities, and by deputies representing the ordinary voters. The members of the lower house are chosen directly by the people. All male citizens of twenty-five, except paupers, and servants who are not householders, are voters.

"The established religion of the state is Lutheran, and the king must be of this church. He nominates the bishops, who have no political power, as in England. They have the general supervision and management of all the affairs of the church in the kingdom. Although there are only about thirteen thousand non-Lutherans in Denmark, entire religious toleration prevails, and no man can be deprived of his civil and political rights on account of his creed.

"Free education is provided by the government for all children whose parents cannot afford to pay for tuition, and attendance at school, between the ages of seven and fourteen, is compulsory. All the people, therefore, are instructed in the elementary branches; and, besides the University of Copenhagen, there is a system of high and middle schools, available for the children of merchants, mechanics, and the more prosperous of the laboring classes.

"Every able-bodied man in Denmark, who has attained the age of twenty-one, is liable to serve as a soldier for eight years in the regular army, and eight more in the army of the reserve. In preparation for this duty, every man is enrolled, and required to drill for a period of from four to six months, according to the arm of the service in which he is placed; and those who do not become proficient in this time are required to drill for another and longer period. The kingdom is divided into military districts, and all the soldiers are required to drill from thirty to forty-five days every year. The navy of Denmark consists of thirty-one steamers of all classes, six of which are iron-clads, carrying three hundred and twelve guns, and manned by nine hundred men.

"Little is known of the history of this country before the eighth century, but the Cimbri occupied it before the time of Christ. The Danes conquered portions of England, and in the eleventh century, Canute, who introduced Christianity into his realm, completed the conquest. Norway was also included in his kingdom, and under him and his successors, during the next two hundred years, Denmark attained the summit of her power and glory. Holstein, Lauenburg, and several other of the northern provinces of Germany, and even a portion of Prussia, were subjected to her sway. Waldemar II., a successor of Canute, with his eldest son, was daringly captured, while resting from the fatigues of the chase, one evening, by Count Schwerin, whom the king had provoked to wrath by some flagrant injustice. This bold act of retaliation was carried to a successful issue, and the king and his son were transported by water to Castle Schwerin, in Mecklenburg, where they were kept as prisoners for three years — a most remarkable instance of retribution, if we consider that Waldemar was the most powerful sovereign of the north. By threats and bribes his release was procured; but during his confinement the conquered provinces had revolted, and the king was unable to recover his lost possessions. Denmark was thus reduced from her lofty position by the injustice of her king.

"Towards the close of the fourteenth century, Margaret — the Semiramis of the North — succeeded to the thrones of Norway and Denmark, and added Sweden to her dominions by conquest, in the compact of Calmar. The Swedes, under Gustavus Vasa, established their independence after the union had existed for one hundred and twenty-five years. At the death of the last of Margaret's line, in 1439, the states of Denmark elected the count of Oldenburg their king, who reigned as Christian I. He was made duke of Schleswig and count of Holstein, and thus the sovereign of

Denmark became the ruler of these duchies, about which there has been so much trouble within the last ten years, and which caused the war of 1866 between Prussia and Austria. He was followed by his son Hans, or John, whose heir was Christian II., deposed in 1523. This prince was a tyrant, and was kept a prisoner for twenty-seven years. His crown was given to Frederick, Duke of Schleswig and Holstein, in whose reign Sweden established her independence. His son Christian III. succeeded him. In the great wars which followed the Reformation, the kings of Denmark took the Protestant side. In repeated conflicts with the Swedes, Denmark lost much of her territory. After Christian III. came Frederick II., and then Christian IV., who was followed by Frederick III., in whose reign the crown, which had been nominally elective, was made hereditary in the Oldenburg line. Under Christian V. the country was at peace; but Frederick IV., who came after him, brought on a war with Sweden by invading the territory of the Duke of Holstein, an ally of the King of Sweden, which continued till 1718. Under Christian VI. and Frederick V. the country was at peace. Christian VII. married the sister of George III. of England, and was followed, in 1808, by Frederick VI., their son.

"In 1780, Russia, Sweden, and Denmark, under the influence of France, established a new code of maritime laws, which operated against the interests of England. This action in convention was called 'Armed Neutrality,' and in 1800, during the reign of Christian VII., its principles were revived, and a new agreement was signed by Russia, Prussia, Denmark, and Sweden. It declared that arms and ammunition alone were contraband of war, that merchandise of belligerents, except contraband of war, was to be protected by a neutral flag, and that 'paper blockades' should be regarded as ineffectual. England immediately laid an embargo on the vessels of the powers signing it. In 1801, a British fleet under Sir Hyde Parker, with Nelson as second in command, bombarded Copenhagen. Again, in 1807, England, fearing that Denmark would be compelled by Napoleon to take part against her, bombarded Copenhagen, and compelled the government to give up its entire fleet, which was sent to England. This ended the armed neutrality. At the final treaty of peace, in 1814, Norway was ceded to Sweden, which, in return, gave to Denmark Pomerania, and the Island of Rügen; but the next year Pomerania was passed over to Prussia, in exchange for the Duchy of Lauenburg.

"Frederick VI. reigned till 1839, when he was followed by Christian VIII. The two Duchies of Schleswig and Holstein were still subjects of dispute. The king claimed them, but the people of Holstien were German in sentiment, and objected to the incorporation of their country in the Kingdom of Denmark, to which the continued efforts of the latter were directed. The Danish language was required to be used to the exclusion of the German. In 1848, Frederick VII. came to the throne, and was more energetic in pushing his claims to the duchies than some of his predecessors had been. The people of Holstein, which was a member of the German Confederation, were in a state of insurrection, when the King of Denmark virtually annexed both duchies to his kingdom. War ensued, and continued for three years. The interference of some of the great powers restored peace, but left the question in dispute unsettled."

"What was the question in dispute?" asked Captain Lincoln.

"I will explain it, though there are so many complications to it, that only a general view of the subject can be given. For four hundred years the line of Oldenburg has occupied the throne of Denmark. Schleswig and Holstein were governed by the same rulers, though each country was separately organized. But the law of succession was different. In Denmark a female could rule, while in the duchies the line was limited to males. Frederick VII. had no children, and it was seen that the direct line of the house of Oldenburg would be extinct at his death. A treaty made by the several powers interested gave the succession to Prince Christian, whose wife was entitled to the throne by right of her descent from Christian III., who died in 1559; but she yielded her right to her husband, who ascended the throne is 1863, as Christian IX., and is the present king. At the death of Frederick VII., the Duke of Augustenburg claimed the duchies. Germany desired to separate Schleswig-Holstein from Denmark. The German troops entered Holstein, which was a member of the Confederation, and entitled to its protection. Denmark refused to yield her title to the duchies, and war ensued. The Danes were overwhelmed, and repeatedly defeated. England declined to assist Denmark, as had been expected by the latter, and Denmark was compelled to renounce all her claims to Schleswig-Holstein and Lauenburg, in favor of Prussia and Austria. The main question in regard to the final disposition of the duchies was left open for future adjustment, and Prussia took temporary possession of Schleswig, and Austria of Holstein. The Duke of Augustenburg was permitted to remain in the latter, but forbidden to get up any demonstration in aid of his own claims.

"Austria favored the claim of the duke. while Prussia denied it, and accused her then powerful rival of encouraging revolutionary movements in Holstein dangerous to the thrones of Europe. Then followed the great war of 1866, which resulted in the utter humiliation of Austria, and the annexation of all the disputed territories to Prussia. Denmark, thus shorn of her territories and her power, has become an insignificant kingdom. With less than two million inhabitants, she supports all the costly trappings of royalty, and keeps an army and navy. The king has a civil list of nearly three hundred thousand dollars, and the heir apparent has an allowance exceeding the salary of the President of the United States, while the entire revenue of the nation is only about thirteen million dollars. Prince Frederick, the king's oldest son, who succeeds to the throne, married the daughter of the King of Sweden and Norway. The princess Alexandra, the oldest daughter, is the wife of the Prince of Wales. Prince Wilhelm, the second son, was elected King of Greece, under the title of Georgios I. in 1863. The Princess Dagmar is the wife of the Grand Duke Alexander, of Russia, heir of the throne. By their connections two of the sons are, or will be, kings, one daughter Queen of England, and another Empress of Russia.

"In 1348, the King of Denmark levied duties on all vessels passing through the Sound, at the Fortress of Kronberg, which were applied to the expenses of the light-houses, and the protection of shipping from pirates. The United States first objected to the payment of this tax, and called the attention of the commercial nations of Europe to the annoyance. All vessels were obliged to anchor, and submit to vexatious delays; but none doubted the right to levy the dues, which had been formally regulated by treaties. Denmark consented to abandon her claims on the payment of about fifteen millions of dollars by the nations of Europe, and about four hundred thousand on the part of the United States."

The professor completed his lecture, and the students separated. Most of them climbed into the rigging, or seated themselves on the rail, where they could see the city and the various objects of interest in the harbor. The view shoreward from the ship was very unsatisfactory, for the city, built on a dead level, presented but little to challenge the attention of the voyager. While they were observing the surroundings, a shore boat approached the vessel, in which were two persons wearing the uniform of the squadron. One of them was a stout man, in whom the students soon recognized Peaks.

"But who is that with him?" asked Norwood.

"It's one of the second cutter's crew, I suppose," replied De Forrest. "I didn't think, when I went ashore with them, that I shouldn't see any of them again for so long a time. I wonder where the rest of them are."

"That's not one of the second cutters," added Judson. "It is the English fellow."

"So it is."

Peaks came alongside, and directed Clyde Blacklock to mount the accommodation ladder, which he did without making any objection. They had arrived the day before. The prisoner seemed to have lost some portion of his stubborn spirit. The boatswain followed him to the deck, and touching his cap to the captain and other officers on the quarter-deck, went aft, where the principal was talking with the surgeon.

"We have come on board, sir," said the boatswain, as he took off his cap and pointed to Clyde.

"I see you have," replied Mr. Lowington. "I'm glad to see you again, Clyde."

The young Briton nodded his head with a jerk, but made no reply.

"Have you seen Mr. Blaine, Peaks?" asked the principal.

"Yes, sir; I met him on the wharf night before last at Gottenburg."

"But where are the crew of the second cutter? I expected you to bring them."

"They came back to Christiania on Friday, and took the steamer for Gottenburg the same evening; but Mr. Blaine had not seen them. Their steamer arrived in the forenoon, and the ship did not sail till night."

"I am afraid there is something wrong about it."

"I left Mr. Blaine in Gottenburg. I suppose he will find them."

Peaks reported in detail the result of his mission on shore. So far as Clyde was concerned it was entirely satisfactory; but the continued absence of the second cutter's crew was very annoying to the principal.

"How do you feel, Clyde?" asked Mr. Lowington, turning to the new student.

"I feel well enough," replied the runaway, roughly.

"I am glad you do. I hope you feel better than when you left the ship."

"I don't."

"While you were on board before, I neglected to explain to you the consequences of leaving the ship without permission."

"It wouldn't have made any difference. I should have gone just the same," answered Clyde, doggedly.

"The less trouble you make, the better it will be for you."

"Perhaps it will; but I don't intend to stay in this ship a great while."

"I intend that you shall stay here; and since you avow your purpose to run away again, I must see that you are put in a safe place. Peaks, the brig."

"The brig? What's that?" demanded Clyde, who was very suspicious of the calm, unmoved tones of the principal.

"Come with me, my lad, and I will show you," replied the boatswain.

The Briton knew by sad experience how useless it was to contend against his tyrant, who, however, always used him well when he behaved in a reasonable manner. He followed the boatswain into the steerage, and the door of the brig, which was a small prison formed of plank slats, set upright under the steps, about three inches apart, was opened.

"That's the brig, my boy," said Peaks. "It's a a regular institution on board a man-of-war; but this one has not been opened for months."

"Well, what's it for?" asked Clyde, who even yet did not seem to comprehend its use.

"Walk in, and I will make it all plain to you in a moment."

"I don't know what you mean."

"Sail in!" shouted a student, who, with others, was observing the treatment.

"On deck, sir!" said the boatswain, sternly, to the speaker. "Report yourself."

It was a principle in the discipline of the ship that no person should say or do anything to irritate a student undergoing punishment, and no one was permitted, on such occasions, to take part on either side, unless called upon by the officer or instructor to do so. In ordinary cases no boy was required, or permitted, to be a "tell-tale," and all were expected to remain neutral. The student who had spoken left the steerage, and went on deck, before Clyde had time to "open upon him," as he intended to do.

"Step in, my lad," added Peaks.

"What for?" asked the Briton, as he obeyed the order, but not without a suspicion that he was to step upon a red-hot gridiron, or be precipitated through some opening in the deck into the dark depths beneath.

No such calamity happened to him, and he was rather astonished to find that no harsher punishment was used for the flagrant offence he had committed. He had pushed the boatswain overboard, and then run away. Peaks had never manifested any resentment towards him on account of his cowardly trick; but he anticipated some severe discipline on board of the ship. The boatswain closed and locked the door of the brig, and then looked in at the prisoner through the slats.

"Do you understand what the brig is for now?" asked Peaks.

"You have locked me in — that's all."

"That's all, my lad."

"How long am I to stay here?"

"Till you make up your mind not to run away."

"This isn't a bad place, and I shall stay here till I grow gray before I promise not to be off when I get a chance."

"All right, my hearty. Think of it a few weeks."

To one who had expected some horrible punishment for his misdemeanors, the brig seemed like very mild discipline. Clyde seated himself on the stool in his prison, and leisurely surveyed the surroundings. He was an enterprising youth, and the bars of his cage looked small and weak. At dinner time, the meal was handed in to him, and he ate with an excellent appetite. Soon after, he heard the call for all hands, and then the waiter in the steerage told him they had gone on shore to see the city. Everything was quiet and still, and he devoted himself to a more particular examination of the bars of the brig. They were two inches thick, but the case looked hopeful. Pursuing his investigations still farther, he found, under the steps, a saw, a hammer, a chisel, and some other tools, which Bitts, the carpenter, had placed there a few days before, and forgotten to remove. Clyde took up the saw; but just then, Peaks, with a book in his hand, seated himself at a table near the brig, and began to read.

CHAPTER XV.

COPENHAGEN AND TIVOLI.

ALL the boats of the squadron came into line, each with the flag in the bow and stern. They pulled along the water front of the city, around a couple of Danish men-of-war, and of course created a sensation. One by one the boats rowed up to the landing, and the students went on shore, each crew securing its cutter at the wharf, near the steps. The custom-house officers were on the alert; but as no one had parcels of any kind, the students were not detained. Mr. and Mrs. Kendall landed, and as they intended to spend a few days in the city, they had a couple of valises, which the porters, who are always in waiting at all the ports in Europe, conveyed into the custom-house. The Toldbod, as this edifice is called by the Danes, is surrounded by a high wall, which also encloses the entire landing-place, so that none can visit the city from the sea without passing through its gates.

One of the officers spoke English very well, and evidently took pride in doing so, for he asked a great many questions so pleasantly, that it was impossible to explain his object in any other way. He wished to know whether the travellers had any clothing they had not worn, and whether Mrs. Kendall had any tobacco or liquor. She protested that she did not use tobacco or liquor; and the actual examination of the baggage was a mere form. The man was so polite, that Paul at once concluded he was only practising his English. A carriage was procured, and Dr. Winstock and Captain Lincoln were invited to join the party. The inquiring students deemed it a great privilege to be permitted to go with the surgeon, for he was a walking encyclopædia of every city and country in Europe. As Paul Kendall had been before, Captain Lincoln was now, the favorite of the doctor, and the little party were to see the city together.

The carriage went out at the gate, and passed into Amaliegade. The houses were plain and substantial, without much ornament. They were of brick, but most of them were covered with stucco.

"What's this?" asked Paul, as the carriage entered an open space, with an equestrian statue in the centre.

"Frederiksplads," replied the doctor; "and that is the statue of Frederik V., who came to the throne in 1746, and in whose reign this palace was erected."

The place was an octagon, surrounded on all sides by public buildings.

"This is the residence of the king on the left. On the other side is the palace of the crown prince. There is the foreign office, and on the other side lives the queen dowager."

"They are not very elegant buildings," said Captain Lincoln.

"No; there are no very fine buildings in Copenhagen, though the Exchange is a very curious structure, and some are very large and unwieldy. There's the Casino," added the doctor.

"What's a casino?" inquired the captain.

"Here it is a building for dancing, concerts, theatrical performances, and similar amusements in the winter season. Everything is cheap here, and the price of admission to the Casino, where one joins the dance or sees a play, is two or three marks."

"How much is that? I haven't looked up the money yet," said Paul.

"A rigsbank dollar is the unit, worth about fifty-four cents of our money. It is divided into six marks, of nine cents each, and a mark into sixteen skillings, of about half a cent each. When the Italian opera is at the Casino, the prices are only three or four marks. This is Gothersgade," added Dr. Winstock, as the carriage turned into another street. "In plain English, Gothic street."

"There's another equestrian statue," added Captain Lincoln, pointing to a large, irregular space, surrounded by public buildings.

"The statue of Christian V. This is Kongens, or King's Square. There are the Academy of Arts, the Royal Theatre, the Guard House, the New Market — none of them very fine, as you can see for yourselves."

The carriage crossed this square, and came out at a canal, on the other side of which was the vast palace of Christiansborg. A short distance farther brought the party to the Royal Hotel. The carriage stopped at the door in the arch, and the two landlords, the porter, the waiters, and the clerk, half a score strong, turned out to receive its occupants. All of them bowed low, and all of them led the way up stairs. Paul took a parlor and chamber for himself and lady.

"Now, where's Joseph?" asked Dr. Winstock.

"Who's Joseph?" inquired the captain.

"He is the guide at this hotel, if he is still living."

Joseph was sent for, and soon made his appearance. He was an elderly man, with gray hair and whiskers, neatly dressed in black. His manners were very agreeable, and he exhibited a lively zeal to serve the tourists. Mr. Lowington had been courteously waited upon by an officer of the government, who had volunteered to have the various palaces, museums, and other places of interest, opened during the afternoon and the next day. Joseph had procured a two-horse carriage, and the party at the hotel seated themselves in it, with the guide on the box with the driver.

"That's the Slot," said Joseph, pointing across the canal.

"The what?" exclaimed Captain Lincoln.

"The Slot, or Palace of Christiansborg."

"Slot! What a name!"

"But not any worse than the German word *Schloss*," added Joseph, laughing. "Do you speak German, sir?"

"Not much."

The guide uttered a few sentences in German, evidently for the purpose of demonstrating that he spoke the language.

"The palace is on an island called Slotsholm, and is as big as it is ugly. Shall we go there now?"

"No; we want a general view of the city first,"

replied Dr. Winstock. "I think we had better ascend to the top of the Round Tower."

Joseph gave the order, and the carriage proceeded to the tower. The canal in front of the hotel was filled with small craft, which had brought pottery and various wares from other parts of Denmark, to sell. The goods were arranged on the decks and on the shore of the canal. Near were groups of women, who were selling fish, vegetables, and other articles, around whom was a crowd of purchasers.

"I suppose you have heard of Andersen?" said Joseph to the captain.

"Heard of him! I have read all his books which have been translated into English," replied Captain Lincoln.

"He has rooms in that building some of the time. Do you see that sign — Melchoir?"

"Yes."

"This Melchoir is a very dear friend of Andersen, who lives with him a portion of the time."

"Is it possible to see Hans Christian Andersen?" asked Mrs. Kendall.

"Quite possible, madam. I will see about it to-day. He is a very agreeable man, and willing to meet all who wish to see him," answered Joseph. "There's the Town Hall," he added, as the carriage passed a large building, with an extensive colonnade in front.

"'*Med Lov skal man Land bygge*,'" said Lincoln, reading an inscription on the front. "Those are my sentiments exactly."

"'With law must the land be built' is the English of that," laughed Joseph. "All the Jutland laws begin with this phrase, which was spoken by Waldemar II. We Danes believe in law, and everything that is good. Copenhagen is a very fine city, and everything is remarkably cheap here."

"What do you call your city in your own lingo, Joseph?"

"Kjöbenhavn; pronounce it Chép-en-ahn."

"Chepenahn," repeated Lincoln.

"Speak it a little quicker, and you will have it right. It was first called simply the Haven; then in Danish, when many merchants carried on business here, *Kaupmannahöfn*, or merchants' haven, from which it was shortened into *chepenahn*. Here is the Round Tower," added Joseph, as the carriage stopped.

The party alighted and entered the structure, which was the tower of the Church of the Trinity.

"This used to be the watch tower, where men were kept to give the alarm in case of fire; but the observatory has been moved to the tower of St. Nicholas, and now we have a telegraphic fire alarm. Won't you walk up to the top of this tower, where you can have a fine view of the whole city? The ascent is very easy," continued Joseph.

There were no stairs, but an inclined plane, gradual in its rise, permitted the tourists to ascend to the summit with very little labor.

"We might have driven up in the carriage," said Captain Lincoln.

"There would be no difficulty at all in doing so. In fact, Peter the Great, when he was in Copenhagen, in 1716, drove to the top with the Empress Catharine, in a coach and four."

"Is that so?" asked the captain.

"I can't remember so far back myself," chuckled Joseph, "for I'm not much over a hundred years old; but everybody says it is true, and I see no reason to doubt the story. Peter the Great liked to do strange things, and you can see for yourself that a carriage would run very well here."

"If he went up with a coach and four, of course he must have come down, unless the carriage and horses are up there now. How did he turn his team?"

"It is easier to ask some questions than to answer them," replied Joseph. "History does not say that he drove down, only that he drove up."

"Perhaps he backed down, which kings and emperors are sometimes obliged to do, as well as common people," suggested Paul Kendall.

"Very likely he did; I don't see any other way for the team to descend," added Joseph. "This tower was begun in 1639."

At the top of the structure the travellers took a general survey of the city, and then proceeded to examine it in detail.

"Do you remember the latitude of Copenhagen, Captain Lincoln?" asked Dr. Winstock.

"About fifty-five and a half."

"The same as the middle of Labrador. Quebec is about forty-seven, and this is a long way farther north. What is the population of this city, Joseph?" asked the doctor.

"One hundred and eighty-one thousand," replied the guide, giving the census of 1870. "Formerly the city was a walled town, with ramparts and moats. It was built partly on Seeland, and partly on the small island of Amager. The channel between them is the harbor. You can see where the old line of fortifications was. The old town lies nearest to the sea, but the city is now spreading rapidly out into the country."

"What is that broad sheet of water, with two bridges over it?" asked Lincoln, pointing to the land side.

"That is the reservoir. Formerly the water in the city was bad, but now it has an excellent system of water-works. The water comes in from the country, and is pumped up by steam before it is distributed. Beyond that, for miles, the country is covered with beautiful villas and country residences. You must ride out there, for the environs of Copenhagen are as fine as anything in Europe."

"You are right, Joseph," added the doctor. "Some parts of the city are not unlike Holland, you see. The Slotsholm canal gives that part of the town a decidedly Dutch look."

"The part on Amager, called Christianshavn, is all cut up by canals," added the guide.

"Now, we will take a ride around the city," said Paul Kendall.

The party descended, and having driven through some of the principal streets, and obtained a very good idea of the city, returned to the hotel.

"Now you can dismiss the carriage, and we will go to some of the museums and churches," suggested Joseph.

"We don't care to walk far; we will retain the carriage," replied Paul.

"It will be much cheaper to walk, as you have to

pay four marks an hour for the carriage," pleaded the economical guide. "Thorwaldsen's Museum and the Northern Antiquities are only a few steps from here."

"Very well; we will walk, then, if you insist upon it," laughed Paul.

"I thought these guides made you spend as much money as possible," said Captain Lincoln to the surgeon.

"I never found it so. I think they are a very useful class of men. They charge here about two rigsdalers a day, and I remember that Joseph would not let me throw away a single mark. They know the prices for carriages and everything else, and it is for their interest not to let any one cheat their employers. Perhaps it is not well to make purchases with them, for they compel the merchant to pay them a commission, which increases the price charged for the articles. But I think, in many places, I have done better with a *commissionnaire* than without one, in making purchases."

Joseph led the way across the bridge to Slotsholm, which was nearly covered by the immense palace of Christiansborg and its dependencies. The first building was Thorwaldsen's Museum, the outer walls of which were covered with an Etruscan fresco of the arrival and debarkation of the great sculptor and his goods, mostly works of art. The figures are about life size, and the situation in which the pictures are placed is novel and quaint. The work was done by inlaying cement of different colors in the wall. Joseph described the various scenes. Thorwaldsen is still held in the highest regard and veneration by all Denmark, and especially by all Copenhagen; indeed, he seems to be the great genius of the country. He was born in 1770, near the city. His father was an Icelander, and a carver in wood — a calling in which the son assisted him when he was only a dozen years old. At seventeen he received the prize of a silver medal from the Academy of Arts, and at twenty-three the grand prize, which carried with it a royal pension, that enabled him to go abroad for the study of his art. He went to Rome in 1796, where he had but little success, and was reduced almost to despair, when his model of Jason and the Golden Fleece attracted the attention of an English gentleman, who commissioned him to complete the work in marble. This event was the dawn of success, and orders continued to pour in upon him from the rich and the powerful, including kings and emperors, until his fortune was made. His works adorn many of the great cities of Europe, and Canova was his only actual rival. His fame extended to every nation, and a visit to his native land in 1819 was a triumphal progress through Italy and Germany. In 1838 he returned to Copenhagen, to pass the remainder of his days, in a frigate sent to Italy for his use by the Danish government. On one side of his museum are depicted his arrival in this ship, and his reception by the citizens; and on the other side, the conveyance of his works from the ship to their final destination. Thorwaldsen went to Rome again on a visit for his health, and died in Copenhagen in 1844. He was a modest, generous, and amiable man. The museum was erected by subscription, though the sculptor gave a fourth part of the sum necessary for its erection, and in his will bequeathed to it the works of art from his cunning brain, of which its contents are almost entirely composed. His biography has been written by Hans Christian Andersen.

After examining the frescoes on the outer wall, the party entered the building. It is an oblong structure, with a court-yard in the middle. It is two stories in height, with connected rooms extending entirely around it. The works of art, and memorials of the sculptor, are classified in these apartments, forty-two in number.

"That is the grave of Thorwaldsen," said Joseph, leading the way into the court-yard. "His body lies there, surrounded by his works, as he requested."

The grave is an oblong enclosure of polished granite, raised a few inches above the ground, and covered over with ivy. At the foot of it is a black cross, with the date of his death inscribed upon it.

The tourists walked through the various rooms, and examined the works of the immortal genius, most of which were in plaster, being the models of all his great achievements set up in marble in various parts of Europe. His pictures, his library, his collections of coins, vases, and antiquities, are placed in the museum. One room is fitted up with his furniture, precisely as he used it, and various interesting mementos of the man are to be seen there. Among the pictures are some mere daubs, which are preserved only because they belonged to Thorwaldsen; but they have an interest as an illustration of the benevolent character of the great sculptor, who ordered many of them merely to save the artists from starvation.

"Did you ever see Thorwaldsen?" asked Lincoln, as Joseph conducted his charge from the building.

"Often," replied the guide. "He was a venerable-looking old man, with long, white hair. He made a statue of himself, which is very like him. He died suddenly in the theatre, and the king and royal family followed his remains to the church."

The Museum of Northern Antiquities was in the old palace of a prince, on the other side of the canal. On the front of the building were some quaint carvings, which gave it a picturesque appearance. Joseph seemed to be in his element at this museum. He spoke glibly and learnedly of "the stone age," "the bronze age," and "the iron age," each designated by the material of which the implements used for domestic purposes, in war and agriculture, were composed. Numberless utensils of all kinds are contained in the cabinets, classified with rare skill, and arranged with excellent taste. All these objects were found below ground, in various parts of Scandinavia. In Denmark the law requires that all antiquities of metal shall belong to the government, which, however, pays the full value of the articles to the finder. In 1847 a pair of solid gold bracelets, very heavy, and elegantly wrought, were dug up from the earth, and added to this collection. There is a great variety of ornaments, in gold and silver, consisting of necklaces, rings, bracelets, and similar trinkets. One necklace contains three pounds of pure gold.

There are plenty of knives, arrow-heads, hatchets, hammers, chisels, and other implements, skilfully made of stone. Runic writings, the most valuable in the world, are collected here. Joseph said that certain long pieces of wood, with signs carved upon them, were Icelandic Calendars. The remains of a warrior, who had fought and died in the ancient time, with the iron mail of his day, were examined with interest, as were also a number of altars, coffers containing relics, and some gold crosses, one of which is said to contain a splinter from the true cross, which were exhibited as specimens of the Catholic form of worship in remote times.

Recrossing the bridge over the canal, the party entered the great, barn-like palace of Christiansborg. It consists of several connected buildings, containing a theatre, riding-school, stables, coach-houses, bakehouse, and the usual royal apartments. In 1168 a castle was erected on this spot, as a protection against pirates, which was repeatedly demolished, rebuilt, altered, and enlarged, till it was levelled to the ground in 1732, and a new palace erected, but was destroyed by fire in 1784. It was rebuilt, in its present cumbrous proportions, in 1828. The visitors entered the large court-yard, passed through the picture gallery, the "Hall of the Knights," the throne-room, looked into the riding-school, — which is a large, oblong room, with an earth floor, where the royal family may practise equestrianism, — the arsenal, the legislative chambers, and other rooms, none of which were very striking to those who had visited the palaces of Paris, London, Berlin, and St. Petersburg.

In front of the palace is a beautiful green, beyond which is the Exchange, or Börsen, built by Christian IV. It is the most picturesque edifice in the city, though the interior is entirely commonplace. It is long and very narrow, and ornamented with a vast number of figures cut in the stone, with elegantly-wrought portals at the entrances. But the spire is the most remarkable portion of the building, and consists of four dragons, the heads at the apex looking towards the four points of the compass.

From the Exchange the party walked to the Fruekirke, or Church of our Lady, which is interesting only on account of the works of Thorwaldsen which it contains. Behind the altar is the majestic and beautiful statue of Christ, which stretches out its wounded hands, as if he were saying, "Come unto me, ye that labor and are heavy-laden, and I will give you rest." On each side of the church are the figures of the twelve apostles, placed against the walls at equal distances, so as to include the whole extent. In the middle of the choir, in front of the altar, is the figure of an angel, holding a baptismal font, in the shape of a shell, which some call Thorwaldsen's masterpiece. In the sacristy of the church are several other works of the great sculptor, who was first interred in this place, before the museum was ready to receive his remains.

Mrs. Kendall declared she had seen enough for one day, for sight-seeing is the hardest work one can do when it is overdone. After supper, when the lady was rested, she consented to visit Tivoli, where the students were to spend the evening. This celebrated resort of the Copenhageners is situated just outside of the old walls of the city, near the arm of the sea which divides Amager from Seeland. One of the two horse-railways, which the people in Europe generally persist in calling "tramways," extends through the city, passing the gates of this garden. Several of the officers and seamen of the ship came by the cars, which hardly differ from those in use in the principal cities of the United States; but all of them have accommodations for passengers on the top.

Captain Lincoln — who had been on board of the ship since he left the party with whom he had spent the afternoon — and Norwood were passengers in a car; but though they could not speak a word of Norsk, they were not disturbed by the situation. Presently the conductor presented himself, which caused a general sounding of pockets among the occupants of the car. He had a tin box, suspended by a strap, which passed around his neck, to contain the money he received. In his hand he held a compact little roll of yellow paper, an inch and a half in width, across which was printed a succession of little tickets, each with a number. The fare was four skillings, or two and one fourth cents, and, as each person paid, the conductor handed him one of these papers, torn from the roll. Captain Lincoln gave him a piece of money, and held up two fingers, pointing to his companion at the same time, to indicate that he paid for both. The man gave him his change, and two of the yellow tickets.

"What are these for?" asked Lincoln, glancing at the little papers.

"They are tickets, of course," replied Norwood.

"I don't think so," added the captain. "All the people seem to throw them away, and the floor of the car is covered with them."

"O, I know now what they are!" exclaimed Norwood. "I have heard of such things."

"I never did."

"I suppose you know what 'knocking down' means — don't you?" laughed the second lieutenant.

"It means stealing."

"Precisely so. It is said that conductors and omnibus drivers at home 'knock down' a good deal, which is the technical name for taking a portion of the fares. They use 'spotters' in our country to keep the conductors and drivers honest."

"Spotters?"

"Yes, that's the name of them. They are men and women, whom the conductors cannot distinguish from other passengers, employed by the railway companies to ride in the cars, and report the number of passengers on certain trips, so that the agents can tell whether the fares are all paid over. These tickets are used for the same purpose."

"I don't see what good they do. They certainly can't keep the men honest, for almost everybody throws away his ticket."

"They are called control-marks," said a gentleman next to the captain, who had been listening with interest to the conversation, and who spoke good English. "The man has to tear one of them off every time a passenger pays him."

"They are all numbered, I see; mine is nine hundred and four," added Lincoln.

"When the man gives up this roll at night, the next number will show how many he has torn off. If he began at No. 200 this morning, he has taken seven hundred and four fares."

"But he might neglect to tear off fifty or a hundred in the course of a day," suggested Lincoln, "and put the money for them in his pocket."

"If he does so, everybody is watching him, and anybody may report him to the agent. I am a share-owner of the company, and for aught the conductor knows, there may be one in every car. If the man neglects his duty, my interest would prompt me to look after him."

"I see; thank you, sir."

"Here is Tivoli," added the gentleman. "I suppose you are going there."

"Yes, sir."

"It is a fine garden, and very cheap."

The young officers left the car, and bought tickets at the gate, for which they paid one mark, or nine cents, each. Near the entrance they found a man selling programmes of the evening's entertainment, at two skillings each. Captain Lincoln bought one, for he carefully preserved every handbill, ticket, or programme for future reference. He could read a little of it. The performances were varied, and covered the time from six o'clock till midnight. But the young officers preferred to take a general view of the premises. It was an extensive garden, prettily and tastefully laid out, with accommodations for concerts, circus, and theatrical performances. In the centre was a "beer garden," with table and seats, for little parties, who drank their beer and chatted, while a band played in a kiosk. Near it was a bazaar, where all kinds of fancy articles were arranged for sale, with the attendant raffles and lotteries. Farther removed from the centre was a theatre, consisting, however, of only the stage, the audience seating themselves in the open air. The performance, from six to seven, as the captain read in his programme, was

Rl. 6. Entrée gymnastique af Brodrene Hermann.

Or, in plain English, a gymnastic exhibition by the brothers Hermann.

In the circus there was a performance at half past seven, such as one sees in the United States, and " Hr. Wallet" was clown. At half past nine o'clock, another exhibition was given in an enclosed building, to which an extra admission fee was charged. At the theatre, dancing by some "celebrated sisters" was in progress at nine o'clock. A Russian mountain was in operation during the whole evening. It was a railroad down one inclined plane, and up another, and back over the same track, a ride costing a few skillings. The concert was continued at intervals during the entire evening. The "*café chantant*" was in full blast after nine o'clock, in two places, one of which was a small hall, with a bar, and the other the interior of a Swiss cottage, with a gallery surrounding it. In each of these were tables, where the audience seated themselves, and drank brandy, wine, beer, and milder beverages. The singers, who are all females, stood upon a stage, and were accompanied by a piano. After one or two songs had been sung, one of the singers passed around among the audience with a plate to receive their contributions, each person generally giving a small copper coin. This order was continually repeated, and the money thus received is the only salary of the performers, whose singing is villanously vile, and whose character is worse than their singing. A canal, extending from the sea, comes up to Tivoli, and passes around an island. Boats are to let here; and, indeed, there is no end to the variety of amusements, and "all for nine cents," as Joseph had said half a dozen times during the afternoon to his party, and a dozen times more during the evening. At half past ten the students returned to the squadron, for by that time they had seen all they desired.

CHAPTER XVI.

AN EXCURSION TO KLAMPENBORG AND ELSINORE.

PEAKS sat near the brig and read his book, which he had procured from the librarian in anticipation of a dull and heavy afternoon. Clyde sat in his cage, watching the boatswain. The book was evidently a very interesting one, for the reader hardly raised his eyes from it for a full hour, and then only to bestow a single glance upon the occupant of the ship's prison. The volume was Peter Simple, and the boatswain relished the adventures of the hero. Once in a while his stalwart frame was shaken by an earthquake of laughter, for he had a certain sense of dignity which did not permit him to laugh outright all alone by himself, and so the shock was diffused through all his members, and his body quaked like that of a man in the incipient throes of a fever and ague fit. The magnanimous conduct of O'Brien, who flogged Peter for seasickness, simply because he loved him, proved to be almost too much for the settled plan of the boatswain, and it was with the utmost difficulty that he restrained an outbreak of laughter.

For a full quarter of an hour Clyde convinced himself that he was entirely satisfied with the situation. The brig was not a bad place, or, at least, it would not be, if the boatswain would only leave the steerage and allow the prisoner to be by himself. He wished very much to try the carpenter's saw upon the slats of his prison. At the end of the second quarter of an hour, the Briton was slightly nervous; the close of the third found him rather impatient, and at the expiration of an hour, he was decidedly provoked with Peaks for staying where he was so long. When the stout sentinel glanced at him, he flattered himself with a transitory hope; but the boatswain only changed his position slightly, and still appeared to be as deeply absorbed as ever in the book.

Clyde was disgusted, and emphatically angry at the end of another half hour. The brig was a vile place, and putting a free-born Briton into such a den was the greatest indignity which had yet been offered to him. It was even worse than ordering him to be silent, or to go forward. It was an insult which required both redress and vengeance. He rose from his seat, and walked to the door of his prison, but with his gaze still fixed upon his jailer. He had come to the conclusion that, if he moved, Peaks would, at least, look at him; but that worthy did not raise his eyes from his book. Clyde took hold of the barred door and began to shake it, making considerable noise by the act. Peaks took no notice whatever of him, and it seemed just as though the boatswain intended to insult him by thus disregarding him. He shook the door again with more violence, but did not succeed in attracting the attention of his custodian. Then he began to kick the door. Making a run of the length of the brig, he threw himself against it with all the force he could, hoping to break it down; but he might as well have butted against the side of the ship. It yielded a little, and rattled a great deal; but it was too strong to be knocked down in any such manner.

The prisoner was boiling over with wrath, as much because Peaks did not notice him, as on account of the indignity of his confinement. He kicked, wrenched, and twisted at the door, till he had nearly exhausted his own strength, apparently without affecting that of the door. The boatswain still read, and still shook with suppressed laughter at the funny blunders and situations of Peter Simple. He had seen just such fellows as Clyde in the brig; had seen them behave just as the present prisoner did; and he had learned that it was better to let them have their own way till they were satisfied, for boys are always better satisfied when they solve such problems for themselves. .

"I'm not going to stay in this place!" howled Clyde, when he had wasted all his powers upon the obstinate door.

"No?"

The boatswain happened to be at the end of a chapter in his book, and he closed the volume, uttering only the single negative participle, with the interrogative inflection, as he glanced at his charge in the brig.

"No, I'm not!" roared Clyde, rousing from his seat, upon which he had dropped in sheer exhaustion, and throwing himself desperately against the unyielding door. "I won't stay in here any longer!"

"Well, now, I thought you would," added Peaks, with the most provoking calmness.

"I won't!"

"But it seems to me that you do stay there."

"I won't any longer."

"Well?"

"I'll send for the British minister."

"Do."

"I won't stand it any longer."

"Sit down, then."

Clyde dashed himself against the door again with all the remaining force he had; but the boatswain, apparently unmoved, opened his book again. It was terribly lacerating to the feelings of the Briton to be so coolly disregarded and ignored. Clyde had the saw, but he had sense enough left to know that any attempt to use it would attract the attention of his jailer, and end in the loss of the implement, with which he could remove a couple of the slats when left alone, or when all hands were asleep at night. Finding that violence accomplished nothing, he seated himself on his stool, — which, however, was far from being the stool of repentance, — and considered the situation more calmly. He was in a profuse perspiration from the energy of his useless exertions. Perhaps he was conscious that he had made a fool of himself, and that his violence was as impolitic as it was useless. In a few moments he was as quiet as a lamb, and remained so for half an hour, though his bondage was no less galling than before.

"Mr. Peaks," said he, in the gentlest of tones.

"Well, my lad, what shall I do for you?" replied the boatswain, closing his book, and going to the door of the brig.

"I'm very thirsty, and want a glass of water. Will you give me one?"

"Certainly, my boy."

The boatswain passed a mug of water through the bars, and Clyde drank as though he was really thirsty.

"You have worked hard, and it makes you dry," said Peaks. "You can keep a mug of water in the brig if you like."

"I will," replied Clyde, as he placed the mug on the deck, after the boatswain had filled it. "Can't you let me out, Mr. Peaks?"

"Certainly I can."

"You will — won't you?"

"With all my heart."

"Do, if you please."

"On certain conditions, you know."

"What conditions?"

"That you won't attempt to run away. But, my lad, it is only a few hours since you said the brig was a very nice place, and you would grow gray in it before you would promise not to leave when you got a good chance."

"I hadn't tried it, then. But I think it is an insult to a fellow to put him in here. I would rather be flogged outright."

"We don't flog the boys."

"I would rather take a flogging, and have it done with."

"That's one of the reasons why we don't do it. We don't want to have it done with till the boy means to do about right. You are a smart boy, my lad; but you have got a heap of bad blood in your veins, which ought to be worked off. If you would only do your duty like a man, you would be comfortable and happy."

"I never can stay in this ship."

"Why not?"

"I don't understand the duty."

"You will soon learn all the ropes in the ship, and they will all come as handy to you as the key of your own watch."

Clyde pulled out his watch, and glanced at the boatswain.

"That's a nice time-keeper you have, my lad; gold, I suppose."

"Yes; it cost thirty pounds. Wouldn't you like it?"

"I?"

"Yes."

"Well, I have a pretty good silver one, which answers my purpose very well," replied Peaks, smiling.

"I'll give it to you, if you will let me out, and permit me to go on shore," added Clyde, in an insinuating tone.

"Thank you, my lad, I don't want it bad enough to do that."

"You can sell it, you know. Or I will give you thirty pounds in cash, if you prefer."

"I can't afford to do it for that," laughed the boatswain.

"I'll give you fifty pounds then," persisted Clyde.

"Can't afford to do it for that, either."

"Say sixty, then."

"Say a hundred, if you like, my lad; and then say a thousand. I can't afford to do it for all the money your mother is worth. You are on the wrong tack, my lad. I can't be bought at any price."

"I won't ask you to let me out. If you will only go on deck, and keep out of the way, I will manage it all myself."

"No, no; sheer off, my hearty. When I have a duty to do, I always mean to do it; and if it isn't done, it isn't my fault. You can't leave the ship with my consent."

"I can't stay here, I say. I should die in a month."

"Very well, die like a man, then," said Peaks, good-naturedly; for, though he could not be bought at any price, he did not indulge in any righteous indignation against his victim. "Learn your duty, and then do it. There is plenty of fun going on in the ship, and you will enjoy yourself as soon as you get on the right tack. That's the up and down of the whole matter."

"I can't take off my cap to these young squirts of officers, and be ordered around by them. It isn't in an Englishman to do anything of the sort."

"Upon my word, I think it is in them. They make first-rate sailors, and always obey their officers."

"Common sailors do; but I'm a gentleman."

"So am I; but I always obey orders," replied the democratic Peaks, warmly. "The officers of this ship are required to behave like gentlemen, and give their orders in a gentlemanly manner. If they don't do it, they are liable to be reduced. Do your duty, and you may be an officer yourself."

Peaks continued for some time to give the prisoner good advice, assuring him that he was no better than the rest of the crew, and that it would not hurt him any more than others to obey the orders of the officers. But it was sowing seed in stony ground, and Clyde, finding he could make nothing out of the honest boatswain, decided to await his time with what patience he could command, which, however, was not much. Peaks was permitted to follow Peter Simple in his stirring career during the rest of the afternoon. The crew returned from Tivoli at eleven in the evening, and soon the ship was quiet, with only an anchor watch, consisting of an officer on the quarter-deck, and two seamen on the forecastle.

Clyde's supper was given to him in his prison, and a bed made up for his use. He kept awake till all the students came on board, and while he was waiting for the crew to slumber, he dropped asleep himself, and did not wake till all hands were called in the morning. He was vexed with himself for his neglect, and afraid that the carpenter would miss the saw, and remember where he had left it. He was determined to keep awake the next night, and make his escape, even if he was obliged to swim to the land.

After breakfast, all the students went on shore for an excursion to Klampenborg and Elsinore. In the custom-house enclosure, a procession of four in a rank was formed, to march to the railroad station, which was near the Tivoli Garden. The students were generally rather fond of processions, not at home, but in the streets of foreign cities. The parade was quite imposing, when every officer and seaman wore his best uniform. They had been carefully taught to march, and Professor Badois had organized a band of eight pieces, which performed a few tunes very well. Unfortunately, on the present occasion, the band was not available, for Stockwell, the cornet player, and Boyden, the bass drummer, belonged to the absent crew of the second cutter, and the procession moved to the sterling notes of the drum and fife.

On parades of this kind, the first and second pursers acted as the fleet staff of the commodore, who would otherwise have been " alone in his glory," and these two useful officers seemed like " odds and ends " in any other position. As this procession was frequently formed, and marched through the streets of various cities, the order is given to satisfy the reasonable curiosity of the reader.

Music.
The Commodore,
And Staff of the Fleet.
The Captain of the Young America.
The Four Masters.
The Four Midshipmen.
The First Lieutenant.
The First Part of the Starboard Watch,
Consisting of Eighteen Seamen.
The Second Lieutenant.
The Second Part of the Starboard Watch.
The Third Lieutenant.
. The First Part of the Port Watch.
The Fourth Lieutenant.
The Second Part of the Port Watch.
The Captain of the Josephine.
The Four Masters.

The First Lieutenant.
The First Part of the Starboard Watch,
Consisting of Eight Seamen.
The Second Lieutenant.
The Second Part of the Starboard Watch.
The Third Lieutenant.
The First Part of the Port Watch.
The Fourth Lieutenant.
The Second Part of the Port Watch.
The Captain of the Tritonia.
The Four Masters.
The First Lieutenant.
The First Part of the Starboard Watch,
Consisting of Eight Seamen.
The Second Lieutenant.
The Second Part of the Starboard Watch.
The Third Lieutenant.
- The First Part of the Port Watch.
The Fourth Lieutenant.
The Second Part of the Port Watch.

Sometimes the order was varied by placing all the officers at the head of the procession, except the lieutenants in command of sections, as, —

The Commodore and Staff.
The three Captains.
Three ranks of Masters.
One rank of Midshipmen.

But keeping all the officers and seamen of each vessel together, as in the first order, was generally preferred. Of course the ranks were not always full, as on the present occasion; but even when the full band was at the head of the column, there were enough for four full ranks in each half-watch of the ship, and two ranks in those of the other vessels. The students had practised so much that they marched exceedingly well, and being aligned according to their height, the effect was very fine. The Copenhageners left their occupations, and hastened to the doors and windows of their houses and shops to see the procession; and even the king and royal family were spectators at the palace windows, as the column moved through Frederiksplads. As it passed the Royal Hotel, Mr. and Mrs. Kendall, with Dr. Winstock and Joseph, were entering a carriage, in which they intended to ride to Klampenborg, in order to see more of the country. At the railroad station, the officers and seamen took seats in the third-class carriages, which were two stories high, the upper as well as the lower one having a roof. The distance to Klampenborg is eight and a half English miles, and the fare is sixteen skillings, or nine cents, third class; twenty-four skillings, or thirteen and a half cents, second class; and thirty-two skillings, or eighteen cents, first class. The third-class compartments are clean and neat, but there are no cushions on the seats. An aisle extends through the middle of them, but the seats are placed in pairs, on each side, so that half the passengers are compelled to ride backwards. In about half an hour the train arrived at Klampenborg.

Paul Kendall's party drove first to the summer residence of Mr. Melchoir, which was in the suburbs of the city, near the sea-shore. The house was a very pretty one, with a neat garden, not unlike the little country places one sees in the vicinity of the large cities of the United States. Joseph rang the bell, and stated the errand of the party to the servant. They were shown up one flight of stairs, where the girl knocked at the door, which was immediately opened by Hans Christian Andersen, and the tourists were ushered into a plainly-furnished room, with a few engravings on the walls. On a table were the writing-materials of the great author, and Paúl looked with interest at the little pile of letter sheets, closely written over, and the unfinished one, on which the ink was not yet dry.

Mr. Andersen's face was covered with a smile as he greeted the party. Dr. Winstock had met him before, and stated the fact.

" O, I'm very glad to see you again," said the author, grasping the doctor's hand with both of his own.

" My young friend here, and his lady, have both read all your books, and desired to see you even more than to look upon the beautiful works of your great sculptor."

" Ah, you are very kind," added Mr. Andersen, again grasping the doctor's hand with both of his own.

Then, darting nervously to Paul, he seized his hand in the same manner.

" This is Captain Paul Kendall, commander of the yacht Grace," added Dr. Winstock.

" I am so pleased to see you!" said Mr. Andersen.

" I have read all your books with the most intense pleasure."

" O, you are too kind, Captain Kendall," replied the

genial author, smiling all over his face, and once more grasping his hand as before.

"Mrs. Kendall," added Paul, presenting Grace.

"I am so pleased to see you! You are very kind to take so much trouble to visit me."

"Indeed, sir, you are very kind to permit us to trouble you, when you are so busy," continued Paul.

"O, I have plenty of time to see my good friends."

"In America we love your books, and they are in all our libraries and most of our houses."

"You are so kind to speak so pleasantly of my works!" replied Mr. Andersen, grasping Paul's hand again.

"We value them very highly."

The conversation continued for a few moments, in which Paul and the doctor expressed the high appreciation of the reading public of the great writer's works. At least a dozen times more he grasped the hand of the speaker with both his. Mr. Andersen is a tall gentleman, with a thin face, — the features of which are far from handsome, — and iron-gray hair. His countenance is always covered with smiles when he speaks, and his whole manner is child-like and simple. He is full of the love of God and of man, which seems to shine out in his face, and to be the interpretation of his ever-present smile. His dress was scrupulously neat and nice in every detail.

The doctor told him about the Academy squadron, of which he had read a brief notice in the newspapers, and invited him to visit the ship, which he promised to do, on the following day. The party took their leave of him, and continued on the way to Klampenborg. The road was on the margin of the sea, and was lined with small country houses, with pleasant gardens. It was a lovely region, with an occasional large villa, and even a summer palace or two. All along this road, called the Strandway, are small and large houses of entertainment, on the sea-side, each one of which has a bathing establishment on a very small and simple scale.

"Here is Charlottelund Castle, in this park," said Joseph, as they passed what seemed to be merely a grove, with a rather dilapidated fence.

"It was formerly the country-seat of the Landgrave of Hesse, I believe," added Dr. Winstock.

"Yes, sir; but it is now the summer residence of the crown prince. He comes out here in June."

"These carriages are called 'privateers,'" continued the guide, pointing to several vehicles like a small omnibus with no top. "They formerly went by the name of 'coffee-mills,' because they made a noise like those machines."

Constantia Tea-Garden, where the Copenhageners go to spend the evening in hot weather, and several fishing villages, were passed, and then the carriage reached the Deer Park, where the students had already arrived, which is a very extensive enclosure, with a few roads extending through it. A portion of it is covered with groves, and it contains about a thousand deer, which are quite tame, and may be seen grazing in herds on the gentle slopes. There is nothing very attractive in the park, though it is much frequented by the people from the city. Neither the roads nor the grounds are well kept, and the government "turns an honest penny" by the letting of it out for the pasturage of horses. On some rising ground, which Denmarkers call a hill, is a large, square, barn-like building, known as the "Hermitage," which was built by Christian VI. for a hunting lodge. This park and that at Charlottelund contain thousands of acres of excellent land, which is almost useless, and which the government cannot afford to keep in condition as pleasure-grounds. They would make thousands of farms, and thus increase the productive industry and the revenues of the nation, if they could be cut up and sold. Royalty is an expensive luxury, which a small kingdom like Denmark cannot afford to support.

Near the entrance to the park is the garden proper of Klampenborg, where music is provided on summer evenings, and refreshments sold. What is called a Norwegian house is erected in the middle of the grounds, which contains a bar and private rooms, and is surrounded by tables and chairs, where the pleasure-seekers may sit and enjoy their beer and the music. A small fee for admission is paid at the gate, where the ticket-seller is kept honest by the aid of the "control-mark." Near this garden is a hotel built for a water-cure establishment, though it is now mainly used as a summer boarding-house. Close by it is a village of small cottages, devoted to the same use, with concert-rooms and bathing-houses in abundance. This place is a favorite resort of the Copenhageners in summer, — in fact, their Newport or Long Branch. For a couple of hours the students wandered through the park and gardens. The railroad station is very near the entrance, where, indeed, the whole beauty of the place is concentrated.

The railway to Klampenborg is a branch of the one which extends from Copenhagen to Elsinore, and in another hour the entire party were transported to the latter place. This town has nine or ten thousand inhabitants, and is located on a basin of the Sound, nearly landlocked by natural and artificial dikes. The Danish name of the place is Helsingör, and is the scene of Shakespeare's tragedy of Hamlet. The excursionists visited the cathedral, which is the principal object of interest in Elsinore, and contains several very old tombs. Near the town, and on the shore of the Sound, is the Castle of Kronberg, erected in 1580. It is a large, oblong, Gothic structure, built of a whitish stone. It contains a chapel and other apartments. Those occupied by the commandant were the prison of Caroline Matilda, who was confined here for a high crime, of which she is now universally believed to be innocent.

Under the castle are casemates for a thousand men, one of which is said to be the abode of *Holger Danske*, who was the Cid Campeador of Denmark, and the hero of a thousand legends. When the state is in peril, he is supposed to march at the head of the armies, but never shows himself at any other time. A farmer, says the story, happened into his gloomy retreat by accident, and found him seated at a stone table, to which his long white beard had grown. The mystic hero demanded the hand of his visitor, who was afraid to trust flesh and blood in the grasp of one so mighty, and offered the iron bar used to fasten the door. Holger Danske seized it, and squeezed it so hard that he left the print of his fingers on the iron.

"Ha, I see there are still *men* in Denmark!" said he, with a grim smile of satisfaction.

Near the castle are a couple of natural ponds, small and round, which are called "Holger Danske's Spectacles."

"This is where Hamlet lived, I suppose," said Captain Lincoln.

"Where Shakespeare says he lived," replied Dr. Winstock.

"But I was told his grave was here."

"Perhaps Hamlet divided himself up, and occupied a dozen graves, for I think you may find a dozen of them here," laughed the doctor. "A resident of this vicinity had what was called the grave of Hamlet in his grounds, which proved to be a nuisance to him, on account of the great number of visitors who came to see it. In order to relieve himself of this injury to his garden, he got up another 'grave of Hamlet,' in another place, which he proved to be the authentic one."

"It is too bad to trifle with history in that manner," protested the captain.

"There is no history about it, Lincoln. His residence in this part of Denmark is all a fiction. Shakespeare makes terrible blunders in his allusions to this place; for there is no 'eastern hill,' no 'dreadful summit of the cliff,' or anything of the sort. Hamlet lived in Jutland, not in Seeland, about four centuries before Christ, and was the son of a pirate chief, instead of a king, who, with his brother, was governor of the province. He married the daughter of the king, who was Hamlet's mother. The chief was murdered by his brother, who married the widow, and was then the sole governor. Hamlet, in order to avenge his father's death, feigned madness; but his uncle, suspecting the trick, sent him to England, with a message carved in wood, requesting the king to destroy him. During the voyage, he obtained the wooden letter, and altered it so as to make it ask for the killing of the two men, creatures of his uncle, who had charge of him, which was done on their arrival. According to the style of romances, he married the king's daughter, and afterwards returned to Jutland, where, still pretending insanity, he contrived to surprise and slay his uncle. He succeeded his victim as governor, and married a second time, to a queen of Scotland, and was finally killed in battle. The main features of the tragedy correspond with the incidents of the story, but the locality is not correct."

The party walked to Marienlyst, a pleasant watering-place, which contains a small royal chateau. The view from this place, as from the tower of Kronberg, is very beautiful. At four o'clock the party took the steamer, and arrived at Copenhagen before dark.

CHAPTER XVII.

TO STOCKHOLM BY GÖTA CANAL.

THE Wadstena, in which the absentees had taken passage at Gottenburg, was a small steamer, but very well fitted up for one of her size. Forward was the saloon, in which meals were taken, and saloon passengers slept. Aft was the cabin, on each side of which were state-rooms, called "hütte." They were not made with regular berths, but had a sofa on each side of the door, on which the beds were made up at night, with a wash-stand between them. Between this cabin and the forward saloon the main deck was raised about three feet, so as to cover the engine and boilers. On each side of this higher deck were more "hütte," which were the best rooms on board. The hurricane-deck, over the after cabin, was the favorite resort of the passengers.

It was two o'clock in the morning, and the independent excursionists were tired and sleepy. They had taken first-class tickets, and two of them had been assigned to each "hütte." As soon as they went on board, therefore, they retired, and most of them slept, in spite of the fleas and other vermin that revelled in their banquet of blood. None but very tired boys could have slumbered under such unfavorable circumstances, and it is a great pity that a steamer otherwise so neat and comfortable should be given up to the dominion of these sleep-destroying insects.

At seven the party turned out, anxious to see the scenery on the banks of the canal. The steamer was still in the river, a stream not more than a hundred and fifty feet wide, with occasional rapids, which are passed by canals, with locks in them. The scenery was pleasant, with rocky hills on each side. Schooners and other craft were continually met, loaded with lumber and other articles from the lakes. The scene was novel and interesting, and though the boys gaped fearfully, they enjoyed the view.

Presently one of the women, who do all the work of stewards and waiters, appeared with coffee on deck, passing the cups to the passengers first, and then filling them. The coffee was delicious, served with the whitest of sugar and the richest of cream, with some little biscuits. It waked the boys up, and seemed to make new beings of them.

"How's this, Sanford?" said Scott.

"First rate! That's the best coffee I ever drank in my life," replied the coxswain.

"Is it a free blow?"

"I don't know. How is it, Ole?"

"No; you pay at the end of the trip for all you have had," replied the waif.

"But who keeps the account?" asked Scott.

"Nobody," laughed Ole. "On the boats from Christiania every passenger tells what he has had, and pays for it."

"Do they think everybody is honest?"

"Certainly; everybody is honest."

"Not much," added Sanford, shaking his head. "Of course you don't pretend to be honest, Norway."

"But I do."

"You didn't take a sovereign from me, and another from Burchmore — did you?"

"I take what you give me."

"It may be honest, but I don't see it in that light, Norway."

"Never mind that now, Sanford," interposed Burchmore. "He sold out the last time for the public good."

"Do you expect to find the ship in Stockholm when we get there?" asked Scott.

"Of course I do," replied Sanford. "We shall not get there till Tuesday."

"Then our cruise is almost ended."

"I suppose so. I have been trying hard to join the ship ever since we left her at Christiansand," continued the coxswain, solemnly.

"Over the left," chuckled Scott.

"Honor bright! I don't believe in running away."

"Nor I; but Laybold and I have put our foot into it. I suppose we shall have to spend a week in the brig, and make love to Peaks while the rest of the fellows are seeing Russia."

"You will find some way to get out of the scrape."

"I don't know. We have lost Copenhagen and Denmark already, and I suppose we shall not see much of Russia."

"We will help you out."

"I don't think you can do it," added Scott, who

had evidently come to the conclusion that running away "did not pay."

The steamer stopped, and the captain informed the party that passengers usually walked three miles around the series of locks, by which they were enabled to see the Falls of Trollhätten. The carrying of the canal around these falls was the most difficult problem in engineering in the construction of the work. It is cut through the solid rock, and contains sixteen locks. The passage of the steamer occupies an hour and a half, which affords ample time for the voyagers to see the falls. The party immediately landed, and were promptly beset by a dozen ragged boys, who desired to act as guides, where no such persons are needed. Not one of them spoke a word of English; but they led the way to the path, each one selecting his own victims, and trusting to the magnanimity of the passengers for their pay. A walk, covered with saw-dust, has been made by some public-spirited persons, and the excursion is a very pleasant one.

The entire fall of the river is one hundred and twelve feet; but it is made in four principal cataracts, and three smaller ones. The scenery in the vicinity is rather picturesque, and at one point the path goes through a grove, on the banks of a rivulet, where the water dashes over large cobble-stones, with an occasional pretty cascade. The walk leads to various eligible spots for examining the falls and the rapids. On the way, the tourist passes *Kungsgrottan*, or King's Grotto. It is a hole in the solid rock, in the shape of half a globe, on the sides of which are inscribed the names of the various sovereigns of Sweden, and other distinguished persons who have visited the spot. Near the village of Trollhätten, which contains several founderies and saw-mills, the finest part of the falls is seen by crossing an iron foot-bridge, at the gate of which stands a woman, who collects a toll of fifty öre for the passage to the little island.

"I don't think much of these falls," said Scott, as he returned from the island.

"I think they are rather fine," replied Laybold.

"You could cut up the rapids of Niagara into about two hundred just such falls, to say nothing of the big cataract itself," added Scott. "It is pleasant, this walk along the river, but you can't call the Falls of Trollhätten a big thing."

"Of course they don't compare with Niagara."

"Certainly not."

The party walked through the yards of the manufactories, and came to a small hotel on the bank of the canal. The place looked very much like many American villages. The canal steamer did not appear for half an hour, and some of the boys strolled about the place. The regiment of ragged boys who had followed the tourists, or led the way, pointing out the various falls and other points of interest in an unknown tongue, begged lustily for the payment for their services. One of them, who had taken Scott and Laybold under his protection, was particularly urgent in his demands.

"Not a red, my hearty," replied Scott. "I didn't engage you, and I shall not pay you."

The boy still held out his hand, and said something which no one of the party could understand.

"Exactly so," replied Scott. "You told me the names of all the places, but I did not understand a word you said. I say, my lad, when did you escape from the rag-bag?"

The boy uttered a few words in Swedish.

"Is that so?"

The boy spoke again.

"Stick to it, my hearty; but I don't believe a word of it."

"What does he say, Scott?"

"He says the moon is made of green cheese. Didn't you, my lad?"

The boy nodded, and spoke again.

"It is a hard case, Young Sweden; but I can't do anything for you."

"What's a hard case, Scott?" asked Laybold.

"Why, he says he has six fathers and five mothers, and he has to support them all by guiding tourists round the falls."

"Get out!"

"I am afraid they don't have roast beef for dinner every day."

"Here's the steamer," added Laybold.

The boy became more importunate as the time came to go on board, but Scott was obstinate.

"Now, out of my way, my lad. Give my regards to your six fathers and five mothers, and I'll remember you in my will; but I won't give you a solitary red now, because I don't like the principle of the thing. I didn't employ you, and I didn't want you. I told you so, and shook my head at you, and told you to get behind me, Satan, and all that sort of thing;

and now I'm not going to pay you for making a nuisance of yourself. On the naked question of charity, I could do something for you, on account of your numerous fathers and mothers. As it is, good by, Sweden;" and Scott went on board of the steamer.

The boat started again, and soon the bell rang for breakfast. The boys hastened to the forward saloon, where they found two tables spread. At a sideboard was the Swedish lunch, or snack, of herring, sliced salmon, various little fishes, sausage, and similar delicacies, with the universal decanter of "finkel," flanked with a circle of wine glasses. The tourists partook of the eatables, but most of them were wise enough to avoid the drinkable. The Swedish bread, which is a great brown cracker, about seven inches in diameter, was considered very palatable. Ordinary white bread is served on steamers and at hotels, and also a dark-colored bread, which looks like rye, and is generally too sour for the taste of a foreigner. The breakfast at the tables consisted of fried veal, and fish, with vegetables, and all the elements of the snack. When the boys had finished, one of the women handed Scott a long narrow blank book.

"Thank you, marm; I am much obliged to you," said he. "Will you have the kindness to inform me what this is for?".

The woman laughed, and answered him in her native tongue.

"Precisely so," added Scott.

"What does she say?" asked Sanford.

"She wants me to write a love letter in this book

to her; but as she is rather ancient, I shall decline in your favor, Sanford."

"Don't do it, old fellow! Face the music."

"Not for Joseph!"

"What did she say, Ole?" inquired Sanford.

"She said you were to keep your account in that book," replied the interpreter.

"Are we to keep our own reckoning?"

"Yes; every one puts down in this book what he has had."

"That means you, Burchmore. You are the cashier for the party."

"How many fellows had coffee this morning?" asked the cashier, as he took the book.

"All of them, of course."

Burchmore made the entries for the coffee and the breakfasts of the whole party.

"Well, that's one way to do the thing," said Scott. "Every man his own book-keeper. I'll bet everybody doesn't charge what he has had."

Ole was requested to ask the woman about the matter. She said the Swedes were honest, but the waiters were required to see that everybody paid for what he had had before leaving the steamer. The having of this book is certainly a better plan than that of the Norwegian steamers, by which the passenger, if he means to be honest, is compelled to recollect all he has had in a passage of thirty hours.

The Wadstena continued on her course through a rather flat country, just coming into the greenness and beauty of the spring time, till she came to Wenersberg, a town of five thousand inhabitants, which is largely engaged in the lumber and iron trade. The boat stopped there a short time, and the party had an opportunity to examine the lake craft at the wharves; but, after seeing them, it was difficult to believe they were not in some New England coast town. The steamers, however, were very different, all of them being very short, to enable them to pass through the locks in the canal, and most of them having the hurricane deck forward and aft, to afford sufficient space for the cabins. All of them were propellers.

The Wadstena started again, the bridges opening to permit her passage. The great Wenern Lake lay before them, which is the third in size in Europe, Onega and Ladoga alone exceeding it in extent. It is about a hundred miles long by fifty in breadth, very irregular in shape, and portions of it are densely crowded with islands. Its greatest depth is three hundred and sixty feet near the Island of Lurö, but a considerable part of it is very shallow, and difficult of navigation. It is one hundred and forty-five feet above the level of the Baltic. Thirty rivers flow into it, and sometimes cause it to rise ten feet above its ordinary level. But the Göta River is its only outlet, and is always supplied with an abundant volume of water. The wind was fresh when the Wadstena steamed out upon the broad expanse, and the lake had a decidedly stormy aspect.

"Will you be seasick?" asked the captain, as the little steamer began to bob up and down with a very uncomfortable jerk.

"Seasick!" laughed Scott. "We are all sailors, sir, and we don't intend to cave in on a fresh-water pond."

"But the lake is very rough to-day."

"If your little tub can stand it, captain, we can."

"I am very glad, for some people are very sick on this part of the passage. It is sometimes very bad, the worst we have in the whole trip."

"How long are we on the lake?" asked Scott.

"About seven hours; but not all of it is so bad as this. We go among the islands by and by."

Doubtless the Wenern Lake fully maintained its reputation on the present occasion, though none of the young salts were sick. The boat stood to the northward, and the short steamer and the short chop sea would have made the passage very trying to landsmen. Nothing but the distant shores were to be seen, and the monotony of the passage was the only disagreeable circumstance to our tourists. For the want of something better to do, they went below, and, lying down on the sofas in their state-rooms, went to sleep without much difficulty, for the red-backs and fleas kept shady in the daytime. The boys were accustomed to being "rocked in the cradle of the deep;" but at the expiration of three hours, the heavy motion ceased, and the change waked them. Going on the hurricane deck again, they found the steamer was among the islands, which were generally low, rocky, and covered with firs and pines. A crooked channel was carefully buoyed off, and the boat was threading its tortuous way with no little difficulty.

Presently the Wadstena made a landing at a rude pier on an island where only a rough shanty was in sight. Several row-boats at the wharf indicated that passengers came to this station from other islands.

Again the steamer went out upon the open lake, and soon after entered another group of islands, among which she made a landing at a small town. Passing over another open space, the entrance to the canal was discovered, marked by two low light-houses, in the form of the frustum of a pyramid. As the Wadstena entered a lock, the captain told the party they might take a walk if they pleased, as there were several locks to pass in the next three miles. This was a grateful relief to the voyagers, and they gladly availed themselves of the opportunity. The country was a dead level, with an occasional small farm-house, and with many groves and forests. But the walk was interesting, and the boys would gladly have continued it longer; but at the last lock of the series, the gate-man told them, through Ole, that they must wait here in order to go on board, for the steamer could not make a landing again for several miles. The party remained on the hurricane deck till the cold and the darkness drove them below. Turning in at an early hour, they slept as well as the vermin would allow, until six o'clock the next morning, when the steamer was approaching the Wettern Lake, the second in size in Sweden. The boat was on a broad arm of the lake, called the Viken, for the canal is built only across the narrowest section of country, between two natural bodies of water.

The Wettern Lake is ninety miles long and fifteen miles wide, surrounded by hills, from which sudden gusts of wind come, producing violent squalls on the water. This lake is noted for big trout. After crossing the Wettern, the steamer approached Wadstena, which contains an ancient church and convent, and a castle built by Gustavus Vasa, and often occupied by his family. Ten miles farther brought the steamer to Motala, which contains several iron founderies and manufactories. Many iron steamers and steam engines are built at this place. The scenery on this portion of the canal is very beautiful, though not grand. Going through another portion of the artificial canal, the boat enters the Roxen Lake, perhaps the most beautiful in Sweden, and makes a landing at Linköping. There are half a dozen towns with this termination in the country, as Norrköping, Söderköping, Jönköping, the last two syllables being pronounced like *chepping;* as, Lin-chep-ping.

Leaving the Roxen Lake, the steamer passes through more canals into an arm of the Baltic, and then into the sea itself, voyaging among a thousand small islands, stopping at Söderköping and Nyköping, important commercial and manufacturing towns. Night came, and our tourists did not stay up to see the lights on the way. The steamer leaves the Baltic, and passing another piece of canal, enters the waters of the Mäler Lake, seventy-five miles long, and containing fourteen hundred islands. The boys were up in season to see the beauties of this lake. Many of the islands rise to a considerable height above the water, and are so thick that one hardly believes he is sailing on a large lake. For quiet beauty and " eternal stillness," the Mäler can hardly be surpassed. In the middle of the forenoon, the spires of Stockholm were to be seen, and the tourists were all attention. From the lake the city presents a fine appearance. Indeed, Stockholm, seen from either of its water approaches, is hardly excelled in beauty by any city in Europe.

The Wadstena made her landing at the Island of Riddarholm. As the party were not burdened with any baggage, they decided to walk to the hotel. Ole inquired the way to the Hotel Rydberg, where they had agreed to go; and crossing a bridge to the largest of the three islands of the city, called Stadeholm, they arrived at the palace, beyond which is the quay. Between this island and the main land, on which the greater portion of the town is built, is the passage from the Baltic to the Mäler Lake, and in the middle of it is the Island of Helgeandsholm, or Holy Ghost's Island, with two bridges connecting it with either side. On it are the king's stables, and a semicircular garden, improved as a *café*, with a handsome face wall on the water side.

"This isn't bad," said Scott, as the party paused to look down into the garden.

"Not at all," replied Sanford. "I suppose they have music here in the evening, and it would be a capital place to loaf."

"See the steamers!" exclaimed Laybold, as a couple of the miniature craft, which abound in the waters of Stockholm, whisked up to the quay.

"A fellow could put half a dozen of them into his trousers pocket," laughed Scott. "We must go on a cruise in some of them, as soon as we get settled."

"Well, where's the hotel?" asked Sanford.

It was in plain sight from the bridge, which they crossed to the Square of Gustavus Adolphus, on which the hotel faced.

"Good morning, young gentlemen. I am happy to see you," said Mr. Blaine, the head steward of the ship, who was the first person to greet them as they entered the hotel.

"Ah, Mr. Blaine!" exclaimed Sanford, his face glowing with apparent satisfaction, "I am delighted to see you; for I was afraid we should never find the ship."

"Were you, indeed? Well, I had the same fear myself. I have been looking for you ever since the ship sailed."

"We have done our best to find the ship, Mr. Blaine," added Sanford.

"O, of course you have; but of course, as you didn't find her, you were not so babyish as to sit down and cry about it."

"Certainly not; still we were very anxious to find her."

"Mr. Peaks says you came down from Christiania before he did."

"Yes, sir."

"And you were so anxious to find the ship, that you took a train to the interior of the country, expecting, no doubt, to come across her on some hill, or possibly on some of these inland lakes," continued Mr. Blaine.

"We were looking for the ship's company. We met Scott and Laybold, who were going into the interior, and we concluded to join them, as they wanted to find their shipmates," replied Sanford, who was now not entirely confident that "the independent excursion without running away" was a success.

"Ah! so you have picked up those two young gentlemen, who ran away," added the head steward, glancing at Scott and Laybold.

"Not exactly, sir; they picked us up," answered the coxswain.

"I think it was a mutual picking up, and we picked each other up," laughed Scott. "We knew that Sanford and his crew were extremely anxious to find the ship's company, and if we joined them we should be sure to come out right."

"Exactly so," laughed Mr. Blaine. "Let me see; after our first day's run on shore, by some mistake you neglected to come on board at night, with the others."

"That was the case exactly. The fact is, we were too drunk to go on board with the others."

"Drunk!" exclaimed Mr. Blaine.

"Such was our melancholy condition, sir," added Scott, shaking his head. "We were invited, in a restaurant, to drink 'finkel,' and not knowing what finkel was, we did drink; and it boozed us exceedingly."

"You are very honest about it, Scott."

"We are about everything, sir. We slept at a hotel, and when we went down to the wharf to go on board, we learned that the ship's company had gone to Trolldoldiddledy Falls. As we felt pretty well, we thought we would take a train, see a little of the inside of Sweden, and meet the ship's company at Squozzlebogchepping."

"Where's that?" asked Mr. Blaine.

"I can't give you the latitude and longitude of the jaw-breaker, but it was at the junction of the two railways, where the party came down from the canal.

We were sure we should find our fellows there, but the Swedish figures bothered us, and we made a mistake in the hour the train was due.

"But the Swedish figures are the same as ours," suggested the head steward.

"Are they? Well, I don't know what the matter was, except that we were five minutes too late for the train. That's what's the matter."

"How very unfortunate it was you lost that train!"

"It was, indeed; I couldn't have felt any worse if I had lost my great-grandmother, who died fifty years before I was born. These honest fellows felt bad, too."

"Of course they did."

"We took the next train to Gottenburg; but when we arrived, the ship had sailed for Copenhagen, which I was more anxious to see than any other place in Northern Europe."

"And for that reason you came on to Stockholm."

"No, sir; you are too fast, Mr. Blaine. Your consequent does not agree with the antecedent. There was no steamer for Copenhagen for a couple of days."

"There was a steamer within an hour after you reached Gottenburg in that train, and an hour before the sailing of the canal steamer; and Mr. Peaks went down in her," said Mr. Blaine.

"We didn't know it."

"Certainly you did not."

"We knew of no steamer till Monday, and we were afraid, if we went in her, that we should be too late to join the ship in Copenhagen; and with heroic self-denial, we abandoned our fondly-cherished hope of seeing the capital of Denmark, and hastened on to Stockholm, so as to be sure and not miss the ship again. These honest fellows," said Scott, pointing to Sandford and his companions, " agreed with us that this was the only safe course to take."

" I see that you struggled very violently to join your ship, and I only wonder that such superhuman efforts should have failed."

" They have not failed, sir," protested Scott. " The ship will come here, and we will join her then, or perish in the attempt."

" Are you not afraid some untoward event will defeat your honest intentions? "

" If they are defeated it will not be our fault."

" No, I suppose not; but whom have you there?" inquired the head steward, for the first time observing Ole, who had pressed forward to hear Scott's remarks. " Ole? "

" Yes, sir; that's the valiant Ole, of Norway," replied the joker.

His presence was satisfactorily explained by the coxswain.

" Why did you desire to leave the ship, Ole? Didn't we use you well? " asked Mr. Blaine.

" Very well indeed, sir; but I was bashful, and did not wish to see some people in Christiansand," replied the waif.

" What people? "

Ole evaded all inquiries, as he had a dozen times before, and declined to explain anything relating to his past history. Mr. Blaine said he had heard the party had taken the canal steamer, and he immediately proceeded to Stockholm by railroad. He at once telegraphed to Mr. Lowington at Copenhagen, that he had found all the absentees, and asked for instructions.

"Here's a go, and the game is up," said Sanford, in a whisper, when he met Stockwell alone.

"That's so; what will he do with us?"

"I don't know; I rather like this mode of travelling. But we are caught now."

"Perhaps not; we may find some way out of it. According to Blaine's cue we are to be regarded as runaways. If that is the case, I don't join the ship this summer," said Stockwell, very decidedly.

"Nor I either," added Sanford.

Before dark, Mr. Blaine received a despatch from the principal, directing him to take the next train to Malmö, which is the town in Sweden opposite Copenhagen. The head steward did not communicate its contents to his charge that night, but he called all of them at four o'clock the next morning, and by good management on his part, they were on the train which left Stockholm at six o'clock. At Katherineholm, where the party ate an excellent breakfast, Mr. Blaine unhappily missed three of his company.

CHAPTER XVIII.

UP THE BALTIC.

THE excursionists of the squadron slept soundly after their trip to Elsinore, and Clyde Blacklock, true to the promise he had made to himself, kept awake to watch his chances to escape. Not a sound was to be heard in the ship, and the intense silence was even more trying to the prisoner in the brig than the noise and bustle of the whole crew when awake. Ryder, the fourth lieutenant, and two seamen had the anchor watch on deck. Each officer served two hours, and was required at the stroke of the bell, every half hour, to walk through the steerage, where no light was permitted after nine o'clock.

Clyde took the saw from its hiding-place under the stairs, and commenced work on one of the slats. The instrument was very sharp, but the noise it made promised to betray him, and he was obliged to use it with extreme caution. Bracing the slat with one shoulder, he worked the saw very slowly, so that the wood should not vibrate. The process was very slow, and twice he was obliged to conceal his saw and lie down on the bed at the approach of the officer of the watch. After working more than an hour, he succeeded in cutting off one of the slats, just far enough above the deck to avoid the nails with which it was secured. But it was fastened at the top as well as at the bottom, and when he pulled it in to wrench it from its position, it creaked horribly, and he was obliged to labor with it another half hour, before he could pull it in far enough to permit his exit. In the middle of the operation he was obliged to restore it partly to its position, and lie down again, to escape the observation of the officer of the anchor watch.

His care and patience were finally successful, though, if the sleepers around him had not been very tired, some of them must have been disturbed even by the little noise he made. The removal of the single slat gave him an opening of about nine inches, which was narrow even for him; but he contrived to work himself through it. Putting the slat back into its original position, and wedging it down with a copper, so that the means of his escape might not readily be seen, he crept carefully forward to the ladder under the forecastle, where he paused to consider the means by which he should escape from the vessel. He began to realize that this was a more difficult matter than getting out of the brig. He knew that the anchor watch consisted of an officer and two seamen.

While he was thinking of the matter, eight bells struck; and he was aware that the watch was changed at this hour. Retiring to the kitchen to wait for a more favorable moment, he heard the two seamen come down the ladder to call the relief. As they entered one of the mess-rooms, he ran up the ladder, and concealed himself under the top-gallant forecastle. In a few moments he heard the relief on deck, and from his hiding-place saw the officer on the quarter-deck with a lantern in his hand. The two seamen took their places on the top-gallant forecastle, where they could see the entire deck, and any boat or vessel that approached the ship.

Clyde did not regard the situation as very hopeful. The night was chilly, and he did not feel at all inclined to swim ashore, which he had intended to do, as a last resort. The boats were all hoisted up at the davits, as if to provide for just such cases as his own. He listened with interest to the conversation of the watch above him; but he could not identify their voices, and was unable to determine whether it was safe for him to address them. In fact he was unable to determine upon anything, and bell after bell struck without finding him any better prepared to make a move. At four bells, or two o'clock in the morning, the watch was relieved again, and Clyde remained in the same unsettled state of mind. But when the two seamen went below to call the relief, he changed his position, crawling into the waist, where he disposed himself under the lee of the rail. Over his head was the fourth cutter, one of the smallest of the boats.

Clyde could see the dark form of the officer walking to and fro on the quarter-deck, and his presence was not favorable to any movement. He found the cleats where the falls of the boat were made fast, and he was considering the practicability of casting them off, letting the cutter drop into the water, and then sliding down on a rope. The officer of the anchor watch seemed to be the only obstacle in his way. He began to experiment with the falls. Casting off one of them, he carefully let the rope slip over the cleat till he had lowered the bow of the cutter about two feet. He repeated the operation upon the stern fall. He let off the rope so gradually that the noise did not attract the attention of any of the watch.

Five bells struck, and the officer descended to the steerage. While he was absent, Clyde dropped each end of the boat about four feet more, and then coiled himself away until the officer had returned to his station. But it was nearly daylight, and he was compelled to hurry on with his work. Little by little he let out the falls, till the fourth cutter floated in the water. When the officer went below, at six bells, he climbed upon the rail, and slid down on the bow fall into the boat. Casting off the falls, he pushed the cutter astern of the ship, and for the first time began to feel as though he were free. He was afraid to use an oar, lest the noise should attract the attention of the watch on deck. He felt that he had managed his escape with exceeding cleverness, and was unwilling to risk anything now in the moment of success. The wind carried the boat clear of the ship, and he lay down in the stern sheets, so that if the officer on the quarter-deck discovered the cutter, he might suppose no one was in her.

He had occupied this position but a moment before he heard a rushing noise near him, and, raising his head, discovered a small schooner, under full sail, headed directly upon him. He had hardly time to stand up before the bow of the vessel was within his reach.

"Hallo!" shouted he, in terror, for the thought of being carried under the keel of the schooner was appalling.

But the cutter was crowded aside by the vessel, and Clyde sprang upon her deck, while his boat went astern of her.

Too late, the schooner luffed up, and Clyde seated himself on the rail to catch his breath. Two men came to him, and spoke in Norwegian.

"I speak English," replied Clyde.

"You are English?" said the captain.

"Yes; I don't speak anything else."

"I speak English," replied the skipper, as he went back to the helm, and Clyde followed him.

"Where are you bound?" asked the runaway.

"To Stockholm."

"You are Danish, I suppose."

"No, Norwegian."

"All the same."

"What shall I do with you?"

"I will go to Stockholm with you, and pay my passage, if you like," added Clyde, who wished to get as far as possible from the ship.

"You shall, if you like; or you shall work, if you please. I lose a young sailor, and I want another, to work in his place."

"No; I will go as a passenger, or not at all," replied Clyde, very decidedly.

"What you do in a boat so late in the night?" asked the skipper.

"I was going on shore to find a steamer for Stockholm. I will pay you twenty species for my passage," added the runaway.

"You are very kind to pay so much. You shall have my berth; but it will be long time to Stockholm in my vessel."

"No matter; I am satisfied."

"I shall pick up the boat you lose?"

"No; never mind the boat," answered Clyde, impatiently, as he glanced at the ship.

The captain questioned him about the boat more particularly; but the fugitive gave such answers as he pleased. Though the skipper was very rough and savage to the two men who formed his crew, he treated his passenger at first with much consideration. The little cabin of the schooner was a nasty hole, and if Clyde had not been very sleepy, he could hardly have closed his eyes there; but before the vessel was out of sight of Copenhagen, his slumber was deep and heavy.

The shout of the fugitive when he was in danger of being run down had been heard by the officer on the quarter-deck of the Young America. He saw the collision, and discovered the cutter when it went astern of the vessel; but he did not suspect that it belonged to the ship. The schooner filled away on her course again, after she had luffed up, and the boat was adrift. He deemed it his duty to secure it before it was stove by some early steamer from Malmö, or elsewhere, and calling the two seamen, he directed them to lower the fourth cutter. But the fourth cutter was already lowered, and the officer began to think that the boat adrift was the missing one. The third cutter, therefore, was used, and when the two seamen had pulled off in her, the officer went below and called Peaks.

The boatswain took his lantern, and went to the brig, as soon as he was told that the fourth cutter was adrift. The bird had flown. The door was secure, and all the slats were apparently in their place; but the appearance of a small quantity of saw-dust indicated where the breach had been made. A little pressure forced in the sawn slat, and Peaks understood why the prisoner had only desired to be left alone.

"Were you all asleep on deck?" asked Peaks of the officer.

"No, sir; I have not been asleep on duty," replied Beckwith, the officer.

"Didn't you see him lower the boat?"

"Of course I did not."

"I don't see how it was done, then," added Peaks. "But where is the prisoner?"

"I don't know. I suppose he went on board that small schooner that run down the cutter."

"Where is she?"

Beckwith pointed to a sail headed to the south-east, which was just visible in the faint light of the early morning.

"He is out of our reach for the present," said Peaks, in utter disgust, as he descended the steps to the main cabin.

Mr. Lowington was informed of the escape of Clyde, but no steamer could be obtained at that early hour to chase the schooner, and the matter was permitted to rest as it was. When all hands turned out in the morning, a strict investigation was made; but no one who had served on the anchor watch was able to give any information. No one had seen the boat lowered, and no one had heard the saw. Peaks went on shore, and ascertained that the Norwegian schooner Rensdyr had sailed at an early hour. She had cleared for

Stockholm, and was doubtless on her way there. The principal was so much interested in the fate of Clyde, or rather in his reformation, that he determined to follow up the fugitive. The English steamer Newsky, from London to Stockholm, was then in port, and when she sailed that day, Peaks was sent in her to intercept the runaway on his arrival at Stockholm.

After breakfast, Mr. Andersen came on board, inspected the ship, and witnessed some of the evolutions in seamanship, which included the manning of the yards in honor of his visit. At the invitation of Paul Kendall he went on board of the Grace, and took a sail up the Sound, dining on board, and returning in the afternoon. The students again went on shore, and visited the Rosenberg Palace, an irregular structure of red brick, with a high peaked roof and four towers. Connected with it is an extensive and beautiful garden, adorned with statues. The palace was built for Christian IV., in 1604, but is no longer a royal residence, being filled with various national collections of arms, medals, and antiquities, including many historical mementos of kings and other great men of Denmark. Among them are the saddle, bridle, and caparisons, the sword and pistols, presented by King Christian IV. to his eldest son at his marriage. They are adorned with diamonds, pearls, and gold, and cost a million francs in Paris.

In the afternoon the students marched to the Palace of Frederiksberg, whose park is a favorite resort of the people of the city. The building contains nothing worth seeing; indeed, portions of it have been rented for the use of private families; but the garden is beautifully laid out with kiosks, bridges over the winding canal, on which float a great number of white swans, with little islands, studded with groves and pleasant grassy slopes. The palace stands on the only eminence near Copenhagen. On pleasant days, especially on Sundays, this park is filled with family picnics, little parties bringing their own lunch, and spending the day in these delightful groves.

During the remainder of the day the students wandered over the city, each seeking what pleased him most. When they went on board the vessels, they were entirely satisfied with what they had seen of Copenhagen, and were ready to visit some other city. Very early the next morning, Mr. Blaine, with all but three of the absentees, came on board. The head steward told his story, and Scott and Laybold told their story; the former, as usual, being the spokesman. The wag told the whole truth, exactly as it was; that they were ashamed to come on board while so tipsy, and had missed the train at the junction.

"Have you drank any finkel since?" asked the principal.

"No, sir; not a drop. One glass was enough for me," replied Scott.

"And you, Laybold?"

"No, sir."

"You may both return to your duty," added the principal.

Both were astonished at being let off so easily; but Mr. Lowington was satisfied that they spoke the truth, and had not intended to run away. The others were also ordered to attend to their duty, but with the intimation that their conduct would be investigated at the return of Sanford and Stockwell, who, with Ole, had left the party at Katherineholm.

The signal for sailing was flying on board of the Young America, and at seven o'clock the squadron was under way, continuing the voyage "up the Baltic." No notice seemed to be taken of the absence of Sanford and Stockwell, but everybody believed that the principal knew what he was about. The wind was tolerably fresh from the west-south-west, and the squadron made rapid progress through the water, logging ten knots all day. The students watched with interest the villages on the coast of Denmark, with their sharp, red roofs, and the swarms of fishing-boats moored in front of them. The shores of Sweden were in sight all the time, and at three o'clock in the afternoon land was also seen on the starboard bow. But the masters, who were constantly watching the chart, were not at all astonished, though the seamen were.

"What land is that, Scott?" asked Laybold.

"That? Why, don't you know?"

"I'm sure I don't. I know Germany is over there somewhere, but I didn't expect to run into it so near Sweden."

"That's Gabogginholm."

"Is it in Germany?"

"No; it's an island, at least a hundred and fifty miles from Germany. The Baltic is rather a big thing out here."

"How do you remember those long names, Scott?"

"What long names?"

"Such as the name of that island. I couldn't recollect such a word ten minutes."

"Nor I either. I know them by instinct."

"What did you say the name of the island is?"

"Gastringumboggin."

"That isn't what you said before."

"I've forgotten what I did say it was. You musn't ask me twice about a name, for I say I can't remember," laughed Scott.

"You are selling me."

"Of course I am; and you go off cheaper than any fellow I ever saw before. I haven't the least idea what the land is, except that it must be an island not less than a hundred and fifty miles from Prussia."

"That's Bornholm," said Walker, a seamen, who had heard the name from the officers. It's an island twenty-six miles long and fifteen wide, belongs to Denmark, and has thirty-two thousand inhabitants, and a lot of round churches on it. That's what the fellows on the quarter-deck say."

"Precisely so," replied Scott. "You have learned your lesson well. What is the principal town on that island?"

"I don't know," answered Walker.

"Stubbenboggin," said Scott.

"Who told you so?"

"My grandmother," laughed the wag, as he turned on his heel, and walked away.

Towards night the wind subsided, and the squadron was almost becalmed; but a light breeze sprang up after dark, and in the morning the ship was off the southern point of Oland, an island ninety miles long by ten wide, and well covered with forests. On the narrow strait which separates it from the main land is Calmar, a town of historic interest, in Sweden. At noon the southern point of Gottland was seen, and Scott insisted upon calling it "Gabungenboggin," though the real name was soon circulated. It is eighty miles long by thirty-three wide, and contains fifty-four thousand inhabitants. Wisby is the only town. The island is noted for its beautiful climate, which makes it a pleasant resort for summer tourists.

At sunrise on the following morning, the ship leading the squadron was approaching the islands which cover the entrance to the harbor of Stockholm. Pilots were taken by the several vessels, and the fleet entered the archipelago, through which it was to sail for thirty miles. At first the openings were very wide, and not much of the shore could be seen; but soon the distances grew less, and the shores were studded with villages and fine residences. The little steamers — some of them not so large as the ship's first cutter — began to appear; and at eight o'clock the Young America let go her anchor between Staden and Skeppsholm, off the quay near the palace, which was crowded with steamers.

"Here we are, Laybold," said Scott, when the sails had been furled, and every rope coiled away in its place.

"That's so. What's that big building on the shore?"

"That's the Slottenboggin," laughed Scott.

"No, you don't! You can't sell me again with your boggins."

"I'll bet half a pint of salt water it is the king's palace."

"Very likely it is; and here is a fine building on the other side."

"That must be the Wobbleboggin."

"No, it isn't."

"Perhaps it isn't; but twig these little steamers," added Scott, pointing to one of the snorting miniature boats that plied across the arm of the sea opposite the quay. "The pilot and engineer, and a boy to take the fares, seem to be the officers, crew, and all hands."

"And in some of them all hands are boys."

The boats seemed to contain nothing but the engine and boiler, which were in a compact mass, without covering. All around them were seats. Forward of the engine was a little steering-wheel, hardly more than a foot in diameter, at which the pilot — often a boy — was seated.

"I want a complete view of the city," said Captain Lincoln, at this moment coming into the waist with the surgeon and Norwood. "I think I can get it from the main cross-trees."

"I am too stiff to go aloft," replied Dr. Winstock; "but I commend your plan."

"I'm with you," added Norwood, as he followed the captain up the main rigging.

From this lofty position on the cross-trees the two officers obtained a good idea of the situation of the city. The three islands which form the central portion of the city lay in the strait leading to the Mäler Lake. The north and south suburbs were on each side of it. Skeppsholm, Castellholm, and the Djurgården — Deer Garden — were other islands, lying nearer the Baltic. The finest portion of the city seemed to be the northern suburbs. While they were studying the panorama of the place, all hands were called to lecture, and they hastened to their places in the steerage. Professor Mapps was at his post, with the map on the foremast.

"Sweden is called *Sverige* by the natives; *La Suède* by the French; *Schweden* by the Germans; *La Svezia* by the Italians; and *Suecia* by the Spaniards. It contains one hundred and sixty-eight thousand square miles — a territory equal in extent to the six New England States, New York, New Jersey, Pennsylvania, and Delaware united. Its population is a little over four millions — about the same as that of the State of New York. It is nearly a thousand miles long from north to south, with an average breadth of two hundred miles. By far the greater portion of it is very sparsely settled, for it extends from fifty-five degrees of north latitude up to the arctic regions. It contains no important rivers, though its large lakes and arms of the sea are valuable as avenues of navigation. Over eighty lakes are mentioned."

The instructer described the Wenern and Wettern Lakes, and the Göta Canal, which passes through them.

"Sweden is an agricultural country, and its principal manufactures are lumber and iron. It has six hundred and thirty-eight miles of railway, and the steamers which you see at the quay, mostly of iron, and built in Sweden, ply to all parts of the country.

"The average of the temperature in Stockholm is forty-two degrees, or twenty-five degrees for winter, and sixty-two degrees for summer. From what you have already seen of Sweden, I think you will consider it very like New England. The interior has about the same physical features, and you will see there similar houses, barns, and fences.

"The government is a limited monarchy, based on the constitution of 1809, and since amended. The king must be a Lutheran. He has an absolute veto on the acts of the legislature. The Diet, or Parliament, consists of two houses, the upper of which is composed of one hundred and twenty-seven members, or one for every thirty thousand inhabitants. The lower house consists of one hundred and eighty-eight members, fifty-five of whom are elected by the towns, and the rest by the rural districts, at the rate of one for every forty thousand people. Property qualifications are required for either house, and all members must be Protestants. They are paid a salary of three hundred and thirty-five dollars of our money, and their travelling expenses, for the session of four months.

"I have incidentally spoken of the history of Sweden in connection with that of Norway and Denmark. The kingdom was founded by Odin, and for a long period the history of the country is a record of the wars with Norway and Denmark, and it was finally conquered by Margaret, and by the Union of Calmar the three kingdoms were consolidated in 1397. It became a Christian nation early in the eleventh century. Sweden was doubtless the first anti-slavery power; for, during the reign of Birger II., about 1300, a law against the sale of slaves was enacted, with the declaration that it was 'in the highest degree criminal for Christians to sell men whom Christ had redeemed by his blood.'

"In 1520 Gustavus Ericsson excited a rebellion against Christian II., of Denmark, who had murdered his father and many other Swedes. This revolution was successful three years later, and its leader made king, under the title of Gustaf I., often called Gustavus Vasa, or Wasa. He was succeeded by his son, and the throne continued in his family; but the next notable sovereign was Gustaf II., or Gustavus Adolphus. His grandfather, Gustavus Vasa, had established the Protestant religion in Sweden; but his nephew, Sigismond, who had been elected king of Poland, and had become a Catholic, succeeded to the throne. Endeavoring to change the established religion, he was deposed, and the succession changed. This caused a war between Sweden, and Russia, and Poland. Gustavus was only eighteen when he came to the throne, with this war bequeathed to him. He was full of energy, and defeated his enemies on all sides. Austria was the leader of the Catholic party in Europe, which was striving to restore the papal supremacy. Gustavus Adolphus held a similar relation to the Protestant party. He was engaged in the Thirty Years' War, and won many decisive victories. He captured Munich, and overran Bavaria, but was finally killed in the battle of Lützen, in 1632. By his prowess and skill he raised Sweden to the rank of one of the first kingdoms of Europe.

"He was succeeded by his daughter, Christina, then only six years old. She reigned but seven years after she became of age, abdicating in favor of her cousin Charles X. She died in Rome, after a dissolute and shameful life, and was interred in St. Peter's Church. Charles was at war with the Danes during his brief reign, and achieved the daring military feat of crossing the Great and Little Belts on the ice, which enabled him to dictate his own terms of peace with the Danes. The Swedes consider him one of their greatest kings. His son, Charles XI., followed him, and ruled for thirty-seven years. After a brief period of peace, another war with Denmark ensued, which resulted to the ultimate advantage of Sweden. This king contrived to obtain from the Diet the gift of absolute power, which, in the hands of his son and successor, Charles XII., nearly ruined the nation. Russia, Poland, and Denmark combined to rob him of a considerable portion of his kingdom, and Charles XII., at the age of sixteen, displayed an energy and a skill far beyond his years. He conquered a peace with Denmark first, and then turned his attention to the rest of his enemies, whom he overwhelmed and subdued. With nine thousand men he defeated a Russian army of forty thousand, under Peter the Great, at Narva. He vanquished the armies of Poland and Saxony, and attempted the conquest of Russia, but was utterly defeated in the battle of Pultowa, and escaped into Turkish territory, where he remained for five years. Here he brought about a war between Turkey and Russia, and the army of the former shut up that of Peter the Great in the Crimea. The lady who was afterwards Catharine I. bribed the grand vizier with all her jewels to allow the Russians to escape, and this event utterly ruined the hopes of the monarch of Sweden. Finally the Turks drove him from their country, and, after various vicissitudes, he arrived in his own, and was killed, in 1718, at Frederikhald, in Norway. While he was away, his enemies had been appropriating his territory, and Sweden was reduced to a second-class power.

"The Diet elected Ulrica Eleonora, sister of Charles, queen, who resigned in favor of her husband, Fredrik I. Another war with Russia followed, and Sweden lost more of her territory. Adolf Fredrik succeeded to the throne in 1751, who was elected by the Diet. Still another war with Russia was carried on during his reign. His son, Gustaf III., with the aid of his soldiers, increased the powers of the crown; but he was assassinated at a ball, in 1792, and his son, Gustaf Adolf IV., came to the throne. His policy involved the nation in a war with the allies, and he lost Finland and Pomerania. He was so unpopular that he was compelled to abdicate, and his uncle, Charles XIII., was raised to the throne in 1809. He had no children, and the Prince of Holstein-Augustenburg was elected as his successor; but he was assassinated, and one of Napoleon's generals, Bernadotte, was chosen crown prince, and in 1818 he succeeded to the throne as Charles XIV. His reign was a successful one, and his efforts to secure Norway to his adopted country made him popular even before he was king. He espoused the cause of the allies against Napoleon, and was well cared for by them when the affairs of Europe were finally settled.

"His son Oscar was his heir, and came to the throne at the death of his father in 1844. He was followed by his son, Charles XV., the present king, in 1859.

"The army organization is similar to that of Denmark, and about one hundred and fifty thousand men are available for service. The navy contains four monitors on the American plan, which were invented by John Ericsson, a Swede, two iron-clad gunboats, twenty-one steamers, and sixteen sailing vessels, besides a great number of floating batteries, and other stationary craft. Although only about six thousand sailors are actually in the navy, nearly thirty thousand can be had in case of war."

The professor finished his lecture, and the students hastened on deck, to see more of the sights which surrounded them.

CHAPTER XIX.

THE CRUISE IN THE LITTLE STEAMER.

"WHAT'S the use, Stockwell?" said Sanford, as the absentees seated themselves on the train for Malmö, under the charge of the head steward. "Blaine got his despatch from the principal last night, but he didn't say a word to us till this morning. He's playing a sharp game."

"That's so," replied Stockwell. "He don't mean to trust us out of sight again."

"Don't say a word to any fellow," whispered the coxswain. "You and I will fight it out on our own hook."

"I understand. It is plain enough that Blaine regards us as runaways, and I suppose the principal will do the same."

"Very likely; and when we get to Russia, all we shall have to do will be to count our fingers in the steerage, while the rest of the fellows are seeing the Russians," continued Sanford, who now appeared to regard "the independent excursion without running away" as a failure. "We shall not even see anything more of Stockholm. I don't like the idea."

"Well, what are you going to do about it?" asked Stockwell.

"At the first chance we will leave this train, and make our way back to Stockholm," whispered Sanford. "There is a steamer to St. Petersburg twice a week, and we have money enough to carry us through."

"Right; I am with you."

"We will take Ole, if you like, to do the talking for us."

"I don't object."

The train stopped at Katherineholm about half past nine. The boys had taken nothing but the Swedish early breakfast of coffee and a biscuit, and the head steward allowed them to have a more substantial meal, each paying for himself. They entered the restaurant, where, on a large table in the centre of the room, were great dishes of broiled salmon and veal cutlets, with high piles of plates near them. Each passenger helped himself at these dishes, and then seated himself at one of the little tables. When he had finished his salmon, he helped himself to veal cutlets; beer and coffee were served by the waiters. Sanford and Stockwell hurried through the meal, and went to the counter where the woman received payment. She asked them some question and they were obliged to call Ole, to know what she said. She asked if they had had beer or coffee, which was extra, the meal being one and a half rix dalers. She gave them a tin check; for at this place they seemed to be sharper than the Swedes usually are, and the check was to enable them to get out of the restaurant. A man at the door received it, and no one was allowed to pass without it; and thus none could leave without paying for the meal.

"Finished your breakfast, Ole?" said Sanford, carelessly.

"Yes; and that salmon was very good."

"First rate. Come with us, Ole," added the coxswain, as he led the way out of the restaurant.

The trio entered the station, and as no one followed them, they left by the front door. Dodging behind the buildings, they soon cleared the station. Taking the public road, they walked for half an hour at a rapid pace, and then halted to consider the situation. The train had gone, for they had heard its departure; but whether Mr. Blaine had gone or not was an open question.

"What next?" said Sanford, as he seated himself at the side of the road.

"Take the train back to Stockholm," replied Stockwell.

"Perhaps Blaine did not go on, after he missed us."

"Of course he did. But whether he did or not, the train has gone, and he cannot take us to Copenhagen. If we find him at the station, why, we took a little walk, and lost the train, you know."

"That's played out," replied Sanford. "We have missed the train too many times, already. What time does the next one return to Stockholm?"

"I don't know. Let's go back to the station."

This course was adopted, and on their arrival they learned that they could return to Stockholm at half past two in the afternoon. The man in charge said that the gentleman with the young men had been looking for them. Sanford replied, through Ole, that they had lost the train, but would return to Stockholm, and start again the next morning. After dining in the restaurant, the runaways — as they certainly were now, if not before — departed, and arrived at their destination in about three hours. They immediately went to the office on the quay, and learned that a steamer would leave for St. Petersburg at two o'clock on Friday morning.

"Can we engage places now?" asked Sanford, — for the clerk in charge spoke English.

"Certainly."

"We will take three places in one room," added the coxswain.

"Have you passports?" asked the clerk.

"No, sir."

"We cannot sell you tickets then."

"Not without passports?" exclaimed Sanford, appalled at this new difficulty.

"No; and passports must be *visé* by the Russian consul before we can issue a ticket."

"We are down then," added the coxswain. "My passport is on board of the ship."

"So is mine," added Stockwell.

"And I never had any," said Ole.

The party left the steamer's office, and were unable to devise any means of overcoming the obstacle. They went to the Hotel Rydberg again, and consulted the porter, who had been very kind to them before. This functionary is entirely different in European hotels from those of the same name in the United States. He stands at the entrance, usually dressed in uniform, to answer all inquiries of guests, and to do all that is required of the clerks in American hotels.

He assured the anxious inquirers that, even if they got into Russia, their passports would be immediately demanded, and that no one could remain in any city there over night without one. The American minister in Stockholm would give them the required documents.

"But Ole, here, is a Norwegian," suggested Sanford.

"No matter. Have him put into your passport as your courier or servant."

"All right; we will see him to-morrow," replied the coxswain; and the problem seemed to be solved.

The next day they went to the American legation, but the minister had gone to Upsala for a week, and the secretary declined to issue the passports, because the boys could not prove that they were citizens of the United States. Vexed and discouraged, they wandered about the city till Friday noon, when an English steamer came into port. They stood on the quay, watching the movements of the passengers as they landed. They had almost concluded to take a steamer to Stettin, Lübec, or some other port in Germany; but Russia was a strange land, and they were not willing to abandon the idea of seeing its sights.

"I wonder whether this steamer goes any farther," said Stockwell.

"I don't know," added Sanford.

"Perhaps she goes to St. Petersburg. It may be her officers are not so particular about the confounded passports."

"But you can't stay in Russia over night without one, even if you get there."

"The American minister will fit us out with them. I expect to find a letter of credit in St. Petersburg, and that will prove that I am an American."

"Let us go on board of the steamer and ascertain where she is going," continued Sanford, as he led the way across the plank, which had been extended from the deck to the stone pier.

The boys went upon the hurricane deck, where they had seen an officer who looked as though he might be the captain.

"Do you go to St. Petersburg, captain?" asked the coxswain.

"No; we return to London, touching only at Copenhagen," replied the officer.

"That's too bad!" exclaimed Stockwell.

"So it is," said a tall man, who had followed the runaways up the steps from the lower deck. "But you are not going to St. Petersburg without the rest of us — are you?"

Sanford was startled, and turning sharp around, saw Peaks, who had come out of the cabin as the boys stepped on board. He had followed them to the hurricane deck, and suspecting that something was wrong, he had waited till the coxswain's question betrayed their intention.

"No, we are not going to St. Petersburg; we are waiting for the ship," replied Sanford, recovering his self-possession in an instant.

"O, you are? All right, then. But the last I heard of you was, that you were all on your way to Copenhagen to join the ship," added the boatswain.

"So we were, Mr. Peaks; but after we had taken

breakfast at a station on the railroad, we went to have a little walk, and see something of the country. We thought we had time enough, but the train — confound it! — went off without us. We were terribly provoked, but we couldn't help ourselves, you know; so we made our way back to this city."

"I think you must have been very badly provoked," said Peaks.

"O, we were, — honor bright."

"But you thought you would go over to St. Petersburg before the ship arrived?"

"Certainly not; we had no idea of going to St. Petersburg."

"And that's the reason you asked whether this steamer was going there, — because you hadn't any idea of going."

"We know very well that we can't go to St. Petersburg without our passports, which are on board of the ship," protested Sanford.

"Yes, I understand; but who is this?" asked Peaks, as he glanced at Ole.

"That's Ole Amundsen; don't you remember him?"

"I think I do. And he is on a lark with you."

"We are not on a lark. We have been trying with all our might to find the ship, for the last fortnight; and we are bound to do so, or die in the attempt," said Stockwell.

"And Ole has been with you all the time?"

"Yes, sir; we couldn't have done anything without him."

"And would have been on board the ship long

ago, if you hadn't had him to speak the lingo for you."

"When we tell you our story, you will see that we have done our best to find the ship."

"I don't know that I care to hear any more of your story; it's too much story for me, and you can tell it to Mr. Lowington, who will be here by to-morrow, I think. Very likely you can take me to a good hotel."

"Yes, sir; we are staying at the Hotel Rydberg, which is the best in Stockholm."

"Heave ahead, then."

The runaways led the way.

"Do you talk the Swedish lingo, Ole?" asked the boatswain.

"Yes, sir."

"Where did you stow yourself, when we went into Christiansand?"

"In the second cutter, sir," replied the waif, laughing.

"Exactly so; you were to go with her crew when they left."

"No, sir; I didn't know a single one of them."

"What did you hide for, then?"

"Because I didn't want the pilot to see me."

"Why not?" asked the boatswain.

But this was as far as Ole would go in that direction. Neither man nor boy could extort from him the secret he so persistently retained. A short walk brought the party to the Hotel Rydberg.

"This gentleman wants a room," said Sanford to the porter.

"No. 29," said the man, calling a servant. "Did you get your passports, young men?"

Sanford drew back, and made energetic signs to the porter to keep still; but the official failed to understand him.

"No; they haven't got them yet," replied Peaks. "The fact is, all the passports are on board the ship."

"But the young gentlemen were very anxious to obtain new ones, so that they could go to St. Petersburg. They intended to leave by this morning's steamer, but no tickets can be had without passports."

Both Sanford and Stockwell shook their heads to the stupid porter, who was remarkably intelligent on all other points; but somehow he did not see them, or could not comprehend them.

"It's too bad about those passports — isn't it, my lads?" laughed Peaks, turning to the runaways. "Here's more proof that you hadn't the least idea of going to St. Petersburg."

"I was very sorry for the young gentlemen, and did the best I could for them," added the gentlemanly porter.

"No doubt you did; and I'm very much obliged to you for the trouble you took," replied the good-natured boatswain.

"No. 29, sir?" interposed the servant, with the key in his hand.

"Ay, ay, my hearty. But, young gentlemen, I want to save you from any more terrible disappointments and awful vexations in finding the ship. I'm going up to my bunk, and if I don't find you here when I come down, I shall call on the American consul, and ask him to put the police on your track. You shall find the ship this time, or perish in the attempt, sure."

"Here's a go!" exclaimed Stockwell, as the servant conducted the boatswain up the stairs to his chamber.

"What did you say anything to him about the passports for?" snapped Sanford to the porter.

The official in uniform by this time understood the matter, and apologized, promising to make it all right with the tall gentleman, and to swear that not a word had been said to him or any one else about passports. It was his business to please everybody, and his perquisites depended upon his skill in doing so.

"What did Peaks mean about police?" said Sanford, as the trio seated themselves near the front door of the hotel.

"He means what he says; confound him, he always does!" replied Stockwell. "He intends to treat us as runaway seamen, and have us arrested if we attempt to leave."

"We are trapped," muttered Sanford. "What's Peaks doing up here?"

"I don't know, unless he is looking for us."

"It makes no difference now. We are caught, and we may as well make the best of it."

"It's all up with us," added the coxswain. "Peaks knows what he is about, and there isn't much chance of getting the weather-gage of him."

The boatswain came down in a short time. He was cool and good-natured, and knew exactly how to deal with the parties in hand.

"Now, young gentlemen, if you are going to Russia, don't let me detain you. If you wish to go any where else, I shall not meddle myself. I shall let the American consul attend to the matter. I have business here, and I can't keep an eye on you. But if you want to be fair and square, and not break your hearts because you can't find the ship, just be in sight when I want to know where you are."

"We shall be right on your heels all the time, Mr. Peaks. If you don't object, we will go with you. We know the way round Stockholm, and will help you all we can," said Stockwell.

"That's sensible."

"We will show you out to the Djurgarden," added Sanford.

"Never mind the shows. I want Ole to talk for me, and I don't object to your company," replied the boatswain.

"I beg your pardon, sir," said the porter, presenting himself to Peaks at this moment. "I made a bad mistake. It was not these young gentlemen who wanted the passports. It was another party."

"Exactly. I understand," replied the boatswain, turning to the boys with a significant smile on his bronzed face.

"They were waiting for you, and were very anxious to join their ship."

"It was very kind of them to wait for me, when they hadn't the least idea I was coming. All right, my hearty; you needn't trouble yourself to smooth it over. How much did you pay him for those lies, Sanford?"

"Not a cent, sir!"

"Never mind; don't bother your heads any more about it. I understand the matter now as well as I shall after you have explained it for a week," answered Peaks, as he left the hotel, followed by the discomfited trio.

The boatswain did not deem it expedient to explain to them his business in Stockholm. He found people enough who spoke English, so that he was able to dispense with the services of Ole as interpreter. He ascertained that no such vessel as the Rensdyr had yet arrived, and satisfied with this information, he went out to the Djurgarden with his charge, dined at Hasselbacken, and made himself quite comfortable.

After breakfast the next morning, with Ole's assistance, he chartered one of the little steamers, which was about the size of the ship's second cutter, and, taking the trio with him, sailed out towards the Baltic.

"Where are you going, Mr. Peaks?" asked Sanford, deeply mystified by the movements of the boatswain.

"I'm going to make a trip down to the Baltic, to see what I can see," replied Peaks.

"Are you going for the fun of it?"

"Well, that depends upon how you view it. I suppose you are going for the fun of it, whether I am or not."

"But we would like to know what is up," added Sanford.

"Young gentlemen should not be inquisitive," laughed the old salt.

"Because, if you are going out to meet the ship, in order to put us on board—"

"I'm not going for any such purpose," interposed the boatswain. "I shouldn't take all that trouble on your account."

"But where are you going?"

"That's my affair, my lad."

"We don't mean to give you any trouble on our account," said Sanford, who could not readily dispossess himself of the belief that the expedition was to put his party on board of the ship when she hove in sight.

"Of course you don't, my tender lambs. You have been so anxious to find the ship, and get on board, it would be cruel to suspect you of any mischief," laughed Peaks.

"But, honor bright, Mr. Peaks, whatever we intended, we are ready now to do just what you say, and return to the ship as soon as we can."

"You are all nice boys. You have had a good time, and I think you ought to be satisfied."

"We are satisfied; but I suppose we shall have no liberty again, after we go on board."

"Perhaps you will; the principal isn't hard with the boys when they come right square up to the mark; but you can't humbug him."

"But, honestly, Mr. Peaks, we tried to find the ship, and—"

"There, there, lads," interposed the boatswain, "I don't believe you will have any liberty."

"Why not?"

"Because you want to humbug the principal; and

me, too — but that's no account. If you want to make the best of it, toe the mark. Don't have any lies in your heart or on your tongue. Tell the whole truth, and you will make more by it; but tell the truth whether you make anything or not."

"You won't believe anything we say," protested Sanford.

"Of course I won't, when you are lying. I call things by their right names."

"We didn't stave the boat at Christiansand."

"Yes, you did," replied Peaks, plumply.

"If you think so, it's no use talking."

"Certainly not; don't talk, then."

Sanford was not prepared for so grave a charge as that of causing the accident to the second cutter; and if the principal was of the same mind as the boatswain, the case would go hard with the runaways. The coxswain and Stockwell went into the bow of the little steamer to discuss their situation, which they did very earnestly for a couple of hours.

"There's the ship!" exclaimed Sanford, as he identified the Young America, half a mile distant, leading the squadron into the harbor of Stockholm.

"So it is; now we are in for it. Peaks has come out here with us to make sure that we don't get away from him," added Stockwell.

"If I had known as much last night as I know now, I would have cleared out, in spite of consul and police. If we are to be charged with smashing the second cutter, we shall not go on shore again this summer."

"That's so. But this boat is not headed for the ship. Peaks don't see her."

"Yes, he does; there isn't a craft of any sort within five miles of us that he don't see."

"There's the ship, Mr. Peaks," shouted Stockwell.

"I see her."

But the boatswain continued on his course, paying no attention to the ship. The squadron disappeared among the islands, and the steamer went out into the Baltic, keeping well in towards the shore. When any small schooner appeared, he ran up and examined her very carefully, overhauling three in this manner in the course of the forenoon. At noon the boatswain piped all hands to dinner, for he had procured a supply of provisions at the hotel. Though he had chartered the steamer with Ole acting as an interpreter, he gave no hint of his plans or purposes. He made signs to the helmsman where to go, and occasionally gave directions through Ole.

The fourth small schooner that he examined proved to be the Rensdyr, and Peaks identified her by seeing Clyde Blacklock, who stood on the forecastle, looking out for the approaches to Stockholm. Possibly he had seen the Young America, which passed the schooner, though a mile distant.

"Lay her alongside that small vessel," said Peaks to Ole.

"That one!" exclaimed Ole, whose brown face seemed to grow pale, as he looked at the Rensdyr.

"That's what I say, my lad."

The waif actually trembled; but he spoke to the helmsman, who immediately put the boat about, and headed her towards Stockholm.

"No," said Peaks, sternly. "That vessel."

He pointed to her, and Ole spoke again to the steersman, but without any better result. The boatswain was not to be thwarted. Going forward, he took the little wheel into his own hands, and headed the steamer towards the Rensdyr. Indicating by his signs what he wanted, the man at the helm seemed to be quite willing to obey orders when he knew what was wanted.

"Don't go to that vessel, Mr. Peaks," cried Ole, in an agony of terror.

"Why, my lad, what's the matter with you?"

"That's the Rensdyr!"

"I know it."

"He will kill me," groaned Ole.

"Who will?"

"Captain Olaf."

"Well, who's he?"

"He is the captain of the Rensdyr. He will kill me."

"No, he won't, my hearty. You shall have fair play. Who is he?"

"My step-father, Olaf Petersen. He beat me and starved me, and I ran away from the Rensdyr in the boat."

"O, ho! The story is out — is it?"

"That's the whole truth, sir; it is, Mr. Peaks," protested Ole. "Don't go to her!"

"Don't you be alarmed. You shall have fair play," added the stout boatswain, as the steamer ran alongside the schooner, and the man at the bow made her fast.

BOARDING THE RENSDYR. Page 344.

Peaks was on her deck in another instant, and had Clyde by the collar.

"I want you, my lad," said he.

"Let me alone!" cried the Briton, who had not recognized his tyrant till he was in his grasp, for the simple reason that he did not expect to see him at that time and place.

"No use to kick or yell, my jolly Briton. I never let go," added the boatswain.

At this moment there was a yell from the steamer. Captain Olaf no sooner discovered his lost step-son, than he sprang upon him like a tiger. Ole howled in his terror. Peaks dragged Clyde on board the steamer, and tossing him on the seat at the stern, turned his attention to the skipper of the schooner.

"Steady! hold up, my hearty," said he, pulling the old Norwegian from his prey.

"My boy! My son! He steal my boat, and leave me," said Olaf, furiously.

"He says you didn't treat him well; that you starved and beat him."

"I'll bet Ole told the truth," interposed Clyde, who seemed suddenly to have laid aside his wrath. "Captain Olaf is a brute."

"How's that, my lad? Do you know anything about it?" asked Peaks.

"I know the skipper is the ugliest man I ever met in my life," answered Clyde.

"Won't you except me, my bold Briton?"

"No; I paid my passage, and haven't had enough to eat to keep soul and body together. Besides that, he tried to make me work, and I did do some things. If

I had been obliged to stay on board another day, I should have jumped overboard," continued Clyde. " I begin to think I was a fool for leaving the ship."

"I began to think so at the first of it," added Peaks.

"Ole is my son; I must have him," growled the skipper.

"I have nothing to do with Ole; he may go where he pleases," said the boatswain.

Olaf spoke to his step-son in his own language, and for a few moments the dialogue between them was very violent.

"Cast off, forward, there; give them the Swedish of that, Ole," shouted Peaks.

"Must I go on board of the Rensdyr?" asked the trembling waif.

"Do just as you please."

"Then I shall stay, and go to the ship."

"No, he shall not; he shall come with me," said Olaf, making a spring at Ole.

But Peaks, who had promised to see fair play, interfered, and with no more force than was necessary, compelled the skipper to return to the schooner. The steamer shoved off, and amid the fierce yells of Olaf, steamed towards Stockholm. As she went on her way, Ole told his story. At the death of his father, who was the master of a small vessel, he had gone to England with a gentleman who had taken a fancy to him, and worked there a year. The next summer he had accompanied his employer in an excursion through Norway, and found his mother had married Olaf Petersen. She prevailed upon him to leave his master, and he went to sea with her husband. Then his mother died, and the skipper abused him to such a degree, that he determined to leave the vessel. Olaf had twice brought him back, and then watched him so closely, that he could find no opportunity to repeat the attempt when the Rensdyr was in port.

On the day before the ship had picked him up, Olaf had thrashed him soundly, and had refused to let him have his supper. Olaf and his man drank too much finkel that night, and left Ole at the helm. Early in the evening, he lashed the tiller, and taking to the boat, with the north star for his guide, pulled towards the coast of Norway. Before morning he was exhausted with hunger and fatigue. He had lost one oar while asleep, and the other was a broken one. At daylight he saw nothing of the Rensdyr, and feeling tolerably safe, had gone to sleep again, when he was awakened by the hail from the ship.

"But why did you leave the ship?" asked Peaks.

"Because I was afraid of the pilot. I thought he and other people would make me go back to Olaf."

"Olaf has no claim upon you. He is neither your father nor your guardian."

"I was afraid."

"Where was your vessel bound?"

"To Bremen, where she expected to get a cargo for Copenhagen. I suppose she found another cargo there for Stockholm."

"I don't blame you, Ole, for leaving him," said Clyde. "Olaf is the worst man I ever saw. When he got drunk, he abused me and the men. I had to keep out of his way, or I believe he would have killed me, though I was a passenger, and paid my fare."

At three o'clock in the afternoon, the little steamer ran alongside the ship, and the party went on board, though the principal and all the officers and crew were on shore.

CHAPTER XX.

STOCKHOLM AND ITS SURROUNDINGS.

AFTER the professor's lecture on board of the ship, the students were piped to dinner. According to his usual custom, Paul Kendall, with his lady, took rooms at the hotel, and in this instance his example was followed by Shuffles. Dr. Winstock and Captain Lincoln had already accepted an invitation from Paul to spend the afternoon with him in a ride through the city; and as soon as the boats landed at the quay, they hastened to keep the appointment, while the students scattered all over the city to take a general view.

"Well, Paul, how do you find the hotel?" asked the doctor, when the party were seated in the carriage.

"Very good; it is one of the best hotels I have seen in Europe."

"It has an excellent location, but I think there was no such hotel when I was here before, and I staid at the Hôtel Kung Carl."

"This is a bath-house," said the *commissionnaire*, as the carriage turned the corner at the hotel, and he pointed to a large, square building, with a court-yard in the middle.

"That looks well for the cleanliness of the people, if they support such fine establishments as that."

"Three classes of baths, sir," added Möller, the guide. "In the first class you have a dressing-room, and an attendant to scrub you, and showers, douches, and everything of the sort. This is Drottninggatan, the principal street of the city," added the man, as the carriage turned into another street.

"In other words, Queen Street," explained the surgeon.

"It is rather a narrow street for the principal one," said Paul.

"All the streets of Stockholm are narrow, or nearly all; and very few of them have sidewalks."

"This street looks very much like the streets at home. The shops are about the same thing. There's a woman in a queer dress," added Captain Lincoln.

"That's a Dalecarlian woman. They used to row the boats about the waters of the city, coming down from Dalecarlia to spend the summer here; but the little steamers have taken the business all away from them. They hired a boat for the season, and paid the owner one half of the fares."

"Their costume is rather picturesque," added Paul.

"But that woman is far from handsome," laughed Mrs. Kendall.

"None of them are pretty," replied the doctor.

The dress was a rather short petticoat, with a fanciful bodice, in which red predominated. Quite a number of them were seen by the party during their stay in Stockholm, but all of them had coarse features and clumsy forms.

The carriage returned to the centre of the city by

another street, passing through Carl XIII. Torg, or square, where stands the statue of that king.

"There is the Café Blanche, where they have music every afternoon in summer, with beer, coffee, and other refreshments. The Swedes are very fond of these gardens," said Möller. "Here is the Hotel Rydberg. This is Gustaf Adolf Torget, and that is his statue."

Crossing the bridge to the little island in the stream, the carriage stopped, to enable the party to look down into the garden, which is called Strömparterren, where a band plays, and refreshments are dispensed in the warm evenings of summer. Passing the immense palace, the tourists drove along the Skeppsbron, or quay, which is the principal landing-place of the steamers. Crossing another bridge over the south stream, or outlet of Lake Mäler, they entered the southern suburb of the city, called Södermalm. Ascending to the highest point of land, the party were conducted to the roof of a house, where a magnificent view of the city and its surroundings was obtained.

"We will sit down here and rest a while," said the doctor, suiting the action to the words. "This promontory, or some other one near it, was formerly called Agne's Rock, and there is a story connected with it. Agne was the king of Sweden about 220 B. C. In a war with the Finns, he killed their king, and captured his daughter Skiolfa. The princess, according to the custom of those days, became the wife, but practically the slave, of her captor. She was brought to Sweden, where Agne and his retainers got beastly drunk on the occasion of celebrating the memorial rites of her father. Skiolfa, with the assistance of her Finnish companions, passed a rope through the massive gold chain on the neck of the king, and hung him to a tree, beneath which their tent was pitched. Having avenged the death of her father, the princess and her friends embarked in their boats, and escaped to Finland."

"They finished him, then," laughed Captain Lincoln. "But what sort of boats had they?"

"I don't know," replied Dr. Winstock.

"Could they cross the Baltic in boats?"

"Yes. When you go to Finland you will find that the course will be through islands nearly all the way. There is no difficulty in crossing in an open boat."

"What is the population of Stockholm?" asked Paul.

"One hundred and thirty-five thousand," replied Möller. "It was founded by King Birger in 1250."

"There is a monitor," said Paul, pointing to the waters near Castelholmen, not far from the anchorage of the squadron.

"We have four in the Swedish navy, and Russia has plenty of them. Ericsson, who invented them, was a Swede, you know."

After the tourists had surveyed the panorama to their satisfaction, they descended, and entering the carriage, drove over to the Riddarholm, where the guide pointed out the church, the statue of Gustavus Vasa, the house of the Nobles, and other objects of interest. Returning to the quay, they stopped to look at the little steamers which were whisking about in every direction.

"That is the National Museum," said Möller, pointing to a large and elegant building across the stream.

"I should like to sail in one of those little boats," said Mrs. Kendall.

"We can go over and back in ten minutes, if you like," added the guide.

"Let us go."

The party alighted from the carriage, and entered the little boat.

"How much did you pay, Paul?" asked Grace.

"The fare is no larger than the boat. It is three öre each person."

"How much is that?"

"Let me see; eight tenths of a cent, or less than a halfpenny, English."

The excursionists returned without landing.

"I should like to go again," said Grace. "It is delightful sailing in such dear little steamers."

"If you please, we will ride over to the Djurgarden, and return by the steamer, which will land us at the Strömparterre," said the guide.

This proposition was accepted, and by a circuitous route they reached the place indicated, which, in English, is the Deer Garden. It is on an island, separated from the main land by a channel. The southern portion of it is a thickly-populated village, but the principal part of the island is laid out as a park, of which the people of Stockholm are justly proud. It was originally a sterile tract of land: the first improvements converted it into a deer park for the royal use; but Gustaf III. and Charles (XIV.) John, as Bernadotte was styled, turned it into a public park. It is laid out in walks and avenues beautifully shaded with oaks and other trees. The land is undulating, and parts of it command splendid views of the islands and watercourses in the vicinity. On the outskirts is an asylum for the blind and for deaf mutes. Rosendahl, a country house, built by Charles John in 1830, and often occupied by him, is quite near the park.

The party drove through the principal avenues of the garden, and stopped at the bust of Bellman, the great poet of Sweden, whose birthday is annually celebrated here with music and festivities. Around the park are various tea-gardens, cafés, and other places of amusement, including a theatre, circus, and opera-house for summer use. There is an Alhambra, with a restaurant; a Tivoli, with a concert-room; a Novilla, with a winter garden, and a concert hall for summer. The tourists stopped at Hasselbacken, which is celebrated for its good dinners at moderate prices. The visitors seated themselves in a broad veranda, overlooking a garden filled with little tables, in the centre of which was a kiosk for the music. The viands, especially the salmon, were very nice, and the coffee, as usual, was excellent. After dinner a short walk brought the party to the landing-place of the little steamers, where, paying eight öre, or about two cents, each, they embarked. The boat flew along at great speed for such a small craft, whisked under the Skeppsholm bridge, and in a few moments landed the tourists at the circular stone quay, which surrounds the Strömparterre. Paul and his lady walked to the hotel, and the doctor and the captain went to the Skeppsbron, where a boat soon conveyed them to the ship.

Sanford and Stockwell had been on board several hours, and had had time to make up their minds in regard to their future course. They had considered the advice of the boatswain, and finally concluded to adopt it. Clyde Blacklock was as tame as a parlor poodle. His experience in running away, especially after his three days on board of the Rensdyr, was far from satisfactory.

"I suppose I must go into that cage again," said he, when he went on board.

"That depends on yourself," replied Peaks. "If you say that you don't intend to run away again, we shall not put you in the brig."

"I think I won't," added Clyde.

"You think?"

"Well, I know I won't. I will try to do the best I can."

"That's all we ask," said Peaks. "You can say all this to the principal."

Mr. Lowington returned earlier than most of the ship's company, and Peaks reported to him immediately. The coxswain and his associate were called up first.

"We have come on board, sir," said Sanford, touching his cap.

"I see you have. You have been gone a long time, and I have been told that you had some difficulty in finding the ship," added the principal.

"We have concluded to tell the whole truth, sir," said Sanford, hanging his head.

"I am very glad to hear that."

"We didn't wish to find the ship."

"Can you explain the accident by which the second cutter was stove at Christiansand?"

"I did it on purpose; but no other fellow was to blame, or knew anything about it."

"I am astonished to think you should expose the lives of your crew, by pushing your boat right into the path of a steamer."

"I didn't do it, sir, till the steamer had stopped her wheels. I wanted to get on board of her, and leave the ship. In Norway, I cheated the rest of the party, and led them out of the way."

"How could you do that?"

"I told Ole what to say."

"Then you wished to travel alone?"

"Yes, sir."

Sanford and Stockwell made a clean breast of it, explaining how they had lost trains and steamers, and thus avoided returning to the ship.

"Then Ole is a rogue as well as the rest of you, it seems."

"He did what I told him to do, and paid him for doing," replied Sanford.

"He is a runaway, too," interposed the boatswain, who proceeded to tell the story of the waif. "The boy has suffered a good deal from the ill-treatment of his step-father."

"I am sorry for him; but his character does not seem to be up to the average of that of his countrymen. I don't think we want him on board," replied Mr. Lowington. "As you say this Olaf has no claim for his services, we will see about him."

The Rensdyr had by this time arrived at the quay,

and it was not believed that Captain Olaf would permit his step-son, whose services seemed to be of so much value to him, to escape without making an effort to reclaim him. After all hands had returned from the shore, he put in an appearance, and seeing Peaks in the waist, directed his steps towards him. The profusion of fine uniforms, the order and discipline that reigned on deck, and the dignified mien of the instructors who were walking back and forth, seemed to produce an impression upon the mind of the rough skipper, for he took off his hat, and appeared to be as timid as though he had come into the presence of the king.

"Good evening, Captain Olaf," said the boatswain.

"I want the boy Ole," replied the skipper, bowing, and returning the salutation.

"You must talk with the principal about that."

"I don't understand."

Peaks conducted Olaf to the quarter-deck, where Mr. Lowington was conversing with Mr. and Mrs. Kendall, who had come on board to visit their old friends.

"This is the man that claims Ole," said the boatswain.

"I want the boy, sir," added Captain Olaf, bowing as gracefully as he knew how.

"If Ole chooses to go with you, he may go," replied the principal.

"He does not choose to go."

"I certainly shall not compel him to go," continued Mr. Lowington.

"I will make him go."

"I shall allow no violence on board of this ship."

"But he is my boy; the son of my wife that is dead."

"He is not your son, and you have no more claim on him than I have. The boy is an orphan. Have you been appointed his guardian?"

This question was out of Olaf's depth in the English language; but it was translated into Danish by Professor Badois, and the skipper did not pretend that he had any legal authority over the boy.

"But I have fed and clothed him, and he must work for me," said he.

"Ole says you did not feed him, and he had nothing but a few dirty rags on when we picked him up. I have nothing to do with the matter. Ole is free to go or stay, just as he pleases," replied the principal, turning away from the skipper, to intimate that he wished to say nothing more about the matter.

"The boy is here, and I shall make him go with me," said Olaf, looking ugly enough to do anything.

Mr. Lowington glanced at Peaks, and appeared to be satisfied that no harm would come to Ole. Olaf walked back into the waist, and then to the forecastle, glancing at every student he met, in order to identify his boy.

"See here, Norway; there comes your guardian genius," said Scott, who, with a dozen others, had gathered around the trembling waif, determined to protect him if their services were needed. "Bear a hand, and tumble down the fore-hatch. Herr Skippenboggin is after you."

Ole heeded this good advice, and followed by his

supporters, he descended to the steerage. Olaf saw him, and was about to descend the ladder, when Peaks interfered.

"You can't go down there," said he, decidedly.

"I want the boy," replied Olaf.

"No visitors in the steerage without an invitation."

"I will have Ole;" and the skipper began to descend.

"Avast, my hearty," interposed the boatswain, laying violent hands on Olaf, and dragging him to the deck.

Bitts, the carpenter, and Leach, the sailmaker, placed themselves beside the boatswain, as the Norwegian picked himself up.

"You may leave the ship, now," said Peaks, pointing to the accommodation stairs.

Olaf looked at the three stout men before him, and prudence triumphed over his angry passions.

"I will have the boy yet," said he, as he walked to the stairs, closely attended by the three forward officers.

He went down into his boat, declaring that he would seize upon Ole the first time he caught him on shore.

"Where is Clyde?" asked Mr. Lowington, as soon as the savage skipper had gone.

"He is forward, sir; he behaves like a new man, and says he will not run away," replied Peaks.

"Send him aft."

"Ay, ay, sir."

Clyde went aft. He was a boy of quick impulses and violent temper. He had been accustomed to have his own way; and this had done more to spoil him than anything else. He had to learn that there was a power greater than himself, to which he must submit. He had twice run away, and failed both times. Three days of fear and absolute misery on board of the Rensdyr had given him time to think. He determined, when he reached Stockholm, to return to his mother, and try to be a better boy. Peaks, in the little steamer, had come upon him like a ghost. He had expected never again to see the ship, or his particular tormentor; and to have the latter appear to him in such an extraordinary manner was very impressive, to say the least. He realized that he must submit; but this thought, like that of resistance before, was only an impulse.

Clyde submitted, and was even candid enough to say so to the principal, who talked to him very gently and kindly for an hour, pointing out to him the ruin which he was seeking.

"We will try you again, Clyde," said Mr. Lowington. "We will wipe out the past, and begin again. You may go forward."

The next day was Sunday, and for a change, the officers and crews of the several vessels were permitted to land, and march to the English church in Stockholm. The neat and pleasant little church was crowded to its utmost capacity by the attendance of such a large number. Mr. Agneau, the chaplain, was invited to take a part in the service, and as Mrs. Kendall, Mrs. Shuffles, and many of the ship's company were good singers, the vocal music was better than usual.

On Monday morning commenced the serious business of sight-seeing in Stockholm. The royal palace, one of the largest and finest in Europe, and the most prominent building in the city, was the first place to be visited. It is four hundred and eighteen feet long, by three hundred and ninety-one wide, with a large court-yard in the middle, from which are the principal entrances. The lower story is of granite; the rest of brick, covered with stucco. The students walked through the vast number of apartments it contains; through red chambers, green chambers, blue chambers, and yellow chambers, as they are designated, through the royal chapel, which is as large as a good-sized church, and through the throne-room, where the king opens the sessions of the Diet. Several were devoted to the Swedish orders of knighthood. The ceilings and walls of the state apartments are beautifully adorned with allegorical and mythological paintings.

The chamber of Bernadotte, or Charles John, remains just as it was during his last sickness. On the bed lies his military cloak, which he wore in his great campaigns. His cane, the gift of Charles XIII., stands in the room. The walls are covered with green silk, and adorned with portraits of the royal family. The apartments actually occupied by the present king were found to be far inferior in elegance to many republican rooms. His chamber has a pine floor, with no carpet; but it looked more home-like than the great barn-like state-rooms. In a series of small and rather low apartments are several collections of curious and antique articles, such as a collection of arms, including a pair of pistols presented to the king by President Lincoln; and of pipes, containing every variety in use, in the smoking-room. The king's library looks like business, for its volumes seemed to be for use rather than ornament. The billiard-room is quite cosy, and his chamber contains photographs of various royal personages, as the Prince of Wales, the Queen of England, and others, which look as though the king had friends, and valued them like common people. His majesty paints very well for a king, and the red cabinet contains pictures by him, and by Oscar I. The queen's apartments, as well as the king's, seemed to the boys like a mockery of royalty, for they were quite plain and comfortable. The entire palace contains five hundred and eighty-three rooms.

The whole forenoon was employed in visiting the palace, and the students went on board the vessels to dinner. As the day was pleasant, a boat excursion to Drottningholm was planned, and the fourteen boats of the squadron were soon in line. A pilot was in the commodore's barge, to indicate the course. Passing under the North Bridge, the excursion entered the waters of the Mäler Lake. A pull of two hours among beautiful islands, covered with the fresh green of spring, through narrow and romantic passages, brought them to their destination. In some places, within five miles of Stockholm, the scene was so quiet, and nature so primitive, that the excursionists could have believed they were hundreds of miles from the homes of civilization. Two or three of the islands had a house or two upon them; but generally they seemed to be unimproved. The boats varied their order at the command of Commodore Cumberland, and when there were any spectators, nothing could exceed their astonishment at the display.

At Drottningholm, or Queen's Island, there is a fine palace, built by the widow of Charles X., and afterwards improved and embellished by the kings of Sweden. Attached to it is a beautiful garden, adorned with fountains and statues. The party went through the palace, which contains a great many historical paintings, and some rooms fitted up in Chinese style. As the students were about to embark, a char-a-banc, a kind of open omnibus, drawn by four horses, drove up to the palace, and a plainly-dressed lady alighted. She stood on the portico, looking at the students; and the pilot said she was the Queen Dowager, wife of Oscar I. Of course the boys looked at her with quite as much interest as she regarded them. The commodore called for three cheers for the royal lady, who was the daughter of Eugene Beauharnais, and granddaughter of the Empress Josephine. She waved her handkerchief in return for the salute, and the students were soon pulling down the lake towards Stockholm.

The next forenoon was devoted to the Royal Museum, which has been recently erected. It contains a vast quantity of Swedish antiquities and curiosities, with illustrations of national manners and customs. It contains specimens of the various implements used in the ages of wood, stone, bronze, and iron, collections of coins and medals, armor, engravings, sculptures, and paintings, including a few works of the great masters of every school in Europe. The students were particularly interested in what Scott irreverently called the "Old Clothes Room," in which were deposited in glass cases the garments and other articles belonging to the Swedish kings and queens, such as the cradle and toys of Charles XII., and the huge sword with which he defended himself against the Turks at Bender; the sword of Gustavus Vasa; the costume of Gustaf III., which he wore when he was shot in the opera-house by Ankarström; the baton of Gustaf Adolf, and the watch of Queen Christina.

In the afternoon the students made an excursion by steamer to Ulriksdal, the summer residence of Bernadotte, Oscar I., and of the present king. It is a beautiful place, and is filled with objects of historical interest. The furniture is neat, pretty, and comfortable. The chamber of the king is the plainest of all, but the bed was used by Gustaf II. in Germany. Every chair, table, and mirror has its history. There is a collection of beer mugs in one chamber, and of pipes in another. The place is full of interest to the curious. In the water in front of the palace were several gilded pleasure-boats, and a fanciful steamer for the use of the royal family.

The steamer in which the party had gone to Ulriksdal was one of the larger class, though the company was all she could carry. She made her way through the several arms of the sea, between the islands, passing through two drawbridges. For the return trip four of the smaller steamers had been engaged, each of which would carry about fifty boys. A short distance from the palace, the boats turned into a narrow stream, passing under bridges, in places so contracted that the engine had to be stopped, and the banks were thoroughly washed. Then they entered a lagoon, bordered with villas, and surrounded by pleasant scenery.

Landing at a point in the northern suburb, most of the students walked through the city to the quay, though several omnibuses ply between this point and the centre of the city.

The next day opened with a visit to Riddarholm. The church, or Riddarholmskyrkan, on this island, was formerly a convent, but is now the mausoleum of the most celebrated kings of Sweden. It was once a Gothic structure; but the addition of several chapels on the sides, for monuments, has completely changed the appearance of the structure. It is remarkable for nothing except the tombs within it. Formerly it contained a number of equestrian figures, clothed in armor, which was valued as relics of the ancient time, including that of Birger Jarl, the founder of the city, and of Charles IX.; but all these have been removed to the National Museum, which is certainly a more appropriate place for them. On each side of the church are the sepulchral chapels of Gustavus Adolphus, Charles XII., Bernadotte, and Oscar I. The Queen Désirée, wife of Bernadotte, and sister-in-law of Joseph Bonaparte, with others of the royal family, and some of the great captains of the Thirty Years' War, are buried here. In the chapels of Gustavus and Charles XII. are placed many of the trophies of their victories, such as flags, drums, swords, and keys.

The party then visited the Riddarhus, where the nobles meet, which is the scene of several great historical events, and contains the shields of three thousand Swedish nobles. From this point the tourists went to Mosebacke, a celebrated tea garden, on the high land in the southern suburb, where they ascended to the roof of the theatre in order to obtain a view of the city and its surroundings.

On Thursday, the students made an excursion to Upsala, the ancient capital of Sweden, which contains a fine old cathedral, where Gustavus Vasa and two of his wives are buried. His tomb was hardly more interesting to the Americans than that of Linnæus, the great botanist, who was born in Upsala, and buried in this church. Other Swedish kings are also buried here. The party visited the university, which contains some curious old books and manuscripts, such as an old Icelandic Edda; the Bible, with written notes by Luther and Melanchthon; the Journal of Linnæus, and the first book ever printed in Sweden, in 1483. The house of the great botanist and the botanical garden were not neglected. The tourists returned to Stockholm in a special steamer, through an arm of Lake Mäler, and landed at the Riddarholm. On Friday some of the students went to the Navy Yard, and on board of a monitor, while others wandered about the city and its suburbs.

After spending a week in the harbor, the voyagers felt that they had seen enough of Sweden; and early on Saturday morning, with a pilot on board of each vessel, the squadron sailed for the Aland Islands, in the Baltic, where the principal decided to pass a week. The vessels lay in the channels between the islands, and the students attended to the regular routine of study and seamanship. Occasional excursions were made on shore, mostly at the uninhabited islands.

Journals of what had been seen in Norway, Denmark, and Sweden were written up; but the students were very anxious to visit Russia.

Ole Amundsen was very careful to avoid his stepfather while he remained in Stockholm. He hardly went on shore, so great was his dread of the cruel skipper of the Rensdyr; and no one rejoiced more heartily than he to leave the Swedish waters. Mr. Lowington did not desire to retain him on board; but the waif begged so hard to remain, and the students liked him so well, that he was finally engaged as an assistant steward in the steerage, at twelve dollars a month; but he made double this sum, besides, out of the boys, by the exercise of his genius in mending clothes, cleaning shoes, and similar services, which the students preferred to pay for, rather than do themselves.

Clyde Blacklock kept his promise as well as he could, and soon learned his duty as a seaman. Though he certainly improved, his violent temper and imperious manners kept him continually in hot water. He could not forget his old grudge against Burchmore, and during an excursion on one of the Aland Islands, he attacked him, but was soundly thrashed for his trouble, and punished on board when his black eye betrayed him. While he is improving there is hope for him.

The runaways promised so much and behaved so well, that none of them were punished as yet, though Sanford was deprived of his position as coxswain of the second cutter; but whether they were to be allowed any liberty in Russia, they were not informed.

At the close of the week among the islands, the squadron was headed for Abo, in Finland, which is now a province of Russia; and what they saw and did there, and in other parts of the vast empire, will be related in NORTHERN LANDS, OR YOUNG AMERICA IN RUSSIA AND PRUSSIA.

www.ingramcontent.com/pod-product-compliance
Lightning Source LLC
Chambersburg PA
CBHW020218240426
43672CB00006B/346